IMAGES OF WAR

UNITED STATES MARINE CORPS IN THE SECOND WORLD WAR

RARE PHOTOGRAPHS FROM WARTIME ARCHIVES

Michael Green

Pen & Sword
MILITARY

First published in Great Britain in 2018 by
PEN & SWORD MILITARY
An imprint of
Pen & Sword Books Ltd
47 Church Street
Barnsley
South Yorkshire
S70 2AS

Copyright © Michael Green, 2018

ISBN 978-1-52670-250-0

The right of Michael Green to be identified as author of this work has been asserted by him in accordance with the Copyright, Designs and Patents Act 1988.

A CIP catalogue record for this book is available from the British Library.

All rights reserved. No part of this book may be reproduced or transmitted in any form or by any means, electronic or mechanical including photocopying, recording or by any information storage and retrieval system, without permission from the Publisher in writing.

Typeset by Concept, Huddersfield, West Yorkshire HD4 5JL.
Printed and bound in India by Replika Press Pvt. Ltd.

Pen & Sword Books Limited incorporates the imprints of Atlas, Archaeology, Aviation, Discovery, Family History, Fiction, History, Maritime, Military, Military Classics, Politics, Select, Transport, True Crime, Air World, Frontline Publishing, Leo Cooper, Remember When, Seaforth Publishing, The Praetorian Press, Wharncliffe Local History, Wharncliffe Transport, Wharncliffe True Crime and White Owl.

For a complete list of Pen & Sword titles please contact
PEN & SWORD BOOKS LIMITED
47 Church Street, Barnsley, South Yorkshire S70 2AS, England
E-mail: enquiries@pen-and-sword.co.uk
Website: www.pen-and-sword.co.uk

Contents

Foreword **5**

Acknowledgements **6**

Chapter One
   The Opening Acts **7**

Chapter Two
   Early Central Pacific Battles **60**

Chapter Three
   Getting Ever Closer **109**

Chapter Four
   The Last Few Battles **158**

Dedication

The author would like to dedicate this book to Marine John Basilone, winner of the Medal of Honor and the Navy Cross during the Second World War.

Foreword

In most respects, the modern United States Marine Corps remains a creation of the Second World War. The unprecedented expansion of the corps in size, composition and mission orientation brought major challenges to a relatively small military organization.

The short pre-war period saw the corps forming its first two divisions and two aircraft wings mere months before the United States entered the war. What followed was a six-fold enlargement by 1944 to field the six divisions, four wings, and corps and force troops to support two amphibious corps, which were the Fleet Marine Forces' highest combat formations. At the same time, Marines continued to form detachments for all US Navy ships of cruiser size and above, and secure naval bases at home and overseas. The corps' top strength was 471,905.

As usual, numbers alone scarcely suffice to tell the story. The Marine Corps provided specialized amphibious forces in the Pacific, making significant changes to equipment, organizations and doctrine to meet the challenges posed by the air, sea and land forces of the Japanese Empire. In doing so, the concept of close air support advanced as were naval fire support, amphibious vehicle development and a host of tactics, techniques and procedures, most of which remain today in recognizable form.

Michael Green's succinct history of the major Second World War operations in which the Marine Corps participated contributes well to our understanding of why such a wholesale organizational evolution took place at a crucial time in our national epic. In the eyes of the American public, the Marine Corps was second to none and seemed destined for a long and useful career.

Kenneth W. Estes
Lieutenant Colonel, US Marines

Acknowledgements

The bulk of the historical images in this work came from the files of the United States Marine Corps Historical Center and will be credited 'USMC'. As with all published works, authors depend on friends for assistance in reviewing their work. Especially helpful as always were Randy Talbot and Peter Shyvers.

Chapter One

The Opening Acts

On Sunday morning, 7 December 1941, there were approximately 4,500 Marines stationed at Naval Station Pearl Harbor and the surrounding area. About 900 of those Marines were stationed on board warships of the United States Pacific Fleet that were docked at Pearl Harbor.

In addition, there was a Marine Corps aviation unit with forty-seven fighters and dive-bombers at Marine Corps Air Station Ewa. When the surprise Japanese aerial attack on Pearl Harbor began on 7 December 1941 at 7.55 am, Ewa was their first target. All the Marine Corps aircraft were destroyed during the attack.

At the Marine Barracks at Pearl Harbor, Samuel R. Shaw, who commanded one of the two barracks companies, remembered that fateful Sunday morning in his oral interview filed in the Marine Corps Historical Collection:

> The boat guards were in place, and the music was out there, and the old and new officer of the day. And we had music, and a hell of a fine sergeant bugler who had been in Shanghai. He would stand beside the officers of the day, and there came the airplanes, and he looked up and he said, 'Captain, those are Japanese war planes.' And one of the two of them said, 'My God, they are, sound the call to arms.' So, the bugler started sounding the call to arms before the first bomb hit.

Only four shore-based Marines were wounded during the Japanese attack on Pearl Harbor. Of the Marines posted to the US Navy warships at the naval base during the attack, 108 were killed and another 49 wounded.

Fears abounded following the Japanese aerial attack on Pearl Harbor. Many assumed that this attack would be followed by an invasion of the Hawaiian Island of Oahu, location of Naval Base Pearl Harbor. However, that was never a Japanese plan. Concerns about the possibility of Japanese landings did not subside until 1943.

More Japanese Attacks

Also on 7 December 1941, Japanese aircraft attacked the American protectorate of Guam, one of the Marianas Islands. A few days later a force of approximately 4,000 Japanese soldiers landed on the island and quickly overwhelmed the 145 Marines assigned to defend Marine Barracks, Naval Station Guam. Thirteen Marines were killed and thirty-seven wounded in the lop sided one-day struggle.

A less dramatic engagement between the Japanese Navy and the Marine Corps also took place on 7 December 1941. Two Japanese destroyers bombarded the Central Pacific island of Midway for fifty-four minutes. The coastal artillery guns of a Marine Corps defence battalion engaged one of the destroyers without striking it. Two Marines died during that brief struggle in what was a very minor footnote in the history of the Second World War.

The Battle for Wake Island

Japanese aerial attacks were launched on the American-occupied Central Pacific island of Wake between 7 and 10 December. On 11 December, a Japanese force of three cruisers, six destroyers and a number of troop transports attempted to land an invasion force of 450 troops on the island.

Unfortunately for the over-confident Japanese invasion force, the approximately 500 Marines of a defence battalion tasked with protecting Wake and surrounding islands were better armed than their Guam comrades. They had anti-aircraft guns, coast artillery guns and a few Wildcat fighters in support. They would employ these weapons to take a heavy toll on the enemy armada, sinking two destroyers and damaging a cruiser.

From a wartime report by a Marine Corps officer who commanded one of the coast artillery batteries at Wake on 11 December comes this extract describing what took place when one of the Japanese warships escorting the troop transports came within range of his guns:

> The first salvo from our guns which hit her [the Japanese cruiser] was fired at a range of 5,500-6,000 yards, bearing about 180 to 190. Both shells entered her port side about amidships just above the waterline. The ship immediately belched smoke and steam through the side and her speed diminished. At 7,000 yards two more hit her in about the same place, but more probably slightly aft of the first two. Her whole side was now engulfed in smoke and steam and she turned to starboard again to try to hide in the smoke ... After we ceased firing, the whole [Japanese] fleet having fled and there being no other targets to engage, the cruiser lay broadside to the sea still pouring steam and smoke from her side. She had a definite port list. After some time, she got slowly under way, going a short distance, stopping, and continuing again; she was engulfed in smoke when she crept over the horizon.

The Japanese learned their lesson. On 23 December 1941, they returned to Wake with a much larger seaborne invasion force transporting 1,500 troops escorted by two aircraft carriers, the *Soryu* and *Hiryu*, which had attacked Pearl Harbor on

> **Marine Defence Battalions**
> Intended for the defence of overseas US Navy bases, the corps formed its first independent defence battalion in 1939. By the time the Japanese attacked Pearl Harbor, there were seven defence battalions in existence. Eventually nineteen were formed during the Second World War. Manpower could range from 500 up to 1,400 personnel, depending on the unit's assignment and weaponry issued.
>
> The defence battalions were originally armed with dismounted fixed 5in or 7in naval guns that were subsequently replaced by towed 155mm guns. In addition, anti-aircraft guns ranging from 20mm to 3in (later replaced by 90mm anti-aircraft guns) were found in their Table of Organization and Equipment (TO&E). These weapons were accompanied by associated aircraft detection equipment such as searchlights and later radar units. Based on the experience of Wake Island, defence battalions could also be equipped with light tanks.
>
> By early 1944, a serious manpower shortage forced the corps to rethink the importance of defence battalions. This resulted in two of them being disbanded in April 1944 and the remaining units converted to anti-aircraft battalions. Some of these had 155mm guns as an attachment rather than as standard equipment. With the end of the war, all the remaining defence battalions and those converted to anti-aircraft battalions were disbanded.

7 December 1941. By the day's end, the badly-outnumbered and outgunned Marines were forced to surrender.

Japanese losses were four ships sunk, with a fifth badly damaged. Two patrol boats were also lost. An estimated eight Japanese aircraft were destroyed, with another twenty damaged. Enemy personnel losses amounted to 820 killed and another 300 wounded. The Marines lost 12 fighter planes, with 119 men on the ground killed and 50 wounded. All the surviving Marines entered into captivity.

In August 1942, an American-made movie titled *Wake Island* which dramatized the Marines' resistant defence of the island was released to help build up the American public's morale and mobilize them for war.

The Philippines

On the same day as the attack on Pearl Harbor, the Japanese military launched a massive aerial attack on two United States Army Air Forces (USAAF) airfields in the Philippines, destroying the majority of the aircraft present. On 8 December Japanese troops began landing in the Philippines. A follow-on aerial attack on 9 December destroyed many of the remaining American warplanes.

In addition to the approximately 30,000 US Army personnel assigned to protect the Philippines, there were about 1,500 Marines stationed there. Despite being cut off from both seaborne and aerial resupply, American ground forces held out for almost four months against the Japanese onslaught before succumbing. When the Imperial Japanese Army finally declared victory on 8 May 1942, over half the Marine contingent were either dead or wounded. Of the surviving Marines, a total of 239 would die in Japanese prison camps.

The Battle for Guadalcanal

Within the span of only a few months since the attack on Pearl Harbor, the Japanese had achieved their planned barrier-island strategy intended to attrite any attacking American forces. Thus in the summer of 1942 the armed forces of the United States and its Pacific Allies (Australia and New Zealand) began planning a limited offensive against the Japanese. Two goals were established: to protect the Allies' very long lines of communications in the South-West Pacific Area, and to prevent the Japanese from consolidating their gains.

The first American target in the South-West Pacific Area was Guadalcanal in the southern Solomon Islands. The Imperial Japanese Navy, having occupied the island, was building an airfield on a portion of the island of Guadalcanal which is referred to as Lunga Point. Once completed, it would threaten the vital supply and communications lifeline between the United States and Australia and New Zealand. It was decided to seize the Japanese airfield before it was completed. The small Japanese-occupied islands across the strait at Tulagi and Gavutu near Guadalcanal as well as a connecting islet named Tanambogo were to be seized at the same time.

As there were no US Army divisions available, the entire American invasion force would consist of Marine units. The understrength 1st Division, supplemented by elements of the 2nd Division, was to lead the way. Both had been formed in February 1941. Two Marine raider battalions would also play key roles in the Guadalcanal campaign. The Marines landed on 7 August 1942, meeting some resistance and catching local Japanese forces and their higher headquarters in Tokyo completely by surprise.

The first major Japanese ground force attack against the Marines on Guadalcanal occurred on 20 August 1942. It was repulsed with the assistance of light tanks and artillery, killing approximately 900 Japanese soldiers for the loss of only thirty-four Marines killed and seventy-five wounded. The Japanese military would mount additional ground offensives against the Marines on Guadalcanal between September and November 1942 without success as they persistently underestimated both the size of the Marine forces ashore and the Marines' resolve.

An example of the fierce fighting that took place on Guadalcanal in August 1942 can be found in this extract from the Medal of Honor citation of Marine Sergeant Mitchell Paige for an action that occurred on 26 October 1942:

> When the enemy broke through the line directly in front of his position, Platoon Sergeant Paige, commanding a machine gun position section with fearless

determination, continued to direct fire of his gunners until all his men were either killed or wounded. Alone, against the deadly hail of Japanese shells, he manned his gun and when it was destroyed, took over another, moving from gun to gun, never ceasing his withering fire against the advancing hordes until reinforcements finally arrived. Then, forming a new line, he dauntlessly and aggressively led a bayonet charge, driving the enemy back and preventing a breakthrough in our lines.

A dramatized account of what the Marines endured appeared in *Guadalcanal Diary*, an American-made movie that was released in theatres in November 1943. It was filmed at a southern California Marine Corps base and employed a number of serving Marines in minor speaking roles.

Marine Air Support in the Southern Solomons

The Marines on the ground in Guadalcanal were supported by various Marine aviation squadrons. They were equipped with fighters, dive-bombers and torpedo-bombers. As the American planning code for Guadalcanal was CACTUS, the Marine, Navy and USAAF aircraft squadrons based on the island become known as the 'Cactus Air Force'. They flew from the captured Japanese airfield that had been named 'Henderson Field' in honour of an early-war Marine Corps Medal of Honor recipient.

Well aware of the strategic importance of Henderson Field, the Japanese conducted continual ground, sea and air attacks between August 1942 and November 1942 to take it out of service. During that time the Marine pilots and air crews of the Cactus Air Force sank seventeen large enemy vessels and damaged another eighteen. The best estimate of Japanese aircraft downed during this time period was 263. American losses were put at 118 aircraft.

Six Marine Corps fighter pilots who flew as part of the Cactus Air Force between August and December 1942 were awarded the Medal of Honor in recognition of their exploits. One of those was First Lieutenant James E. Swett. A portion of his citation reads as follows:

In a daring flight to intercept a wave of 150 Japanese planes, First Lieutenant Swett unhesitatingly hurled his four-plane division into action against a formation of fifteen enemy bombers and during his dive personally exploded three hostile planes in mid-air with accurate and deadly fire. Although separated from his division while clearing the heavy concentration of anti-aircraft fire, he boldly attacked six enemy bombers, engaged the first four in turn, and unaided, shot them down in flames. Exhausting his ammunition as he closed the fifth Japanese bomber, he relentlessly drove his attack against terrific opposition which partially disabled his engine, shattered the windscreen and slashed his face. In spite of this, he brought his battered plane down with skillful precision in the water off Tulagi [a small island north of Guadalcanal] without further injury.

During the Guadalcanal campaign the Marine Corps fighter squadron that formed a portion of the Cactus Air Force flew the F4F Wildcat. It was inferior to the Japanese Zero in speed and manoeuvrability. However, Marine Corps pilots flying the Wildcat often prevailed over their counterparts by exploiting its strengths: more rugged construction, faster diving speed, armour protection, self-sealing gas tanks and excellent firepower. By employing tactics that used the plane's advantages against Japanese aircraft weaknesses, far fewer Cactus fliers would prevail against much larger numbers of Japanese forces.

The Guadalcanal Fight Comes to a Close

The first small US Army ground reinforcements began arriving on Guadalcanal in late August 1942. The US Army would play an important part in stopping the final Japanese ground offensive mounted in November 1942. The 1st Marine Division was withdrawn to Australia during December 1942 and January 1943, replaced by the 2nd Marine Division and US Army units.

By early 1943 the Japanese had abandoned hope of retaining the island and successfully evacuated the remainder of their troops by sea during the first week of February 1943. Numbers ranged between 7,000 and 10,000 men, depending on the source. Despite this setback, the successful conquest of Guadalcanal provided the American military with its first large-scale land victory over the Empire of Japan, with the Marine Corps playing an important part.

From a Marine Corps Historical Branch publication titled *The Guadalcanal Campaign* appears this passage explaining the importance of the fight for the island:

> Between August and November of 1942, the seemingly irresistible advance of the Japanese collided head-on with the scanty forces which the United States could throw in their path. By the end of November [1942], the enemy had been halted on the ground, turned back at sea, and virtually driven from the air above Guadalcanal. After 7 August 1942, when U.S. Marines opened the assault, the Japanese never again advanced beyond the Pacific positions which they held at that time. Their succeeding movements throughout the war were always to the rear. This turn of the tide, largely accomplished by the forces of the U.S. Navy and Marine Corps, inflicted at least 27,500 casualties upon the enemy, and cost us 6,111, including 1,752 killed or missing in action. What is more, it gained for the United States a strategic initiative which was never relinquished.

The Battle for the Central Solomons

Following the Japanese evacuation of Guadalcanal, the American military set its sights on the neutralization of the Japanese base of Rabaul. The strategic air and naval hub of the Japanese defensive perimeter in the South-West Pacific Area, Rabaul was located on the north-eastern tip of the island of New Britain.

To reach New Britain the American military's senior leadership put into place a two-pronged advance named Operation CARTWHEEL. US Army forces, the first prong, would push through the island of New Guinea before reaching the island of New Britain, home of Rabaul. The second prong – US Naval forces – was tasked with advancing through the Central Solomons to capture the island of Bougainville in the Northern Solomons. US-built airfields on Bougainville would support single-engine fighter operations against Rabaul.

The Ground Campaign in the Central Solomons

The Japanese Navy decided to build an airfield at Munda Point on New Georgia Island in the Central Solomons in late November 1942. It was eventually decided by the American military that the island and its airfield had to be secured. This would involve Marine raider units, defence battalions, aviation squadrons and two US Army infantry divisions.

The seizure of New Georgia Island, as well as some smaller nearby islands, took from June 1943 until October 1943 in what was referred to as Operation TOE-NAILS. Munda airfield was captured on 5 August 1943 and placed into American military service two days later.

As the bulk of the personnel involved in the campaign to take New Georgia Island were from the US Army, Marine Corps losses were minimal: 192 killed and 534 wounded. The corps first experimented with mounting flame-throwers on their tanks during this campaign.

Marine Corps Aviation in the Central Solomons

Marine Corps aircraft made a significant contribution to the campaign. The air war itself had begun in December 1942 before Operation CARTWHEEL was even put into effect. Consisting of an endless series of fighter sweeps and bombing runs, the effort aimed to neutralize Japanese air power that would have made the American march up the Central Solomons impossible.

One of the best-known Marine pilots from that time was Major Gregory 'Pappy' Boyington. His exploits were dramatized in a very inaccurate American television series that ran from 1976 to 1978 and was titled *Baa-Baa Black Sheep* and later *Black Sheep Squadron*. Boyington was eventually awarded a Medal of Honor for his actions in the Central Solomons. From his citation comes the following description of his accomplishments:

> For extraordinary heroism and valiant devotion to duty as commanding officer of Marine Fighting Squadron 214 in action against enemy Japanese forces in the Central Solomons area from 12 September 1943 to 3 January 1944. Consistently outnumbered throughout successive hazardous flights over heavily defended hostile territory, Major Boyington struck at the enemy with daring and

courageous persistence, leading his squadron into combat with devastating results to Japanese shipping, shore installations, and aerial forces. Resolute in his efforts to inflict crippling damage on the enemy, Major Boyington led a formation of twenty-four fighters over Kahili on 17 October, and, persistently circling the airdrome where sixty hostile aircraft were grounded, boldly challenged the Japanese to send up planes. Under his brilliant command, our fighters shot down twenty enemy craft in the ensuing action without the loss of a single ship. A superb airman and determined fighter against overwhelming odds, Major Boyington personally destroyed 26 of the many Japanese planes shot down by his squadron and, by his forceful leadership developed the combat readiness in his command which was a distinctive factor in the Allied aerial achievements in this vitally strategic area.

The aircraft that Boyington's squadron (VMF-214) flew off various airfields in the Central Solomons was the F4U Corsair. It first showed up in the Pacific with a Marine fighter squadron in February 1943. It had originally entered service with the US Navy but had been rejected due to the difficulty of landing it on aircraft carrier flight decks. This resulted in the US Navy selecting the F6F Hellcat for carrier use and passing the F4U Corsair to the Marine Corps for use from land bases. Eventually some design issues with the F4U Corsair were resolved and Marine Corps squadrons began flying off US Navy aircraft carriers in late 1944.

The Battle for Bougainville

Operation CARTWHEEL was broken down into ten subsidiary operations. Of these, the Marines participated in three led by the US Navy through the Solomons. The largest and most important such subsidiary operation was Operation CHERRY BLOSSOM, the capture of a small portion of the island of Bougainville in the Northern Solomons for the building of airfields. It began on 1 November 1943 and involved elements of the 3rd Marine Division and two attached Marine raider battalions. The 3rd Marine Division was formed in September 1942.

By this point in the war, the senior American military leadership saw no need to capture entire islands in bloody battles with the Japanese. Rather, only enough room to build airfields and a strong defensive perimeter around them were required. This perspective on how to beat the enemy was also applied to the Japanese military base at Rabaul. Physically capturing the base was ruled unnecessary by late 1943. By constant aerial attacks and interdicting resupply, the base would eventually be reduced to military insignificance.

The Japanese anticipated that the Allies would eventually attempt to capture Bougainville in order to build airfields. To mislead them, the 2nd Marine Parachute Battalion carried out a raid on the nearby Japanese-occupied island of Choiseul, which

> **Marine Raiders**
> Impressed by the British commandos in 1940 and their numerous exploits behind German lines, the president of the United States and some like-minded senior Marines Corps officers formed the 1st and 2nd Raider Battalions in early 1942. It was envisioned that these lightly-equipped units would create havoc in Japanese rear areas.
>
> Of the first two missions conducted by the 1st and 2nd Raider Battalions in August 1942, one was considered a moderate success (Tulagi), with the other (Makin Atoll) a painful failure. During that second mission nine raiders were captured and beheaded by the Japanese troops. Those that made it off Makin island left behind most of their weapons and equipment.
>
> The mixed fortunes of these two initial raider battalion endeavours badly soured a number of high-level senior officers towards the concept. Nevertheless, two more units were formed in 1942. They would arrive in the South-West Pacific in February 1943 and consolidated the following month with the original raider battalions to form the 1st Raider Regiment. However, at this time the biggest demand was for more front-line infantrymen. This led to the reflagging of the 1st Raider Regiment and all its battalions as the new 4th Marine Regiment in January 1944. The approximately 6,000 raiders thus replaced the regiment lost in the fall of the Philippines in May 1942.

was also considered part of the Northern Solomons. The raid by the parachute battalion lasted from 28 October 1943 to 3 November 1943 and killed 143 Japanese troops. Marine losses were twelve killed and two missing in action.

Unlike Guadalcanal, where the corps' initial landings were not expected and therefore went generally unopposed, Japanese troops on Bougainville had built a series of strong defensive positions on likely American landing areas. While one landing was opposed, others were not.

The first US Army units began arriving on Bougainville on 8 November 1943. Their assignment was to secure and expand the area captured by the Marines, thus relieving them – as they were now seen as an elite amphibious assault force – to prepare for the next operation. The first airfield for corps' single-engine fighters became operational on Bougainville on 10 December 1943. They were now close enough to Rabaul to begin the attack.

The Battle for Cape Gloucester

The 1st Marine Division was assigned Operation BACKHANDER, an important and subsidiary part of Operation CARTWHEEL. The division was to seize two Japanese air bases on the western tip of the island of New Britain, named 'Cape Gloucester'.

Marine Paratroopers

The early-war success of German Air Force paratroopers inspired the Marine Corps' senior leadership to call for the formation of similar units. The first battalion of parachutists was formed in May 1941. In March 1943, the first three parachutist battalions were formed into the 1st Parachute Regiment. However, it soon became apparent that a lack of suitable training facilities and transport aircraft made it impossible to raise the number of parachutists needed for large-scale operations.

There were other potential issues that precluded the possible employment of parachutists in the Pacific. Even if enough transport aircraft and parachutists could be massed for such an operation, the distances between the possible objectives exceeded the aircrafts' range. Secondly, the type of close-in fighting that the Marines had experienced in the South-West Pacific did not lend itself well to large-scale airborne operations. That being said, a few hundred of the original parachutists would see action in 1942 as infantrymen on Guadalcanal and on other nearby islands.

After deciding that they had no need for parachute units, the Marine Corps' senior leadership pondered what missions could be performed by the existing paratroopers. Some thought that the parachute units could be employed in commando-type raids. However, this duplicated the role (or mission) envisioned for the raider battalions. Thus the 1st Parachute Regiment was disbanded in February 1944, with the personnel forming cadres for the 5th Marine Division's 26th Marine Regiment.

Their seizure would serve two purposes: first, to deny their use to the Japanese who could have used them to mount aerial attacks on the right flank of Allied troops advancing through New Guinea; second, their capture would allow Allied aircraft to neutralize Rabul.

Although most of the corps' activities in the South-West Pacific from 1942 until 1944 were centred around the Solomons and under US Navy command, the taking of Cape Gloucester by the 1st Marine Division fell under the command of the US Army. The division was chosen as it had been rested and built up to strength in Australia following its withdrawal from Guadalcanal.

The 1st Marine Division's landings on Cape Gloucester were on 26 December 1943 and initially met with limited enemy resistance. Casualties were light, as only 21 men were killed and 23 wounded of 11,000 men put ashore that day. The Japanese, in response, quickly sent reinforcements in the direction of Cape Gloucester to counter-attack. However, despite their most determined efforts, they could not dislodge the Marines from the ground they occupied.

Besides fighting the Japanese, the Marines on Cape Gloucester battled inhospitable terrain and horrendous weather. Cape Gloucester is considered one of the rainiest locations on the planet. In a Marine Corps historical publication titled *Cape Gloucester: The Green Inferno* by Bernard C. Nalty appears the following passage describing the battlefield conditions endured by the Marines:

> Rains brought by seasonal monsoons seemed to fall with the velocity of a fire hose, soaking everyone, sending streams from their banks, and turning trails into quagmire. The terrain of the volcanic island varied from coastal plain to mountains that rose as high as 7,000 feet above sea level. A variety of forest covered the island, punctuated by patches of grassland, a few large coconut plantations, and garden plots near the scattered villages.
>
> Much of the fighting, especially during the early days, raged in swamp forest, sometimes erroneously described as damp flat. The swamp forest consisted of scattered trees growing as high as a hundred feet from a plain that remained flooded throughout the rainy season, if not for the entire year. Tangled roots buttressed the towering trees, but could not anchor them against gale-force winds, while vines and undergrowth reduced visibility on the flooded surface to a few yards.

By early February 1944, the Japanese began withdrawing their ground forces from eastern New Britain to their base at Rabaul on the other side of the island. One of the key factors that allowed the Marines to prevail over the Japanese included the almost complete American domination of both the air and sea space around the battlefield. The last Marine unit departed from the island in May 1944 with their defence obligations taken over by US Army units.

The Destruction of Rabaul

The first Allied air-raid on Rabaul took place in February 1942. It was conducted by six USAAF four-engine heavy bombers flying out of Australia. This type of air-raid would be repeated about once a month thereafter. To the Japanese, these were nuisance raids that did little to hamper the operations of the air and naval facilities at the base. Besides its own planes, Rabaul was defended by hundreds of anti-aircraft guns of all sizes supported by land-based radar units.

The tempo and size of the air-raids on Rabaul escalated in October 1943. Hundreds of Allied multi-engine bombers, escorted by USAAF twin-engine fighters, attacked the Japanese base on six occasions. On 2 November 1943, an aerial raid on Rabaul harbour resulted in the sinking of two enemy warships and eight merchant ships. Three days later another aerial raid damaged seven Japanese Navy warships in Rabaul's harbour. That was enough for the Japanese Navy and on 6 November 1943 they decided to withdraw all their ships from Rabaul, never to return.

Marine Aviation Organization

One month prior to the German invasion of Poland in September 1939, Marine Corps aviation consisted of two 'aircraft groups' comprising a total of nine squadrons. The number of aircraft in a squadron depended on the mission and the aircraft assigned to it. A pre-war fighter squadron had eighteen aircraft, with a wartime fighter squadron having up to twenty-four.

The major expansion of the corps in early 1941 included an increase of the size of the aircraft groups; a larger unit of organization called a 'wing' was established. The first two aircraft wings (1st and 2nd Marine Aircraft Wings, abbreviated to MAW-1 and MAW-2) were formed; groups now served under wings. By December 1944 three more wings had been formed, giving a grand total of 31 groups comprising 145 squadrons. Aviation personnel strength in December totalled 102,216 including 10,349 pilots.

The most common type of aviation squadron was the Fighter Squadron (VMF). It was considered a multi-purpose unit capable of air-to-air combat, bomber escort, anti-ship attack and close air support (CAS). There were also two specialized types of fighter squadrons: the radar-equipped Night Fighting Squadron VMF(N) and the Fighter-Bombing Squadron (VMBF or VMFB), which was optimized for the CAS or anti-ship role. All these fighter units were land-based until early 1945 when they first began flying off US Navy aircraft carriers. Marine aviation accounted for 2,355 Japanese aircraft, losing 573 of their own during the Second World War.

In addition, there were other squadrons equipped with a wide variety of aircraft. These included the Scout Bombing Squadron (VMSB), the Torpedo Bombing Squadron (VMTB) and the Scouting Squadron (VBM). They all flew single-engine aircraft supplied by the US Navy. By contrast, Bombing Squadron (VBM), Observation Squadron (VMO), Photographic Squadron (VMD/VMP), Utility/Transport Squadron (VMJ/VMR) and Target Towing Detachment (VMTD/VMJ) flew both single-engine and multi-engine aircraft which were also flown by the US Navy and USAAF. All Marine Corps aircraft have been and continue to be purchased and supported by the US Navy.

Marine Aviation Joins the Final Fight

On 7 December 1943 Bougainville-based Marine single-engine fighters joined other Allied fighters to attack Rabaul. The continuing raids conducted through to 19 February 1944 destroyed a large number of enemy aircraft. The Marine fighter pilots claimed the destruction of 342 aircraft with most being fighters. These aircraft would not be available to the Japanese as the American military pushed forward to their ultimate goal, the Japanese home islands.

Despite Rabaul being rendered impotent by early 1944, Marine aircraft were still tasked with attacking the base until August 1945. In spite of the perceived uselessness of the job, there was one advantage to be gained by the Marine pilots assigned, as described in a Marine Corps historical publication titled *The Isolation of Rabaul*:

> The monotonous pattern of attacks on the same targets, day after day, went on regardless of the pending deployment of various wing units. One virtue of the situation was that many Marine pilots and aircrew got their first taste of combat flying during these months of strikes against bypassed objectives. The flying, gunnery, and bombing experience gained while hitting Rabaul and Kavieng and tackling the Japanese positions in the northern Solomons was invaluable.

Pre-war a Marine scans the horizon for any threats as he stands next to a coast artillery gun. The weapon itself is a redundant 5in naval gun transferred to the Marine Corps. It would comprise a portion of the armament of a typical Marine Corps defence battalion tasked with guarding an overseas US Navy base. There were seven Marine defence battalions in existence prior to the Japanese attack on Pearl Harbor. (*United States Marine Corps*, hereafter *USMC*)

Taking part in a pre-war training exercise is a Marine Corps artillery crew armed with a 75mm M1A1 pack howitzer. When the Second World War began in September 1939, the Marine Corps had a personnel strength of approximately 66,000. Of that number, roughly 20,000 were on active service with the remainder comprising reservists. Among the active-duty Marines there were 3,367 assigned to 24 Marine barracks and detachments. (*USMC*)

Of the 20,000 Marines on active duty when the Second World War began, a total of 3,793 were assigned to ship guard detachments divided among sixty-eight vessels. US Marines first served on US Navy warships during the Revolutionary War. From the 1930s up until the 1990s, shipboard Marines were tasked with manning some of the anti-aircraft guns on US Navy warships as seen in this photograph. (*USMC*)

The Marine infantryman armed with the Model 1903 Springfield rifle in this pre-war photograph wears the summer service uniform and the M1917A1 helmet. The headgear is very reminiscent of the type worn by Marines during the First World War and was nicknamed the 'tin hat'. However, the M1917A1, introduced in 1939, was a major improvement over the crude original as it had a padded leather liner and a two-piece chin strap. (*USMC*)

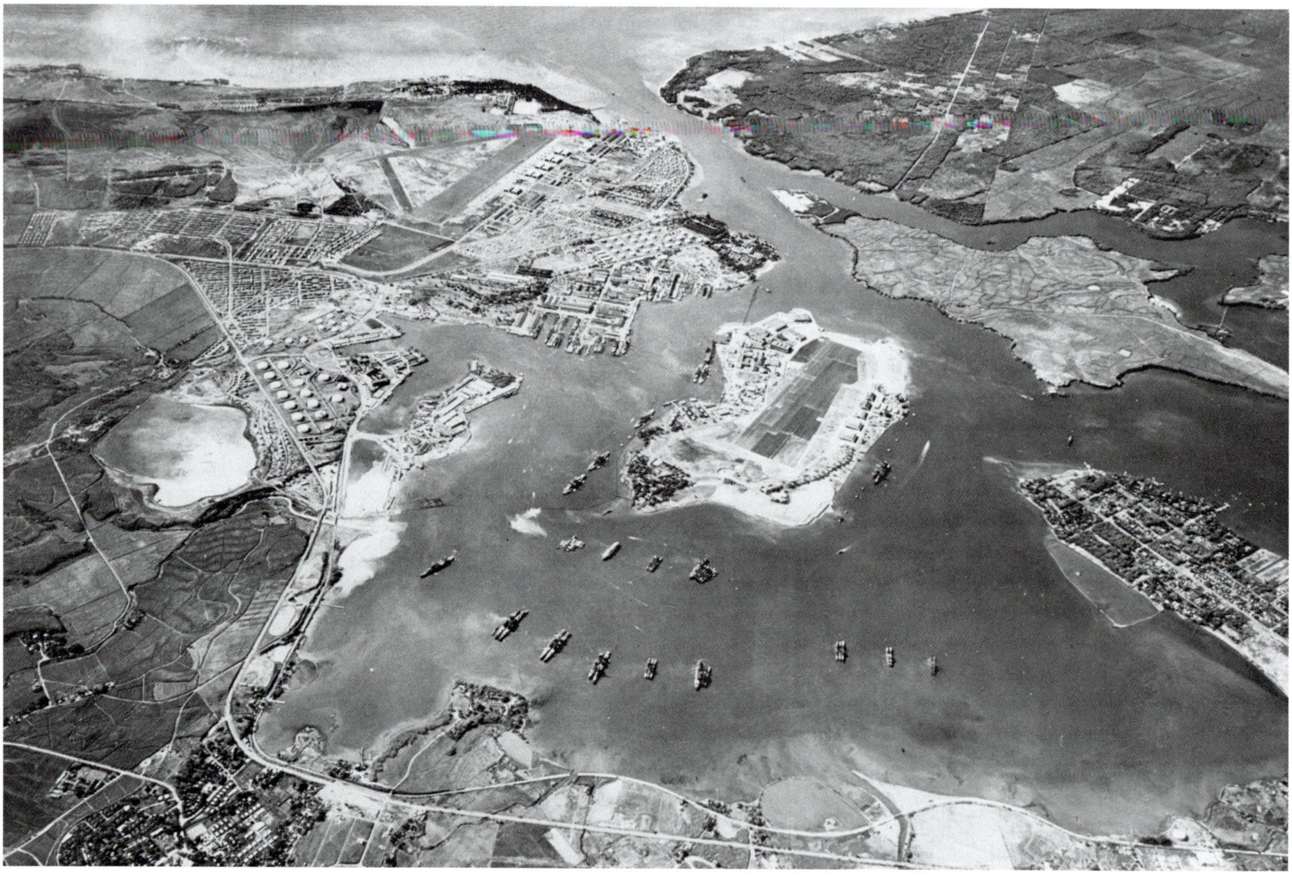

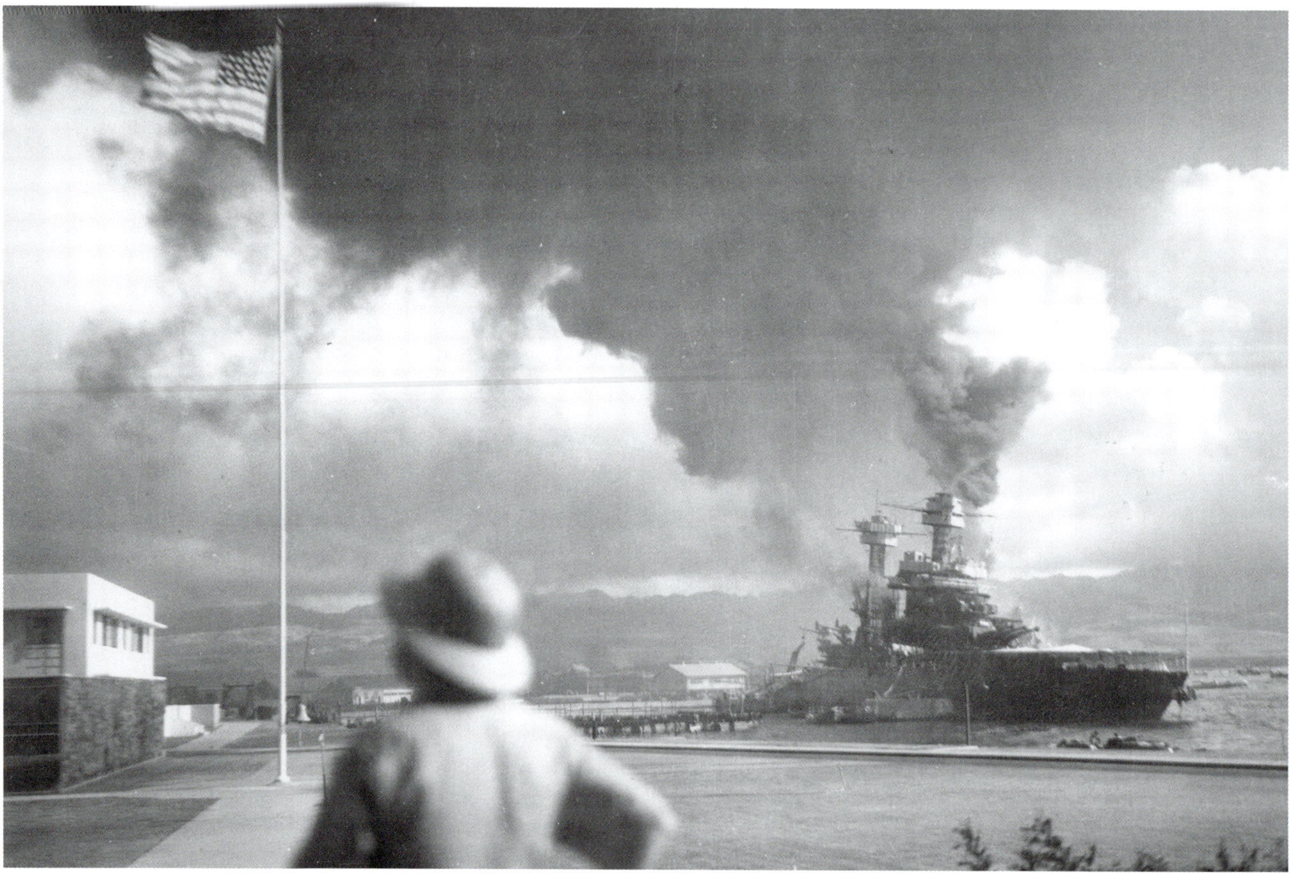

(**Opposite, above**) In this pre-war picture, we see Naval Station Pearl Harbor on the island of Oahu in Hawaii. It was then the home port for the US Navy Pacific Fleet. In the middle of the harbour is Ford Island Naval Air Station with ships arrayed around the island. Visible in the upper left-hand side of the image is Hickam Field, which opened in September 1938, for the United States Army Air Force (USAAF). (*US Navy*)

(**Opposite, below**) In this picture taken from Ford Island during the Japanese attack on Pearl Harbor on 7 December 1941 is the battleship USS *California*, one of eight US Navy battleships attacked. Four of the eight battleships were sunk, one was beached and the remaining three badly damaged. All but two were eventually returned to service. The Pacific Fleet's three aircraft carriers were not present during the enemy attack. (*US Navy*)

(**Above**) The first target of the Japanese attack on Pearl Harbor was Marine Corps Air Station Ewa, located 7 miles west of Pearl Harbor. It is seen here in a pre-war photo composite. Originally opened in 1925 as a facility for airships, it became an airfield in February 1941. Note the aircraft on the field are all neatly lined up to prevent attack by saboteurs. Sadly, this made them easy targets for the attacking Japanese aircraft. (*National Archives*)

(**Above**) From a distance can be seen the thick black smoke caused by the burning of highly flammable aviation fuel stored at Marine Corps Air Station Ewa on the morning of 7 December 1941. Not a single Marine aircraft made it into the air to defend Ewa. Rather, two USAAF fighters showed up and shot down three of the attacking Japanese aircraft. (USMC)

(**Opposite, above**) Pictured is what was left of a Vought SB2U Vindicator dive-bomber of the Marine Scout Bombing Squadron (VMSB) following the Japanese attack on Marine Corps Air Station Ewa on the morning of 7 December 1941. Of the forty-seven Marine aircraft present that morning thirty-three burned, with all but two of the remaining fourteen planes suffering major damage. (USMC)

(**Opposite, below**) Taken on the parade field of the Marine Corps barracks located at Pearl Harbor Naval Base is this shot of Marines looking towards the harbour and the massive palls of black smoke rising in the distance from the burning US Navy ships. It is difficult to discern in the photograph, but the Marines have emplaced a 3in anti-aircraft gun on the parade field. (USMC)

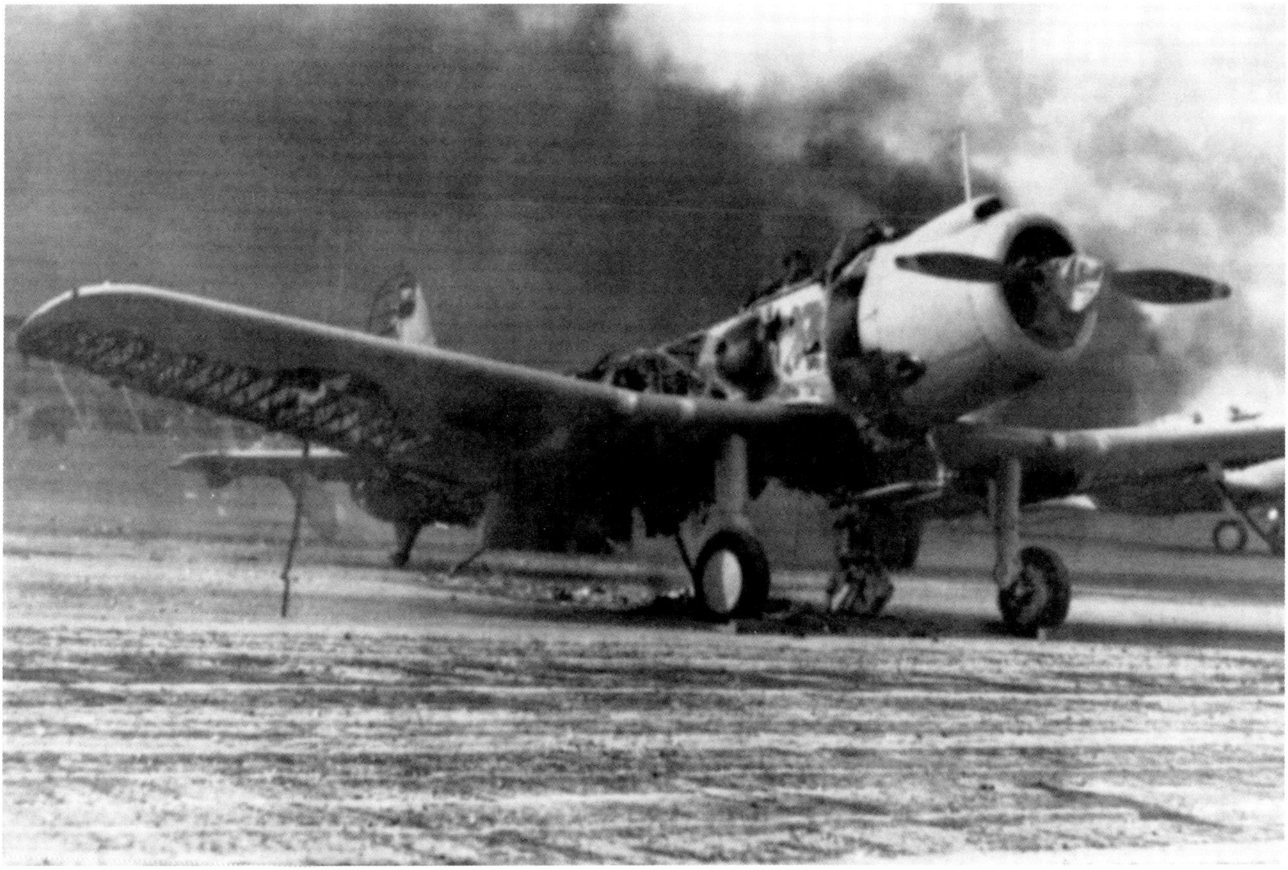

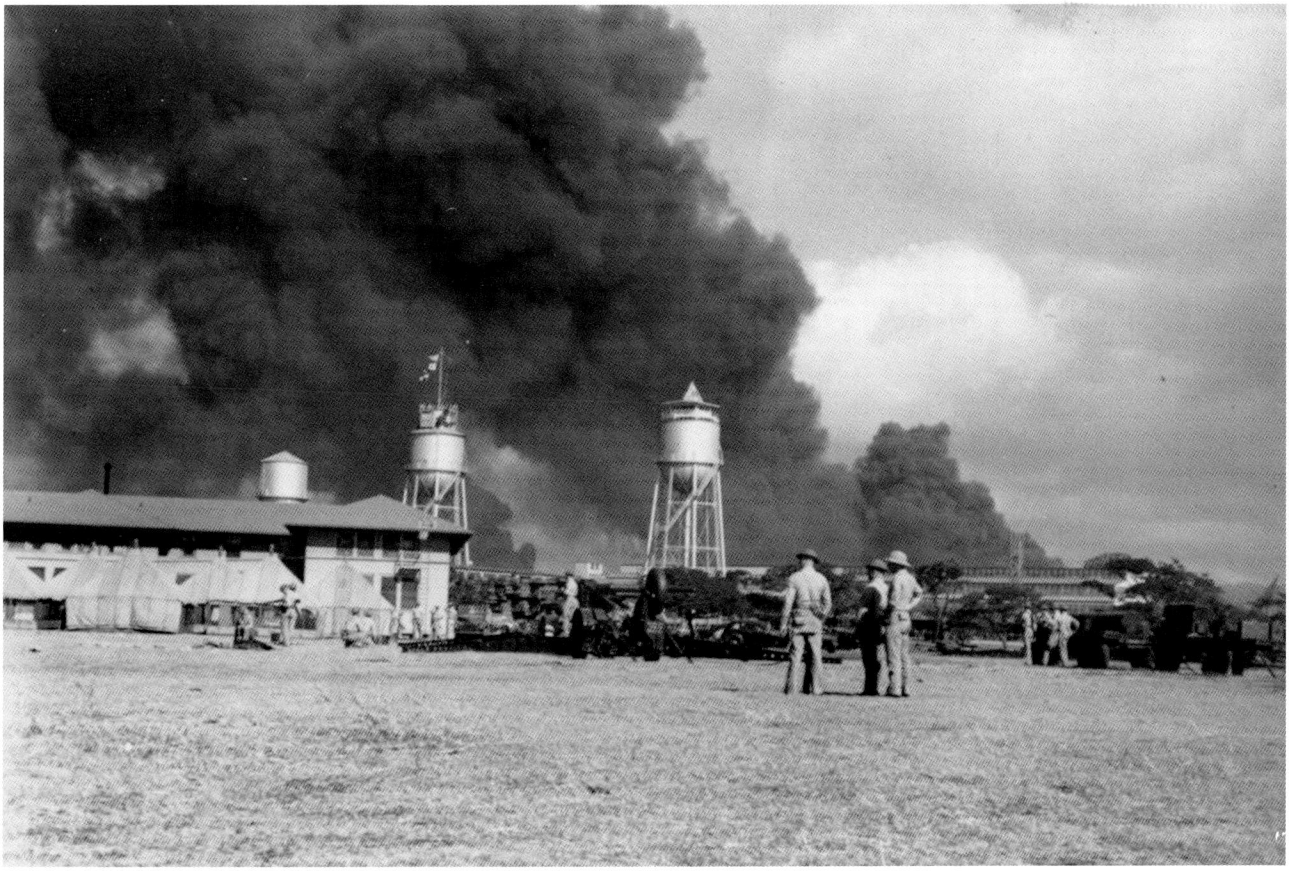

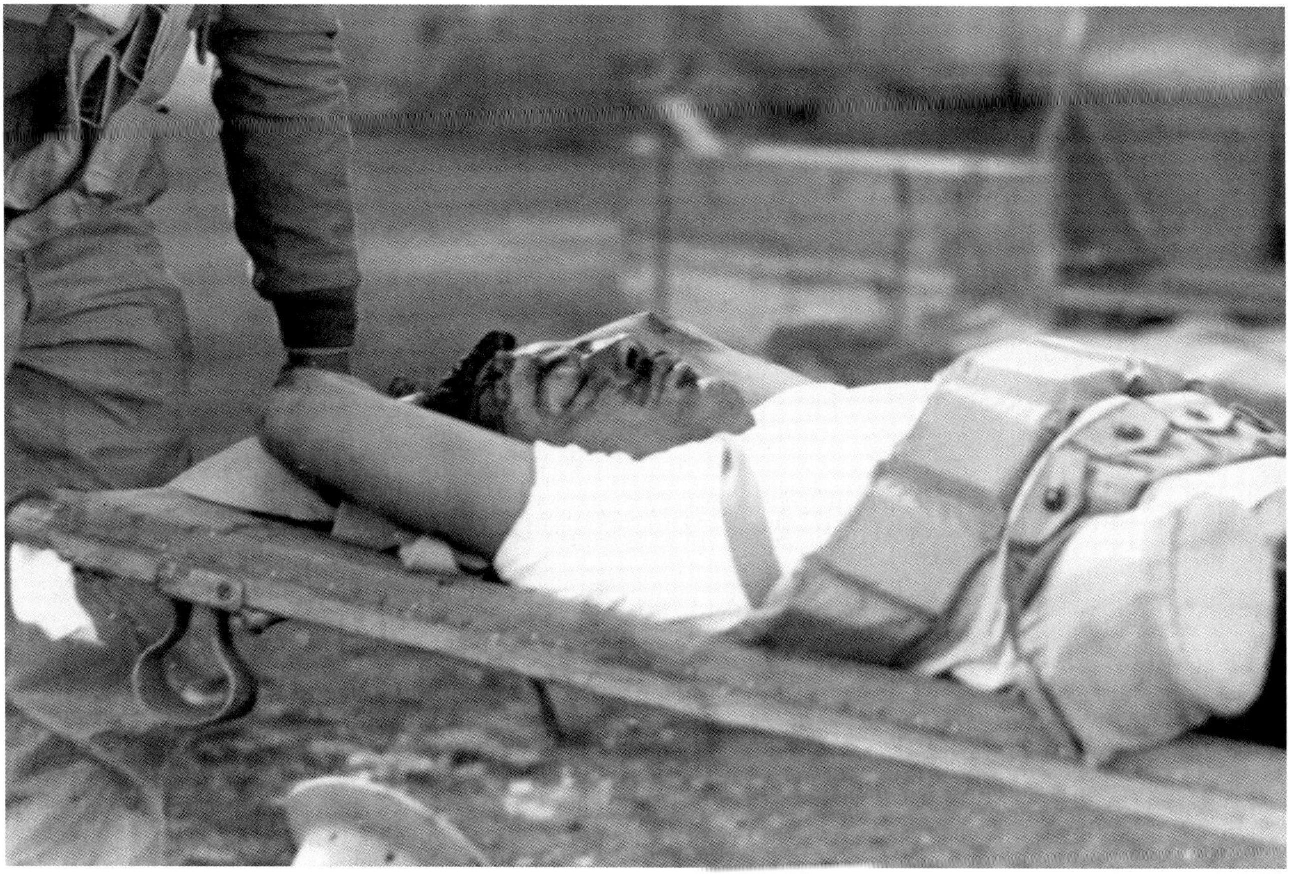

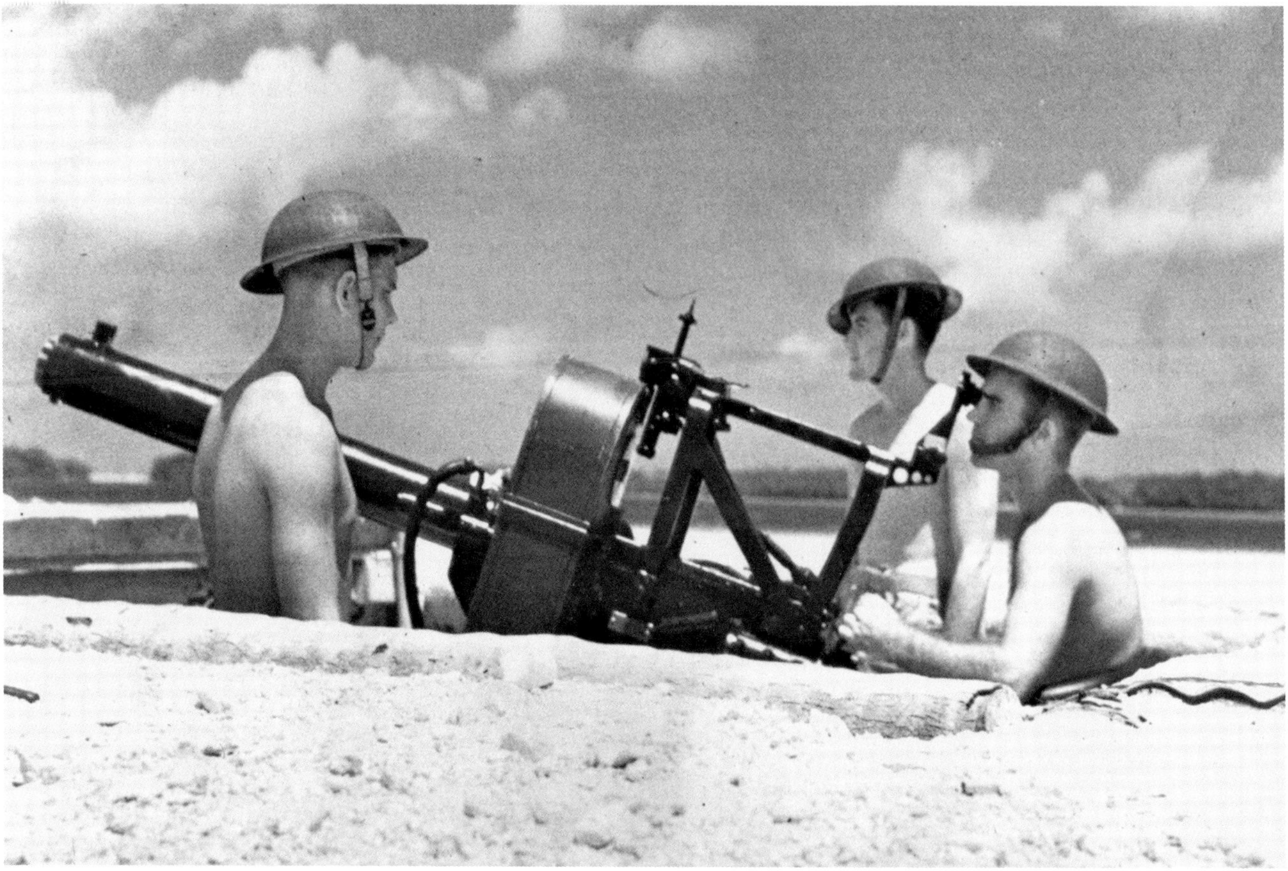

(**Opposite, above**) A wounded Marine is being taken to an aid station on a stretcher with his ammunition pouches still on. As the Japanese attack continued, the Marines of the defence battalions stationed at Pearl Harbor put into service as many machine guns as could be found and manned. As the ammunition for their 3in anti-aircraft gun was stored 27 miles away, it did not reach the Marines until the enemy planes had departed. (USMC)

(**Above**) A Marine rifle squad fires a volley over caskets laid to rest following the Japanese attack on Pearl Harbor the day before. During the attack, the Japanese sank nine US Navy ships and damaged twenty-one more; they also destroyed 188 American military aircraft and damaged a further thirty-one. Total US Marine Corps and US Navy losses were 2,086 killed, with the US Army having 194 men killed. (USMC)

(**Opposite, below**) Fearing another aerial attack by the Japanese Navy, the anti-aircraft defences at Marine Corps Air Station Ewa and Naval Base Pearl Harbor were increased. Here we see the men of a Marine Corps defence battalion at their drill station. They are manning a water-cooled M2 .50-calibre machine gun mounted on the tripod mount M3. The water jacket around the barrel contains 10 gallons of water. (USMC)

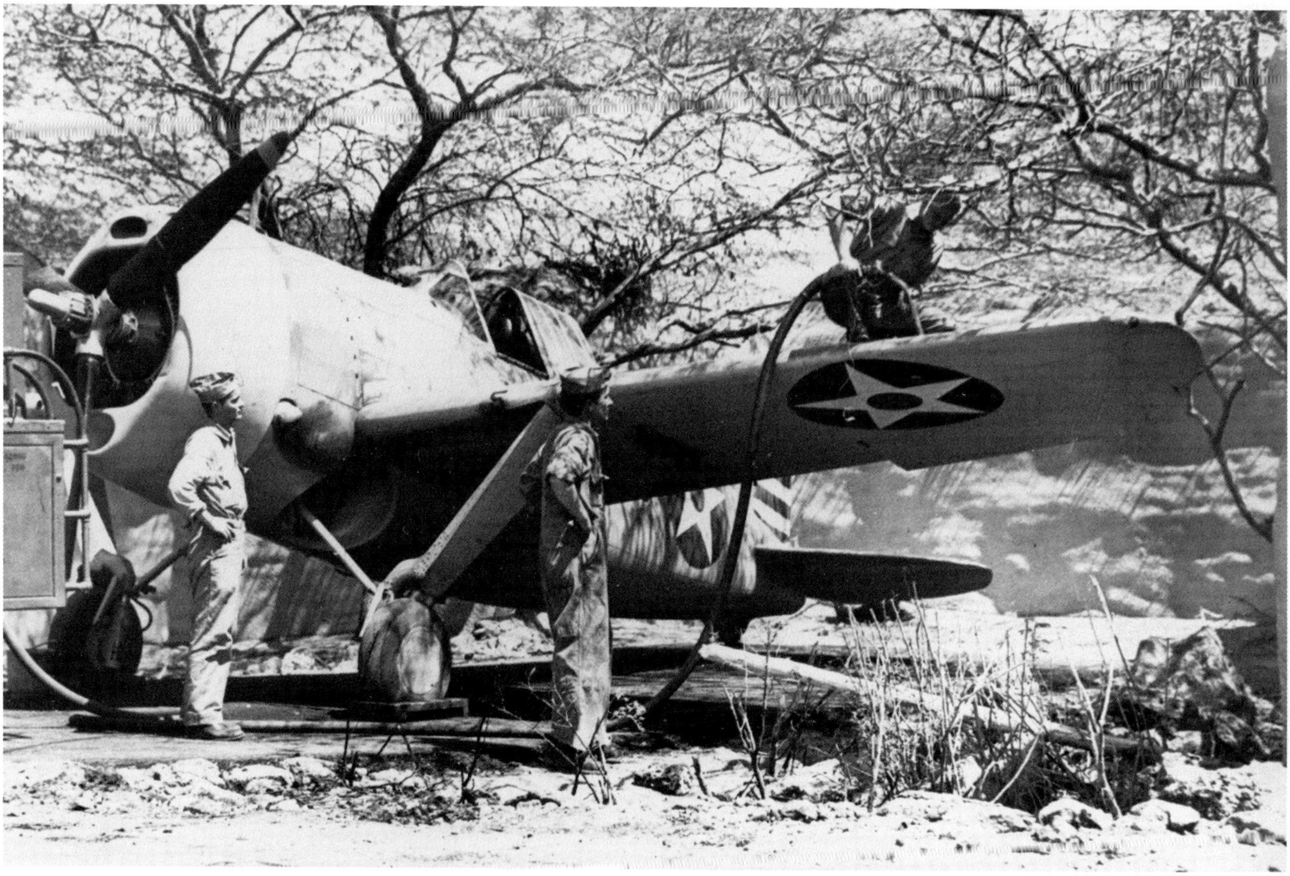

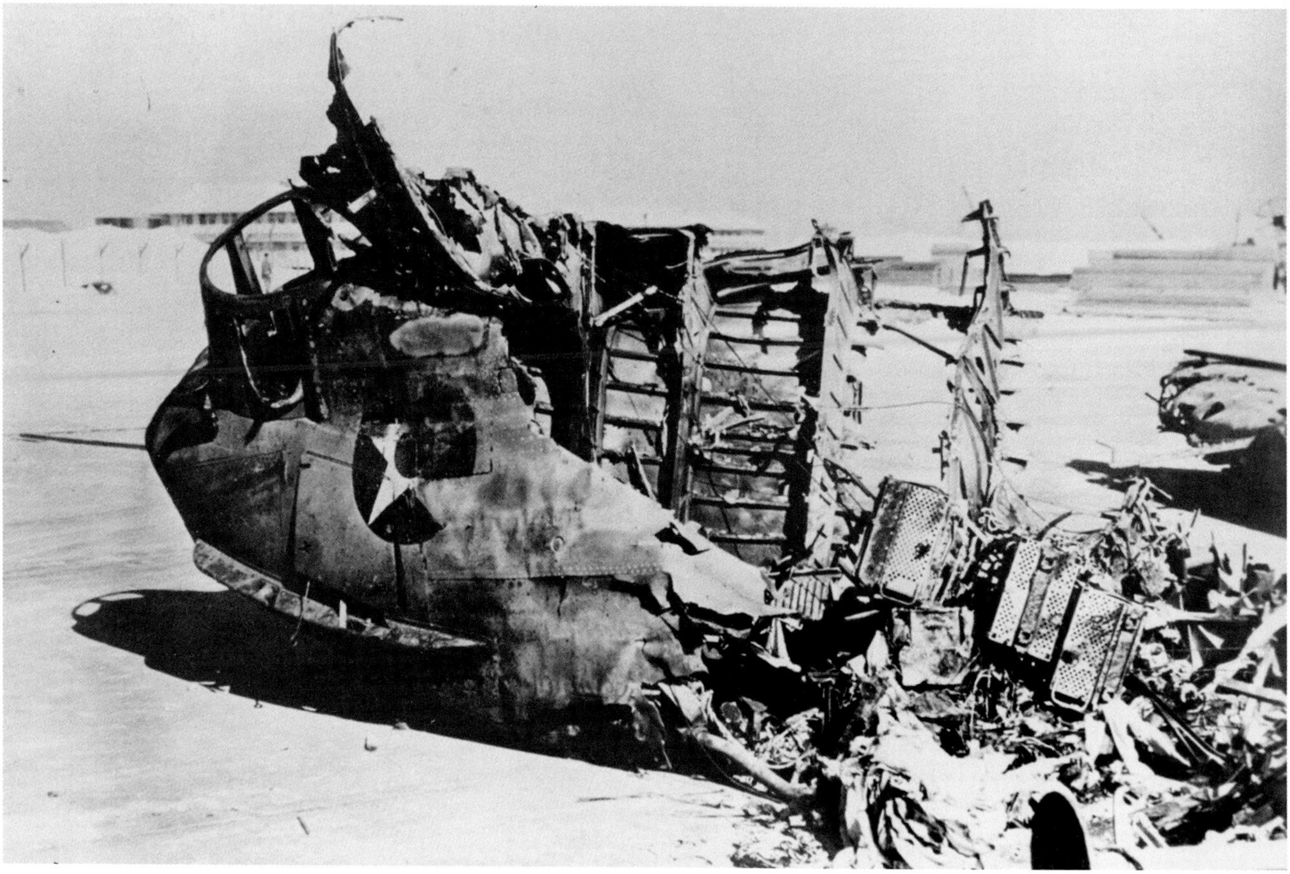

(**Opposite, above**) Following the Japanese attack on Marine Corps Air Station Ewa on 7 December 1941, replacement aircraft were both dispersed and parked in revetments around the field as seen in this picture of a ground crew fuelling a Brewster F2A-3 Buffalo fighter prior to a training mission. Obsolete by 1940, a small number were operated by the Marine Corps until replaced by the Grumman F4F fighter. (USMC)

(**Above**) Shown here in a pictured dated 24 November 1941 is the American-occupied atoll of Midway in the Central Pacific. On the same day that the Japanese Navy attacked Pearl Harbor, two Japanese destroyers bombarded the island. This was done to neutralize the atoll's airfield and seaplane base and prevent any of its aircraft interfering with the withdrawal of the Japanese Navy aircraft carriers whose planes attacked Pearl Harbor. (US Navy)

(**Opposite, below**) The only aircraft based at Midway Atoll prior to the Japanese attack on 7 December 1941 were seven US Navy twin-engine PBY Patrol Bombers. Besides scoring hits on some of the 5in coast artillery guns of a Marine defence battalion and a number of structures on the island, one of the destroyer salvos struck and destroyed one of the parked PBY Patrol Bombers as seen here. (US Navy)

Wake Island seen here in a pre-war picture was the westernmost atoll occupied by the American military in the Central Pacific. It was defended by a Marine defence battalion detachment and a fighter squadron of twelve Grumman F4F Wildcat fighters. On 11 December 1941, the Japanese Navy attempted to land troops on the island but was beaten back with heavy losses. However, they returned on 23 December 1941 with a larger force and successfully captured Wake. (US Navy)

On 12 December 1941, Marine aviator Captain Henry T. Elrod (seen here) single-handedly attacked a formation of twenty-two Japanese planes over Wake Island, shooting down two. He then attacked the Japanese Navy warships off Wake and sank a destroyer when his small bombs detonated the depth-charges on the stern of the ship. When he no longer had a plane to fly he organized and led the Marines on the island to repulse Japanese landings until he was killed. For his fearless exploits, he was posthumously awarded the Medal of Honor. (USMC)

Wrecked Grumman F4F Wildcat fighters of Marine Fighter Squadron 211 (VMF-211), photographed on the Wake airfield sometime after the Japanese captured the island on 23 December 1941. There appear to be at least seven F4Fs in the picture. The plane in the foreground, 211-F-11, was flown by Captain Henry T. Elrod during the 11 December 1941 attack that sank the Japanese destroyer *Kisaragi*. (USMC)

The vast expanse of the Pacific Ocean and the areas over which the American and Japanese military fought during the Second World War are seen in this simplified map. Once the US Navy Pacific Fleet was out of action following Pearl Harbor, the Japanese military quickly moved eastward to take such locations as Wake Island and also southwards to seize the Philippines and South-East Asia. (USMC)

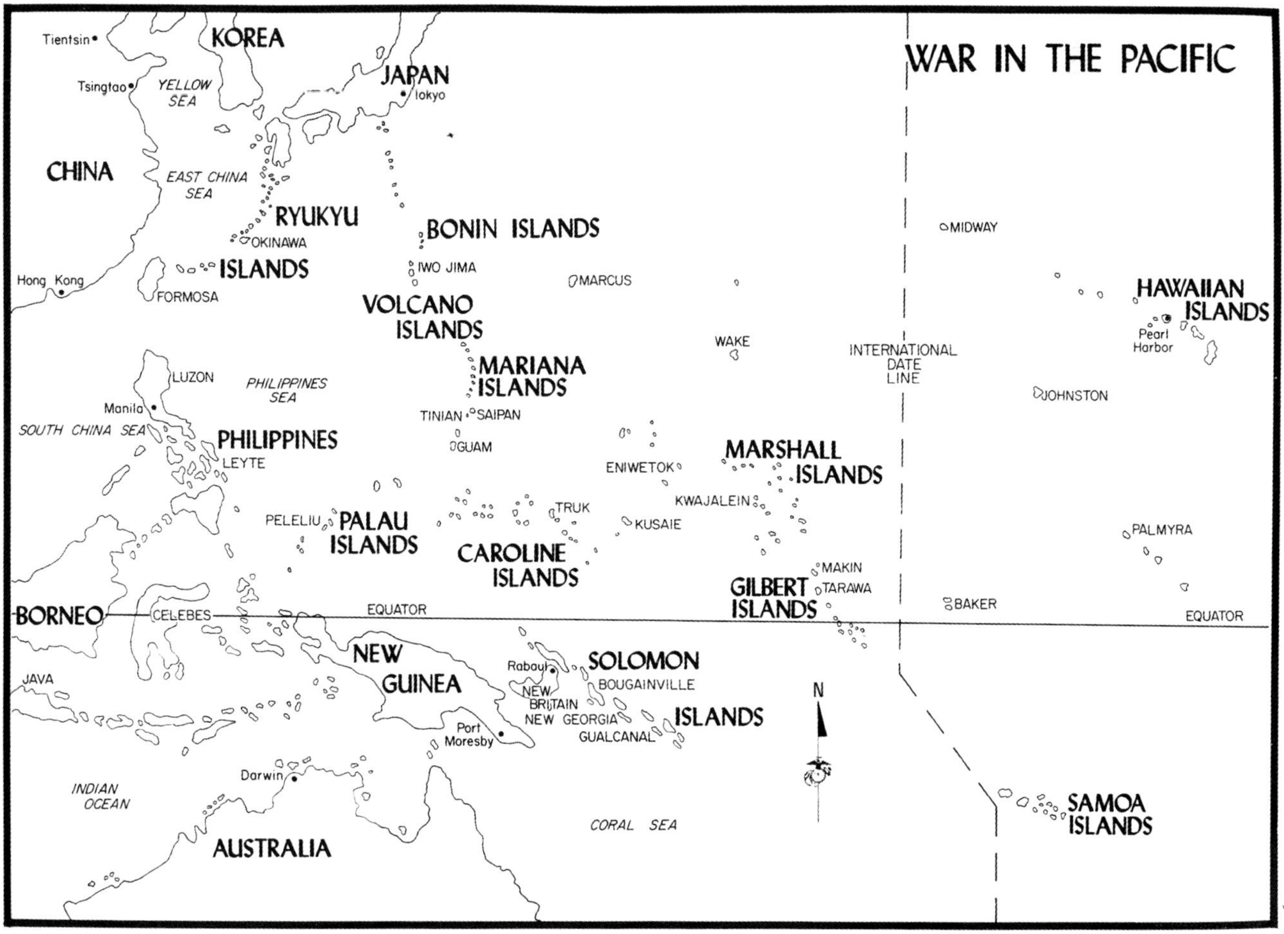

(**Above**) The Japanese invasion of the Philippines had begun on 8 December 1941. Japanese troops secured the main Philippine island of Luzon on 9 April 1942, with their capture of 76,000 American and Filipino troops on the Bataan Peninsula. The last organized American and Filipino military units withdrew to the island of Corregidor, located in Manila Bay. However, it fell on 6 May 1942, as seen in this poor quality picture of Japanese troops and tanks on the island following its surrender. (USMC)

(**Opposite, above**) The Japanese seizure of the small island of Tulagi in the Florida Island chain and the much larger nearby island of Guadalcanal in May 1942 was a threat to the supply lines between the United States and Australia and New Zealand. The 1st Marine Division was ordered to prepare for the capture of Tulagi in June 1942. When it became known that the Japanese might be building an airfield at Lunga Point on Guadalcanal, that island's seizure was given priority and also assigned to the 1st Marine Division. (USMC)

(**Opposite, below**) Marines of the 1st Marine Division pass up the gangway of a transport ship that will take them to Guadalcanal and Operation WATCHTOWER (or SHOESTRING as the Marines called it). When called to action for the planned invasion of the island of Tulagi, elements of the division were located all over the Pacific. The only readily available troops for the upcoming invasions were in New Zealand. (USMC)

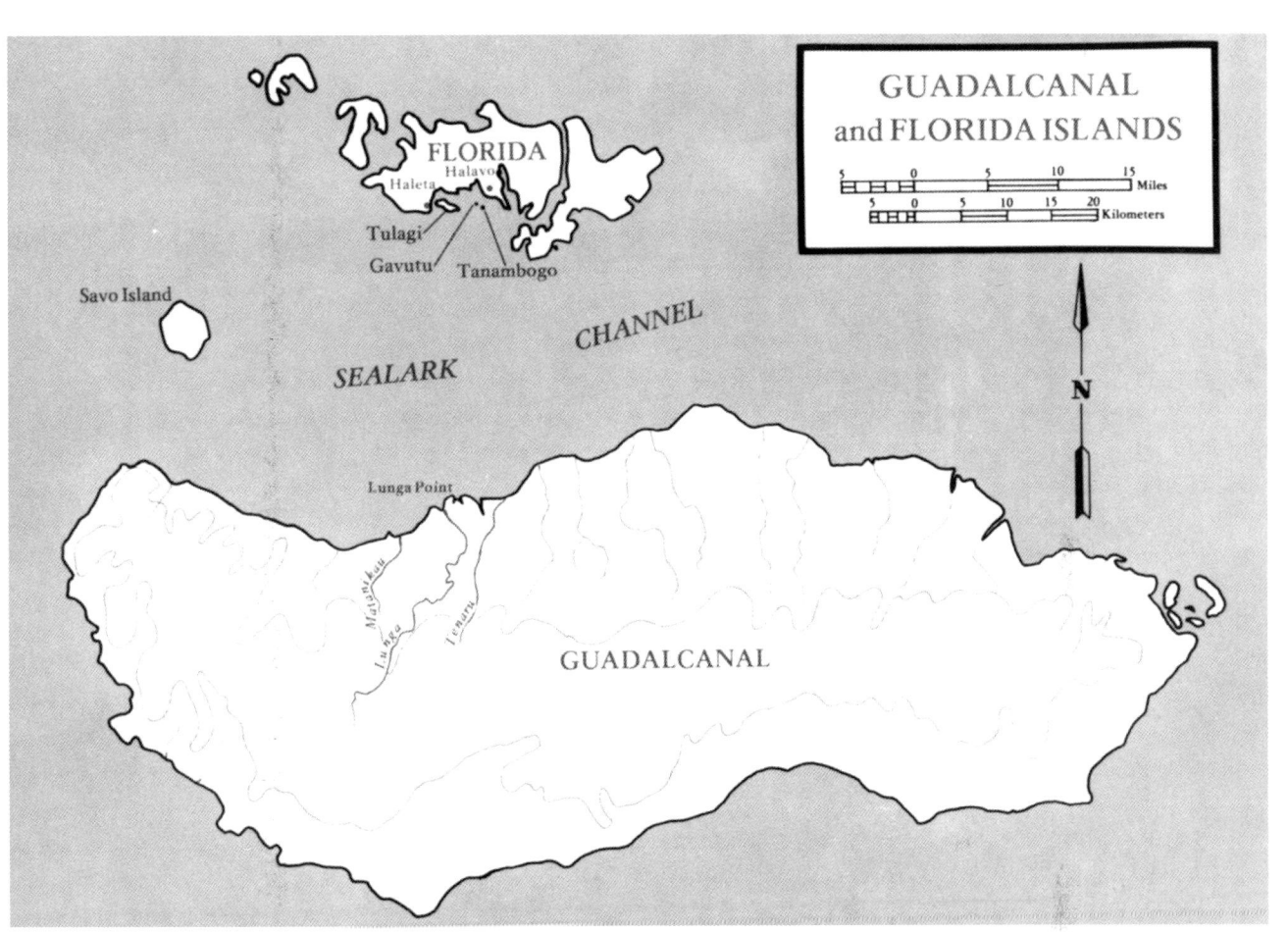

GUADALCANAL and FLORIDA ISLANDS

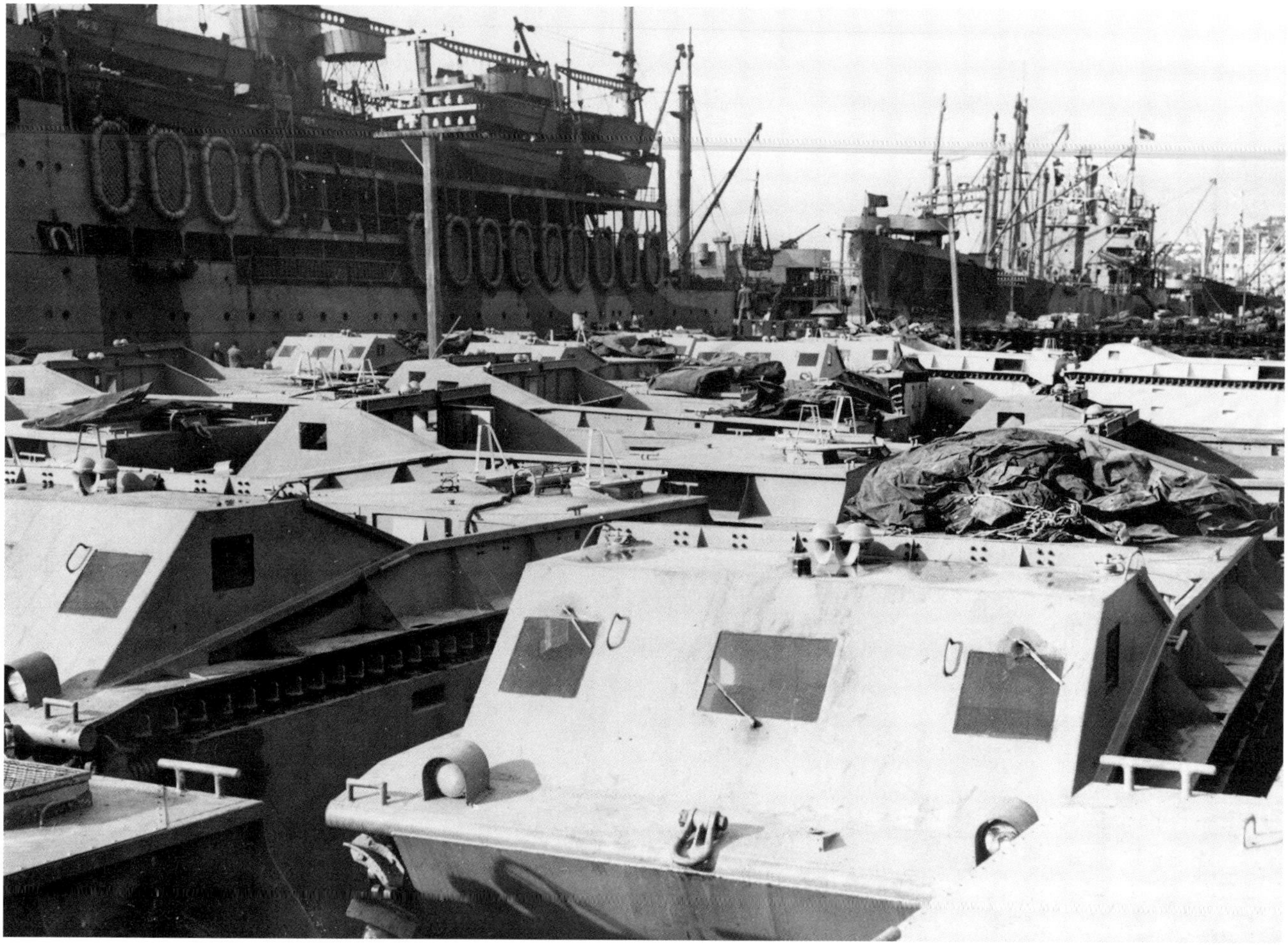

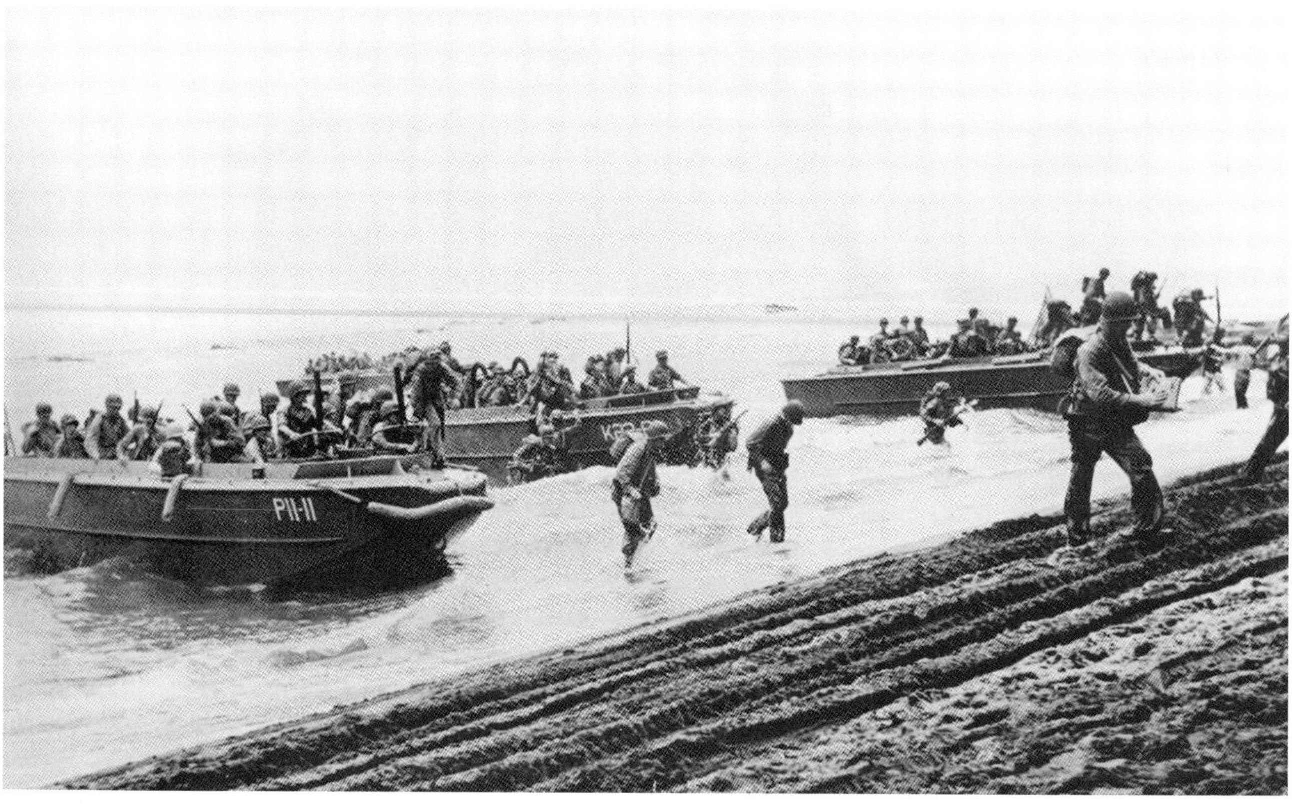
P11-11

(**Opposite, above**) Among the various pieces of equipment to be loaded on the transport ships tasked with taking the 1st Marine Division to Guadalcanal was the brand-new LVT-1 (Landing Vehicle Tracked No. 1) pictured here. It was not seen as a combat vehicle but simply as an unarmoured logistical support vehicle. The cargo compartment of the vehicle could hold up to 4,500lb of matériel or twenty-four Marines. (*USMC*)

(**Above**) On 7 August 1942, Marines of either the 1st or 2nd Division are shown climbing down what were referred to as 'scramble nets' into Landing Craft, Personnel (Large) (LCP(L)). It was these boats that would transport them to the beaches of Guadalcanal at a maximum speed of 8 knots. The LCP(L) had a crew of three and could accommodate up to thirty-six Marines in combat gear. (*USMC*)

(**Opposite, below**) The Marines seen here are disembarking from the bow and sides of the LCP(L) on to Guadalcanal. The wooden boat did not have a hinged ramp at its bow as did subsequent shallow-water landing craft. It had entered US Navy service in 1940 and was based on a design by the Eureka Tug-Boat Company of New Orleans. Actual construction of the LCP(L) was awarded to Higgins Industries of New Orleans. (*USMC*)

Taken from an American aircraft is this picture of Henderson Field located at Lunga Point on the island of Guadalcanal. It had been seized by the Marines without any enemy resistance on 8 August 1942 incomplete and undamaged. It was placed into operational service on 20 August 1942 when nineteen F4F Wildcat fighters of VMF-223 and twelve SBD Dauntless dive-bombers of VMSB-232 landed. They had been brought to Guadalcanal by the prototype US Navy 'aircraft escort vessel' USS *Long Island* AVG-1. *(USMC)*

Despite the lack of resistance to the initial landings of the Marines on Guadalcanal on 7 August 1942, the Marines knew that Japanese counter-attacks were to be expected. No time was wasted and the task of building a defensive perimeter around the landing zones and Henderson Field began. Here we see Marines laying out barbed wire, an item that was in short supply throughout the campaign. They are wearing the new two-piece M1 helmet introduced into service in the spring and summer of 1941. (USMC)

Major General Alexander A. Vandergrift seen here was appointed commander of the 1st Marine Division in early 1942 and led it throughout the Guadalcanal campaign. He was awarded the Medal of Honor for his 'tenacity, courage and resourcefulness' during the operation that took place between August and December 1942. He became commandant of the Marine Corps on 1 January 1944. (USMC)

The 37mm gun M3A1 pictured in this Marine Corps sandbagged emplacement on Guadalcanal was primarily designed as an anti-tank gun. However, it was also provided with a very useful canister round designated the M2 that contained 122 0.375in steel balls packed in resin. When firing the canister round the 37mm gun had a maximum effective range of 250 yards and proved deadly against massed Japanese infantry attacks. (USMC)

Marines on Guadalcanal are shown here armed with a .30 Browning air-cooled light machine gun designated the M1919A4. The Marine general in charge of the island had assumed in the weeks after the American landings that he was facing only stragglers rather than any organized resistance. Unbeknown to him, the Japanese had begun landing thousands of troops on Guadalcanal as of 12 August 1942. (*USMC*)

The first major attempt to retake Guadalcanal from the Marines was assigned to Colonel Kiyonao Ichiki of the Japanese Army seen here, who selected approximately 2,000 men from the 28th Infantry Regiment for the task. However, only half his force had been landed on the island when the Marines encountered some of them at midday on 19 August 1942. This prompted Colonel Ichiki to prematurely launch his assault on the Marine defensive lines on the nights of 20 and 21 August 1942. (*National Archives*)

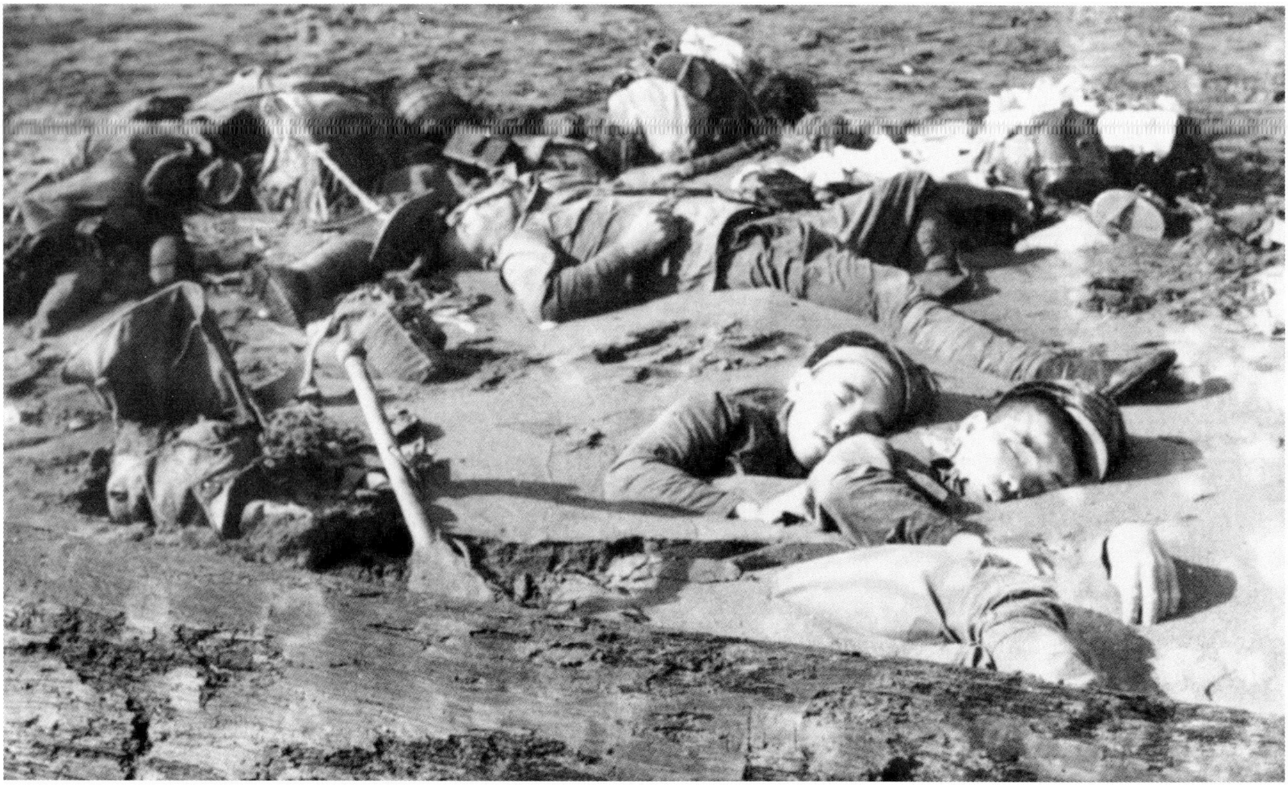

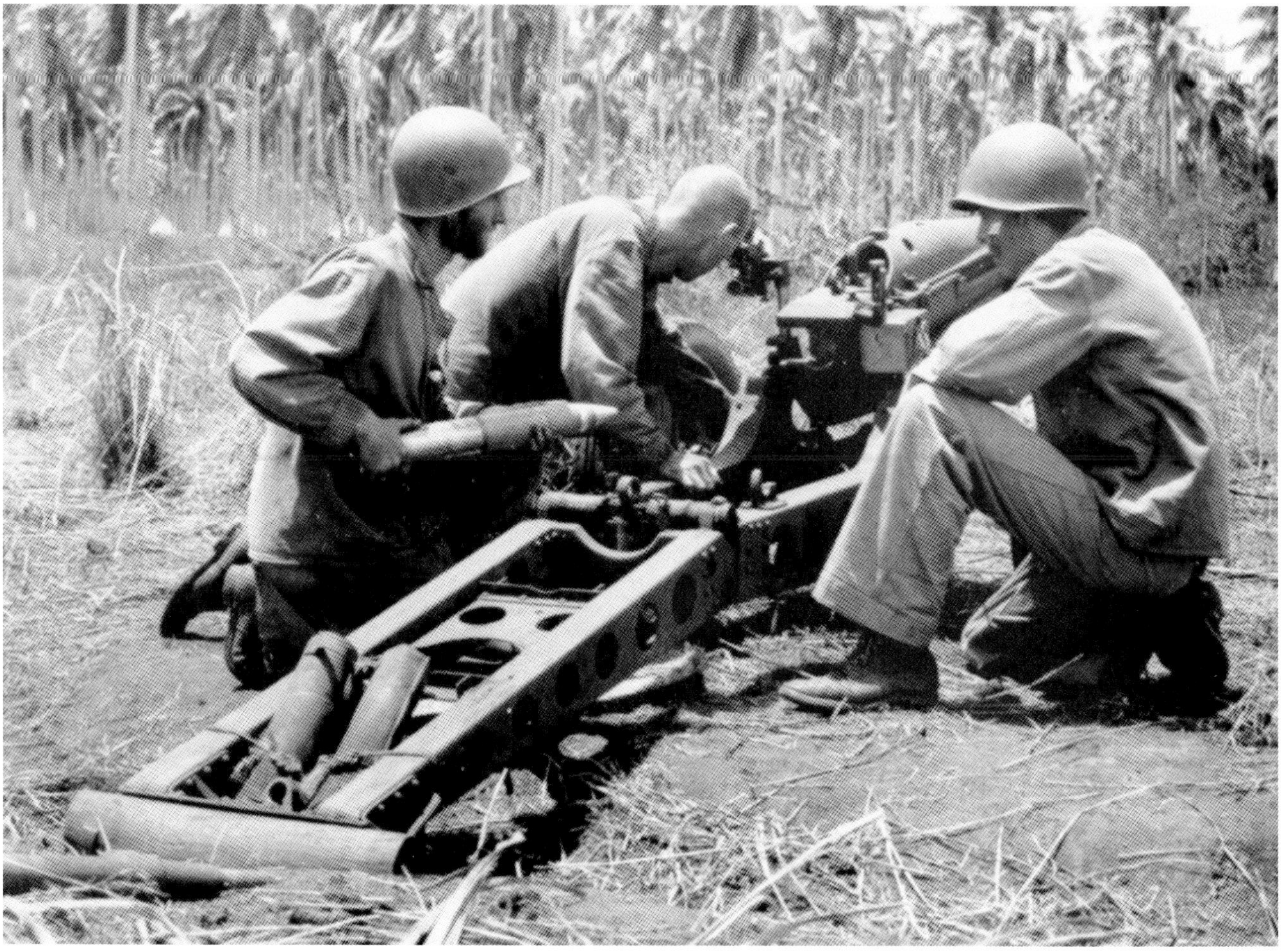

(**Opposite, above**) Colonel Ichiki's 1,000 men began their attack along a waterway known to the Marines as the Tenaru River. His men would run into a wall of fire from Marine machine guns, anti-tank guns and light tanks. In the end, the Marines counted 871 Japanese corpses and took fifteen prisoners. Between 12 and 14 September 1942, the Japanese Army's 35th Infantry Brigade tried to penetrate Marine lines, but failed with heavy losses. (*USMC*)

(**Above**) In response to the failure of their first two ground offensives on Guadalcanal, the Japanese military increased the ground forces committed to battle on the island. By mid-October 1942, the Japanese 17th Army had approximately two divisions on Guadalcanal, including tanks for the first time. On 20 October 1942, a Marine 37mm anti-tank gun disabled a Japanese Type 97 Chi Ha medium tank seen here that was abandoned by its crew. (*USMC*)

(**Opposite, below**) The Japanese 17th Army commander on Guadalcanal had planned for a two-pronged attack on the Marines' defensive perimeter. His initial plans had called for the attacks to begin on 21 October 1942. However, a number of unforeseen delays and communications problems caused the attacks to be delayed, with one prong launched on 23 October 1942 and the second on the following night. Marine artillery pieces such as the 75mm howitzer took a heavy toll on the enemy infantrymen during both Japanese attacks. (*USMC*)

(**Above**) Marines are seen here on Guadalcanal with an M1 81mm mortar. It had a maximum range of 3,290 yards firing a high-explosive (HE) round. The normal rate of fire for the weapon was eighteen rounds per minute. For very short periods of time the maximum rate of fire was thirty to thirty-five rounds per minute. It was mortars like this that played an important role in smashing the Japanese night attacks between 23 and 25 October 1942. *(USMC)*

(**Opposite, above**) The first Japanese attack on 23 October 1942 was aimed at the Marines' positions on the east bank of the Matanikau River. The attack was made by 600 infantrymen and nine tanks. A Marine 37mm anti-tank gun and a Marine half-track armed with a 75mm gun destroyed eight of the enemy tanks and a Marine infantryman employed a hand grenade to knock out the ninth. Supporting Marine artillery and mortars decimated the Japanese infantry, as seen in this picture taken on the following morning. *(USMC)*

(**Opposite, below**) Marine losses in stopping the Japanese attacks from 23 October through to 26 October 1942 stood at eighty killed. By contrast, the Japanese 17th Army lost anywhere between 2,000 and 3,000 men. Despite these defeats, the Japanese senior leadership knew the importance of Guadalcanal and launched more ground attacks on the island in November 1942 without any success. Beginning in early November 1942, the Marines had launched their own offensive operations against the remaining Japanese units on the island. *(USMC)*

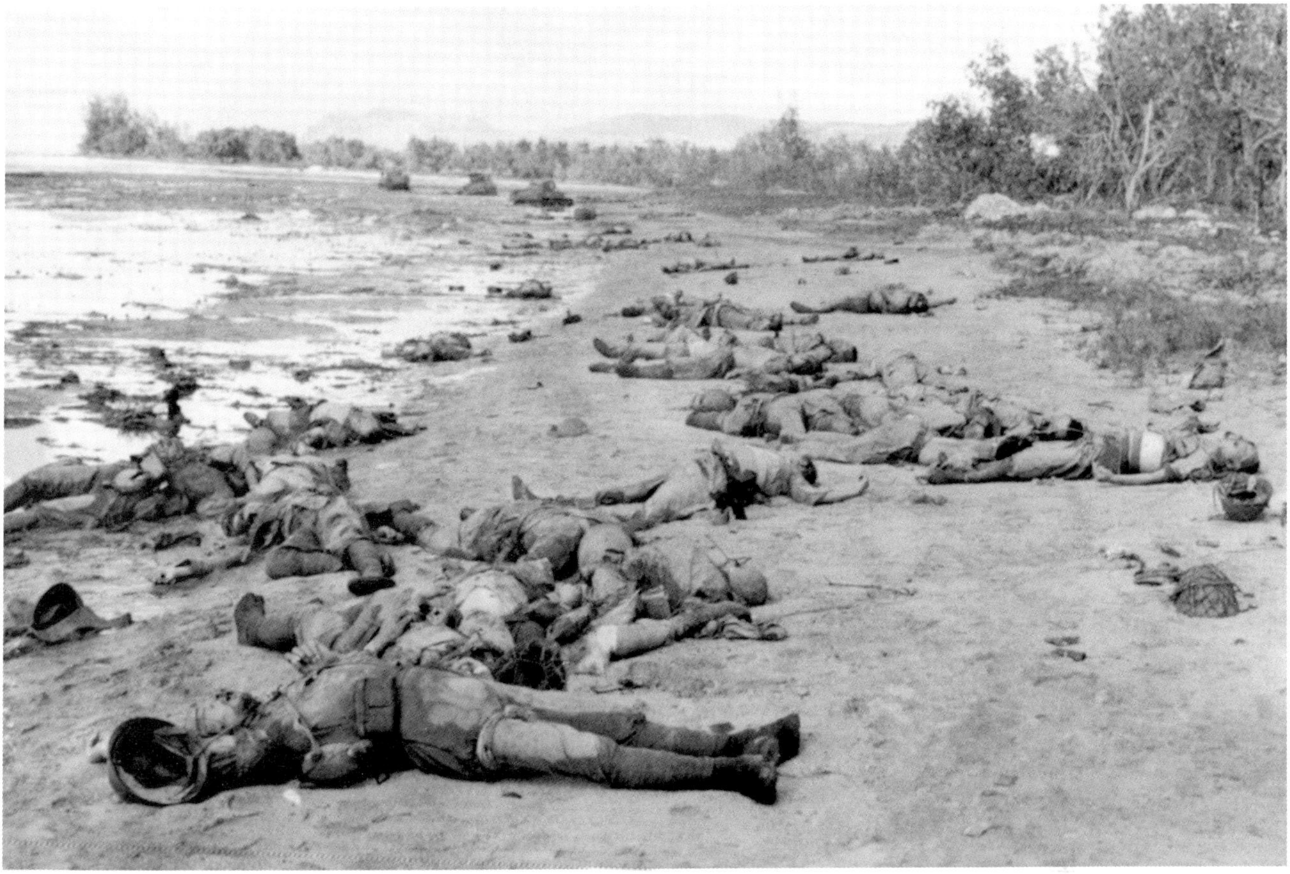

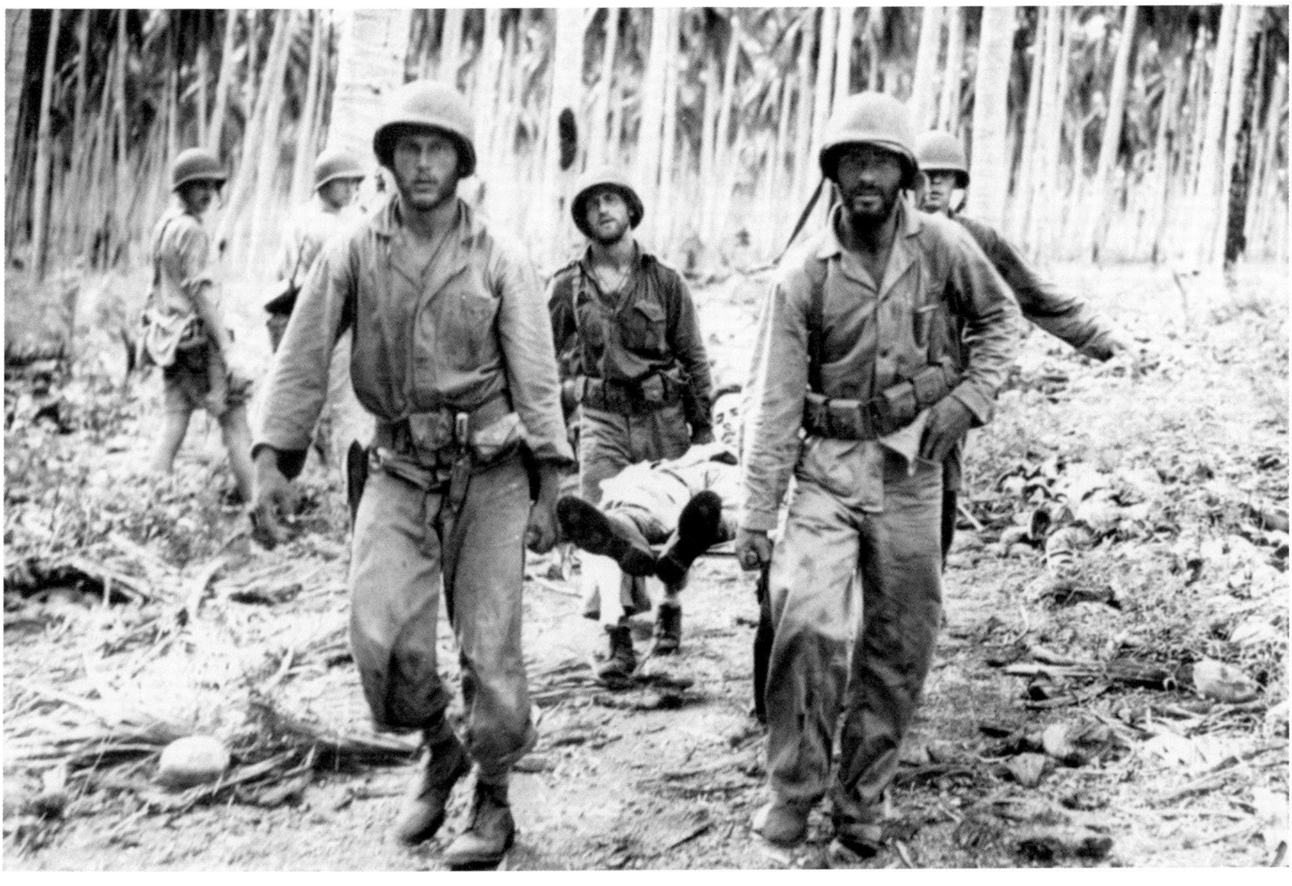

Even before the first Japanese ground offensive on Guadalcanal aimed at recapturing Henderson Field, the Japanese had begun an aerial campaign to neutralize the airfield. To prevent this from happening, an ad hoc force composed of Marine, US Navy and USAAF fighter squadrons nicknamed the 'Cactus Air Force' took up residence on Henderson Field. Shown here is a Marine F4F Wildcat that flew from Henderson Field. (USMC)

Pictured is Medal of Honor recipient Major John L. Smith who commanded Marine Fighting Squadron 223 (VMF-223) between 21 August and 15 September 1942. It comprised part of the multi-service Cactus Air Force that defended Guadalcanal and Henderson Field. His squadron accounted for eighty-three enemy aircraft during his time in command, with sixteen of those credited to him. During the remainder of the war he shot down another three Japanese aircraft. (USMC)

To protect Henderson Field on Guadalcanal from the almost endless Japanese aerial attacks that it endured for almost six months, the Marines employed a range of American-designed and built anti-aircraft weapons. A few abandoned Japanese anti-aircraft guns such as this triple-barrelled 25mm Type 96 were also pressed into service until the on-hand ammunition supply was exhausted. (USMC)

(**Above**) The largest anti-aircraft gun employed by the Marine defence battalions in protecting Henderson Field was the 90mm M1 seen here. It fired a high-explosive (HE) projectile weighing 23.4lb that left the barrel with a muzzle velocity of 2,700 feet per second. The maximum effective ceiling for the weapon was 39,500ft. The combination of gun and mount weighed in at 32,300lb. (USMC)

(**Opposite, above**) To aim the 90mm anti-aircraft gun M1 at approaching enemy aircraft there was the M9A1 Director, a primitive analogue computer, and the 13.5ft-long stereoscopic optical height-finder seen here on Guadalcanal designated the M1A1. It continuously determined the slant range and altitude of aircraft in clear weather and daylight conditions. For poor weather or night-time operations there was a height-finding radar unit designated the SCR-547. (USMC)

(**Opposite, below**) To assist in defending Guadalcanal from Japanese Naval bombardment, the Marine defence battalions assigned to the island were equipped with fixed 5in guns as seen here. Due to their weight and size, they were time-consuming to move and emplace. They would eventually be replaced in the Marine defence battalions by towed 155mm guns: initially the First World War-era M1918M1 and then the modernized M1A1. (USMC)

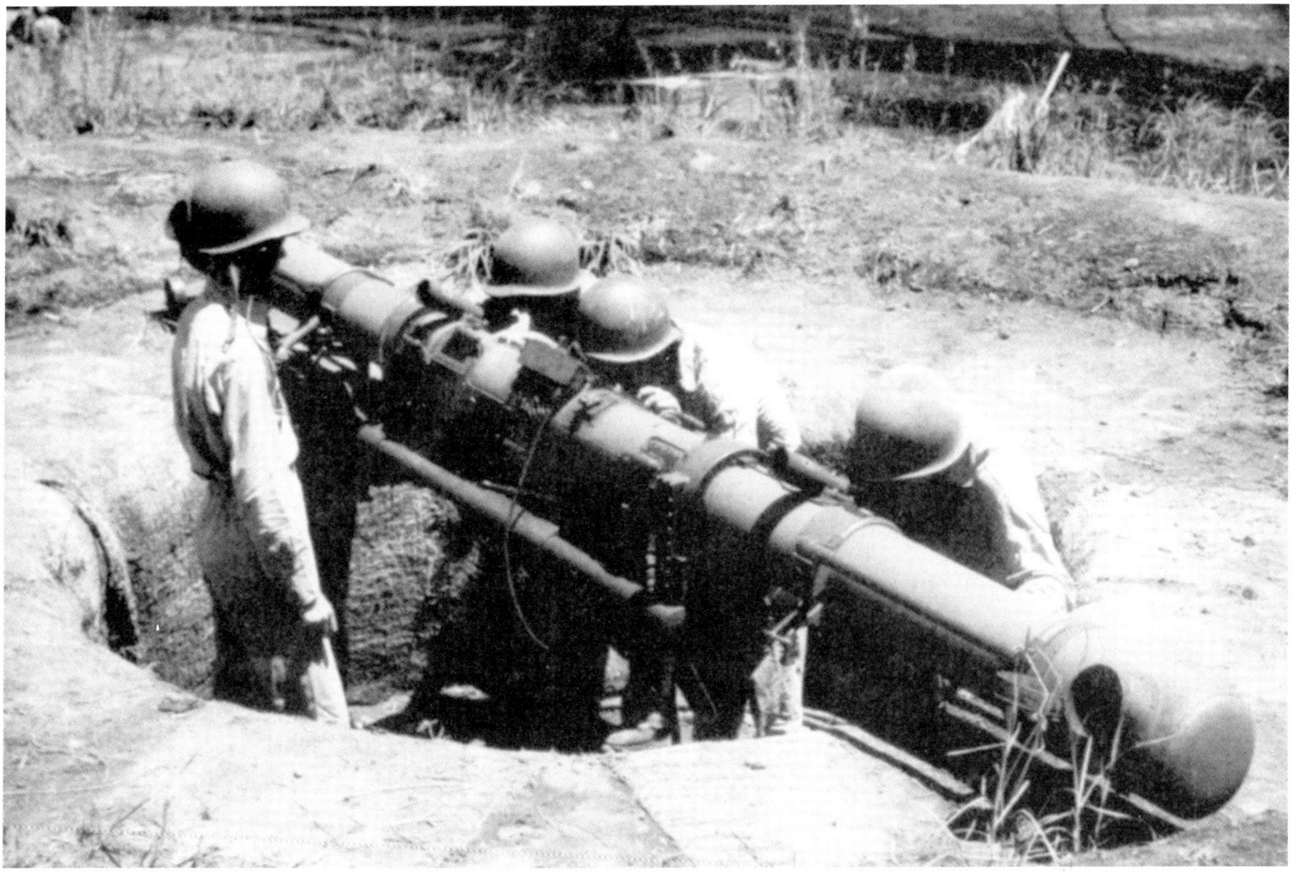

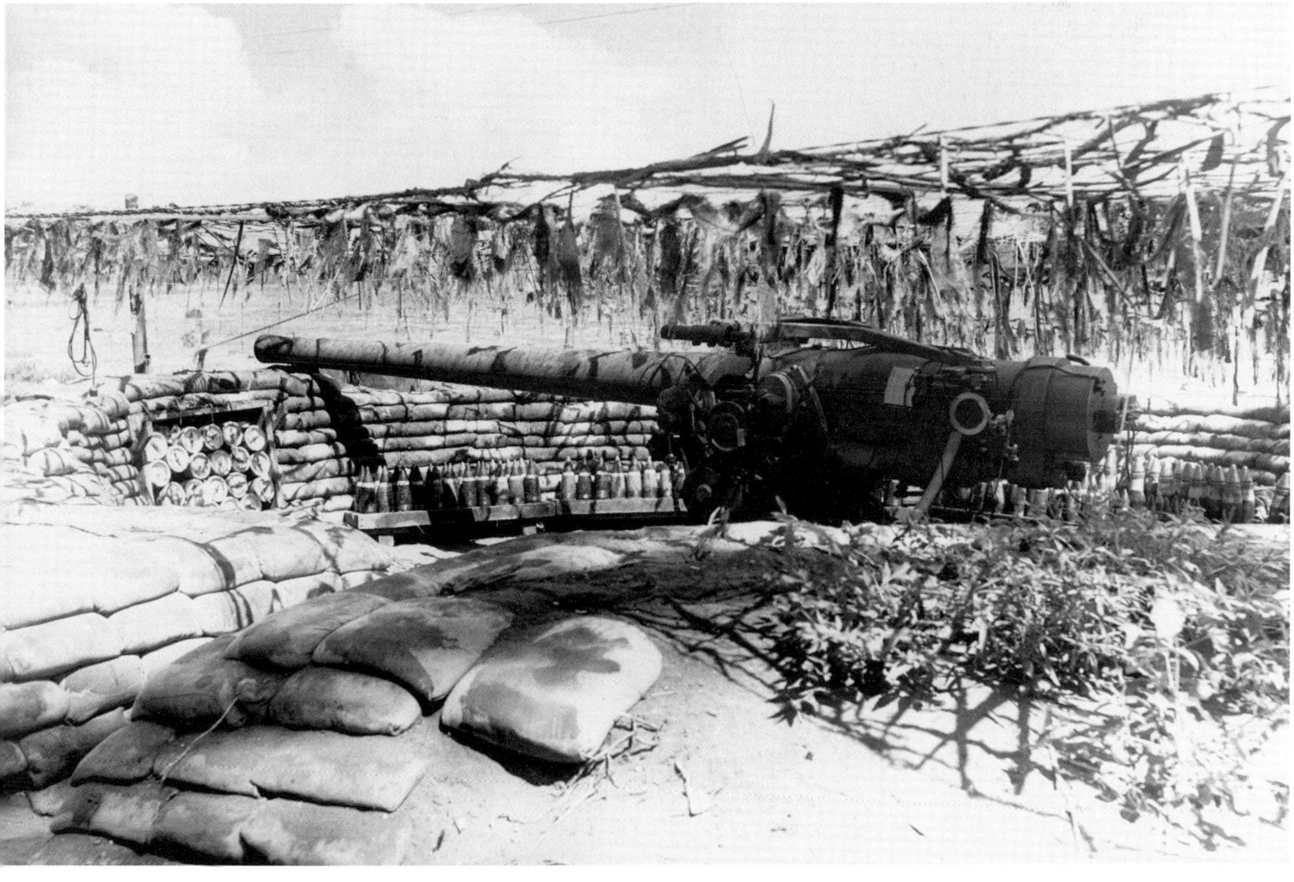

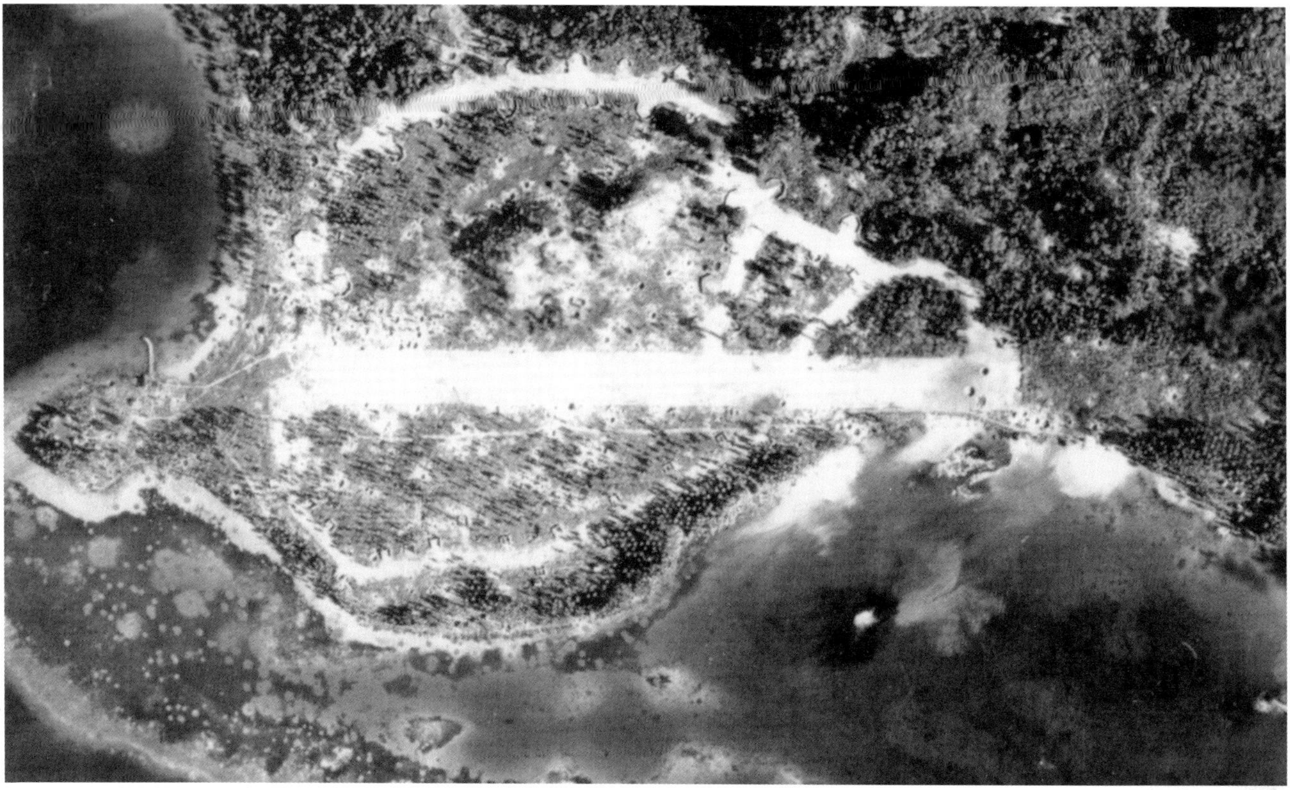

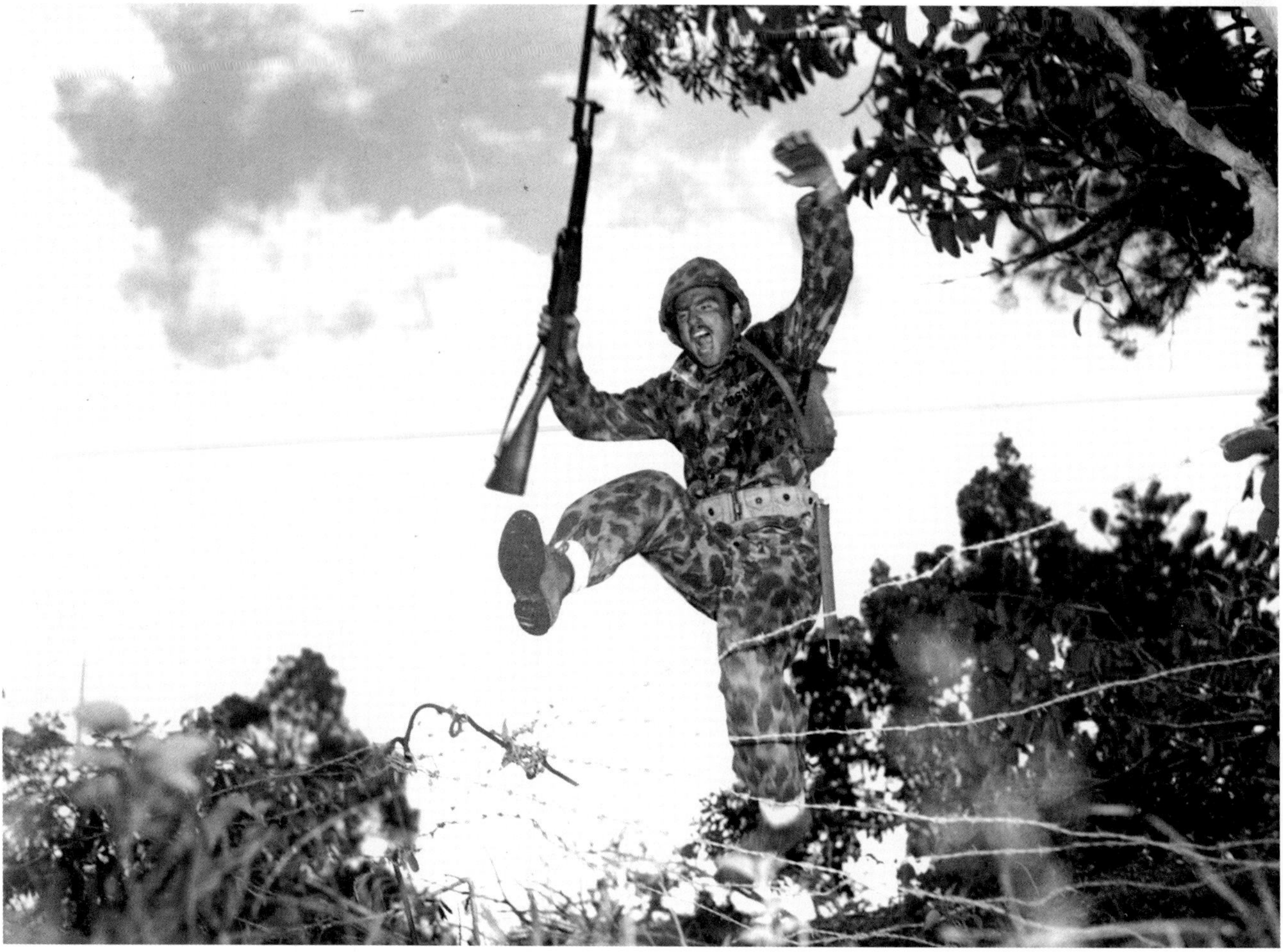

(**Opposite, above**) The Japanese Navy began construction of the Munda airfield seen here on New Georgia Island in early November 1942. This new enemy airfield in the Central Solomons posed a threat that could not be ignored by the American military. It was therefore constantly attacked by air. Note the various bomb craters in the picture. The airfield and the island were slated for capture in June 1943 by both Marines and US Army units. (*National Archives*)

(**Opposite, below**) There would be no Marine Corps divisions assigned to the capture of New Georgia Island and the Munda airfield. Rather, the majority of ground troops committed to the seizure of the island would be two US Army divisions under the command of the XIV Corps. They would be assisted by various Marine defence battalions and Marine Raider battalions. Pictured is a Marine Raider during a training exercise. (*USMC*)

(**Above**) Once the US Army XIV Corps landed on New Georgia Island, it began to stockpile the supplies such as ammunition and fuel that would be needed to push on to the Munda airfield. Among the anti-aircraft guns brought to New Georgia by the Marine Corps defence battalions to protect the army's supply dumps was the 40mm Bofors M1 seen here. In the background is an M9A1 Director. (*USMC*)

Contributing to the artillery support for the two US Army divisions assigned to capture the Munda airfield on the island of New Georgia were eight M1 155mm towed guns of the 9th Marine Defense Battalion. In this picture we see the weapon in full recoil at the moment of firing. The towed 155mm guns were also intended to act as anti-ship weapons if the Japanese Navy intended to shell the US Army advance on Munda airfield. (USMC)

Important assets for the US Army two-division drive on Munda airfield on New Georgia were the M3 series light tanks seen here belonging to the 9th, 10th and 11th Marine defence battalions. They were committed to the battle on 16 July 1943. The M3 light tank was an improved version of the M2A4 light tank that the Marines had originally brought to the Guadalcanal campaign. (USMC)

Pictured here is Gregory 'Pappy' Boyington, one of the best-known Marine Corps fighter pilots of the Second World War. He was appointed commander of a Marine Corps fighter squadron (VMF-214) nicknamed the 'Black Sheep' in September 1943. By early January 1944 he had destroyed twenty-six Japanese planes before he himself was shot down and captured. He survived Japanese captivity to be awarded the Medal of Honor by President Harry Truman on 5 October 1945. (USMC)

(**Above**) VMF-214 Commanding Officer Major Gregory Boyington, kneeling on the left-hand side of the photograph, gives pre-flight instructions to his pilots on 11 September 1943. The pilots of VMF-214 all flew the F4U Corsair. Because Boyington was a decade older than the pilots he commanded, they nicknamed him 'Gramps', which later became 'Pappy'. Of the twenty-eight pilots on the first tour of the Black Sheep squadron under Boyington, nine would become aces. (USMC)

(**Opposite, above**) The F4U Corsairs seen here preparing for take-off in the Solomons were faster and could fly higher than any of their Japanese counterparts. The Marine pilots nicknamed it the 'Bent Wing Widow Maker' because of all the enemy planes it downed. The F4U Corsair was also longer and had a wider wing span than any of its opponents with a length of 33ft 4in and a wingspan of 41ft. (USMC)

(**Opposite, below**) Marines are shown disembarking from their Landing Craft, Vehicle, Personnel (LCVP) during the invasion of Bougainville, which began on 1 November 1943. The island formed part of what was referred to as the Northern Solomons. The camouflage helmet covers and one-piece uniforms seen on the Marines pictured were acquired from the US Army for the Solomons campaigns. Eventually, the Marine Corps came up with its own superior two-piece camouflage uniform design. (USMC)

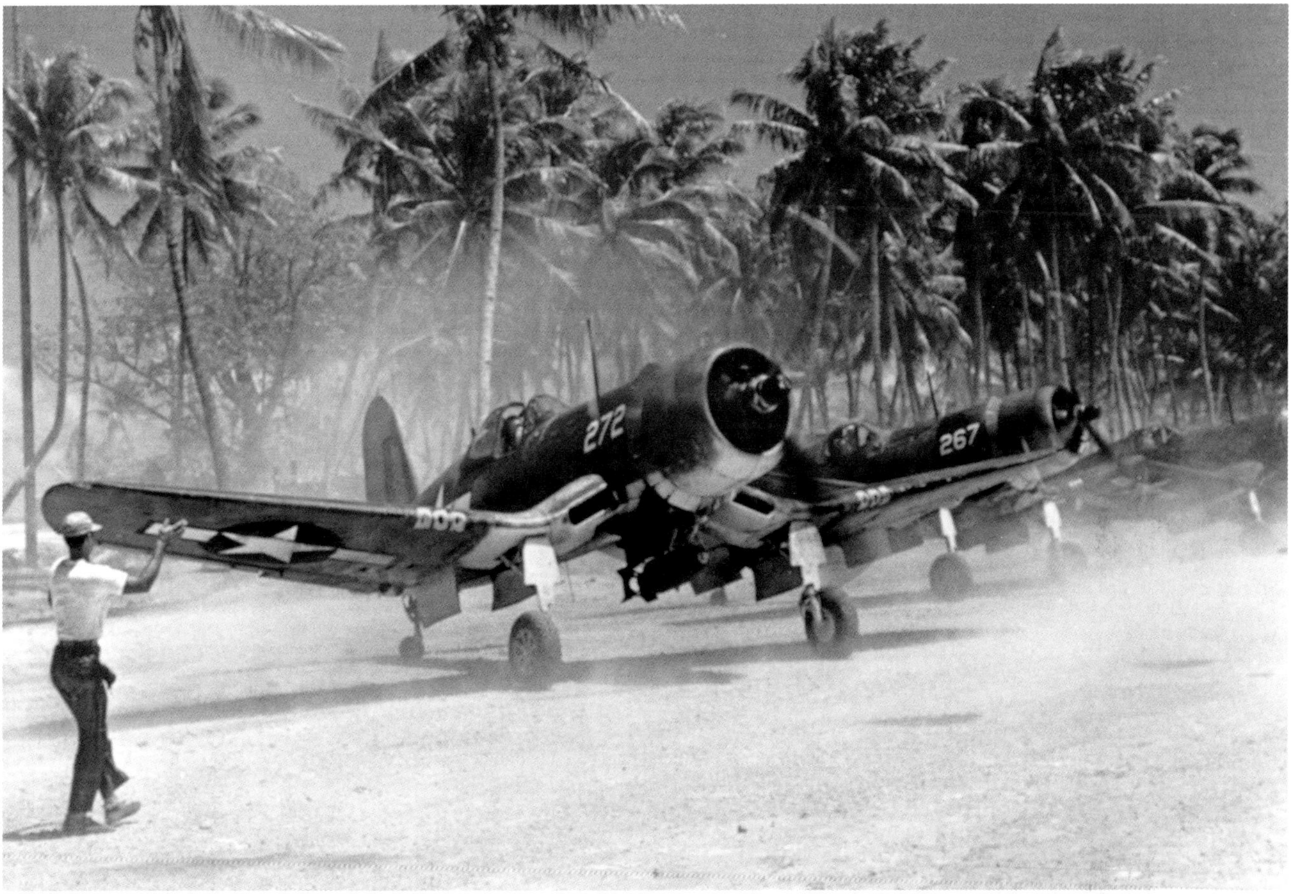
272
267

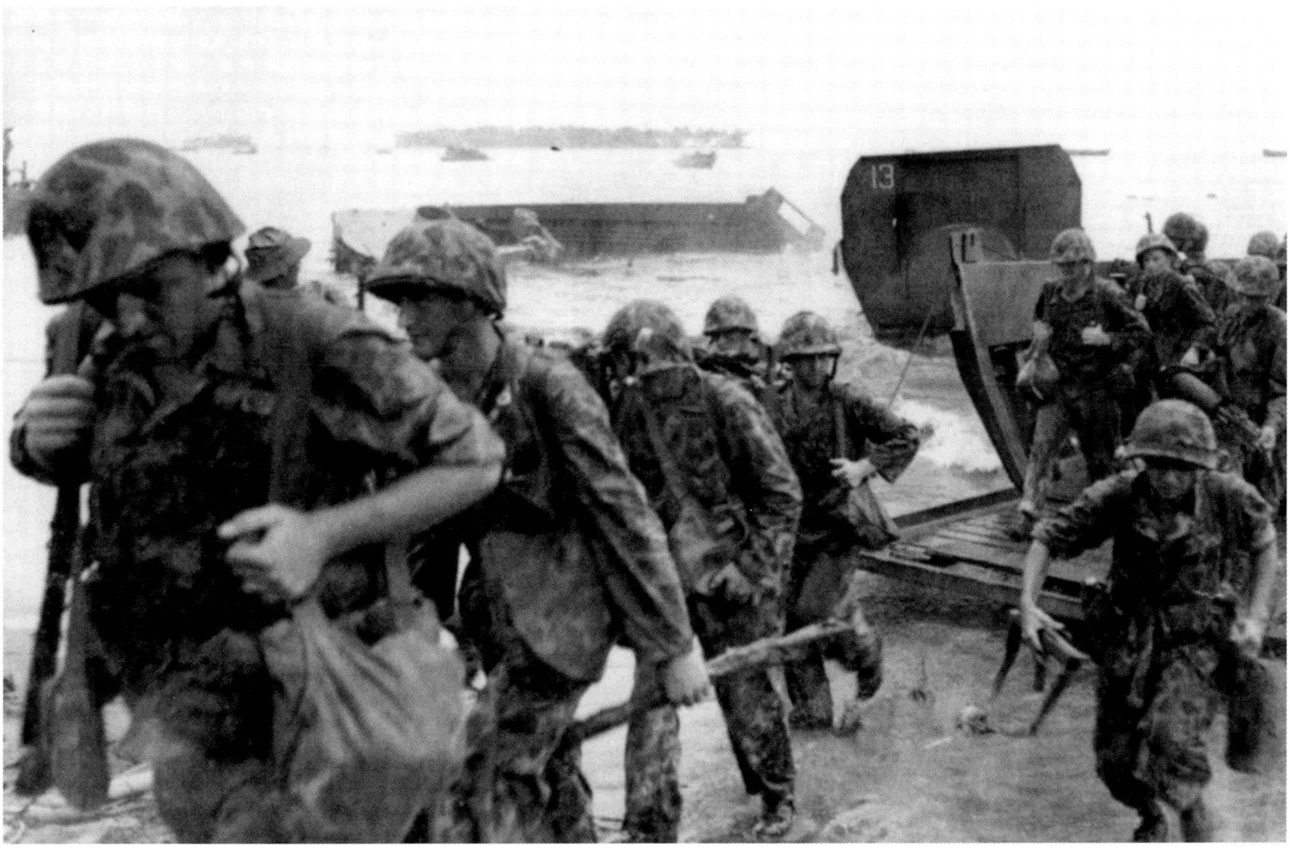
13

During the fighting on Bougainville the Marines found the jungles and swamps of the island as difficult to deal with as the Japanese and just as formidable. As maintaining the correct direction is crucial in the jungle and it is often impossible to march on terrain features, both the Marines and the Japanese relied on the compass a great deal. Here we see two Marines with a compass trying to figure out where they were heading. (USMC)

Shown here in action on Bougainville is a Marine Corps 105mm Howitzer M2A1 with its barrel at full elevation of 66 degrees. Above the barrel (also known as the tube) is a counter-recoil mechanism that returns the barrel from its recoiled position to its firing position and holds it there until fired again. It was estimated that about half the Japanese losses on Bougainville were as a direct result of artillery shelling. (USMC)

As suitable roads could not be built fast enough to keep pace with the Marines fighting in the swamps and jungles of Bougainville, the LVT-1 as seen here was pressed into service to move supplies and artillery pieces where needed. They were also employed as ambulances to pull out the wounded from the front lines. However, there were not enough of the amphibious tractors to meet all the needs of the Marines on the island. (USMC)

The majority of the Marine infantrymen that fought on Guadalcanal were armed with the five-round bolt-action .30 M1903 rifle known by its popular nickname of the '03 Springfield'. By 1943, the majority were armed with the eight-round semi-automatic .30 M1 rifle seen here in the hands of a Marine on Bougainville. The 'M1', as it was nicknamed, had first entered US Army service in 1937. (USMC)

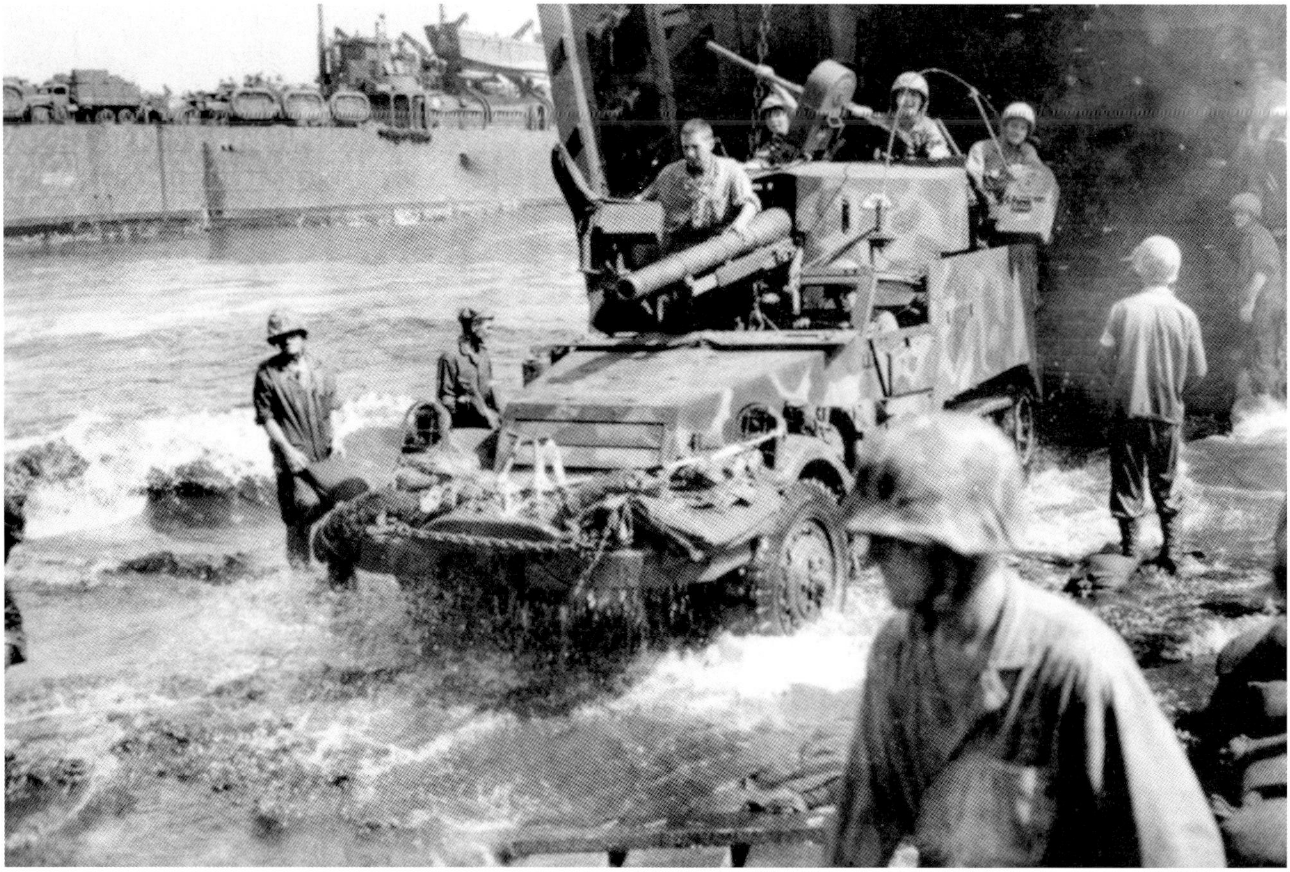

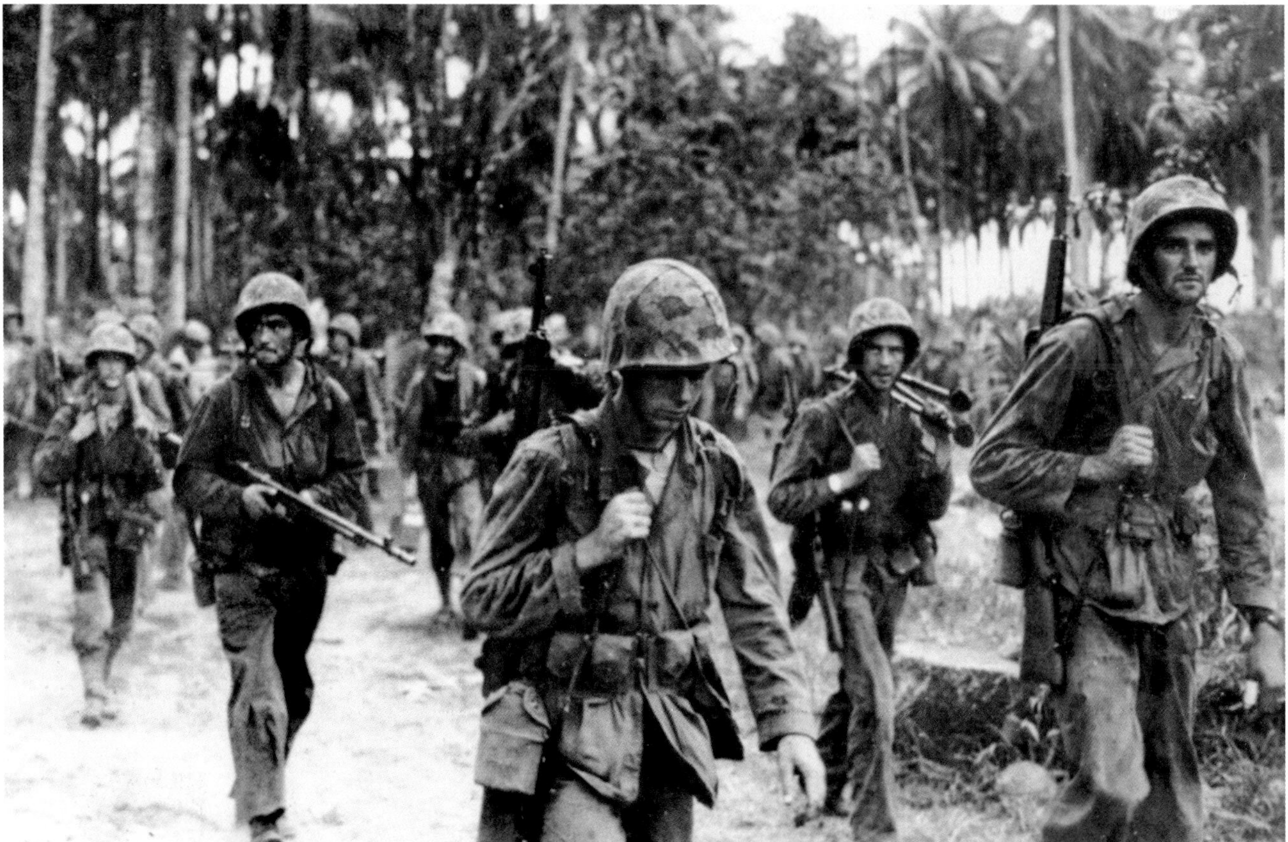

(**Opposite, above**) Coming off a US Navy Landing Ship, Tank (LST) at Cape Gloucester is a Marine Corps M3 Gun Motor Carriage (GMC). It consisted of a modified version of the standard M3 Half-Track Personnel Carrier with a forward-firing 75mm gun designated the M1897. There were two per infantry regiment and twelve per divisional special weapons battalion until early 1945. They had first seen combat on Guadalcanal with the Marines. (*USMC*)

(**Above**) Shown here during the invasion of Cape Gloucester is a platoon of Marine Corps M4 series medium tanks armed with a 75mm main gun. These particular examples are the M4A1 variant powered by a gasoline engine. The Marine Corps requisitioned its first M4 series tank from the US Army in October 1942. (*USMC*)

(**Opposite, below**) By 1943, many of the Marines involved in the battles for the Central and Northern Solomons had been issued with a cotton sage-green herringbone twill utility uniform as seen here. The individual combat equipment was the distinctive Marine Corps 1941 pattern that derived from earlier army M1910 designs. It consisted of a cartridge belt, belt suspenders, haversack and knapsack, supplemented by poncho, shelter half, entrenching tool, gas mask and canteens. It was still in use by the USMC, through Korea and Vietnam, until 1975. (*USMC*)

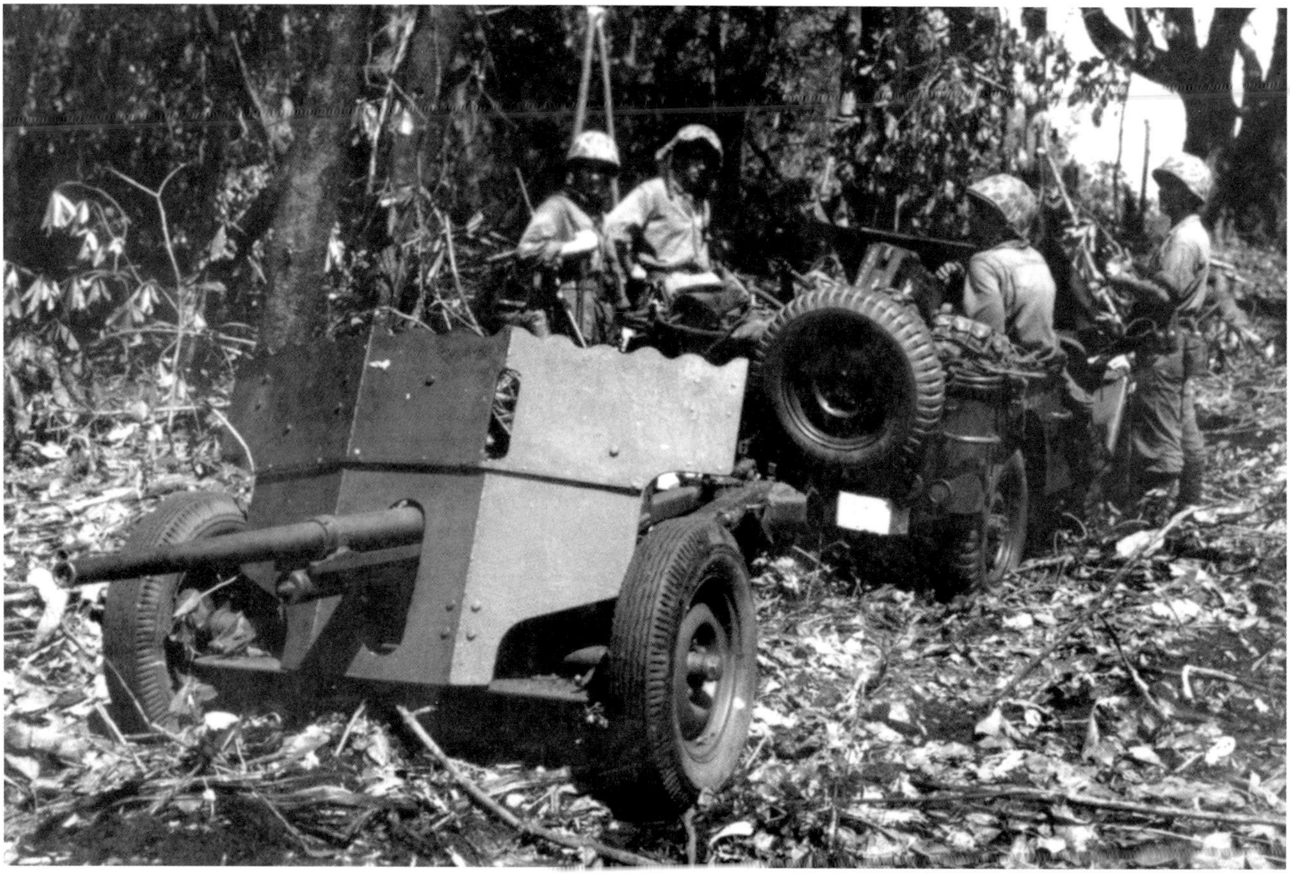

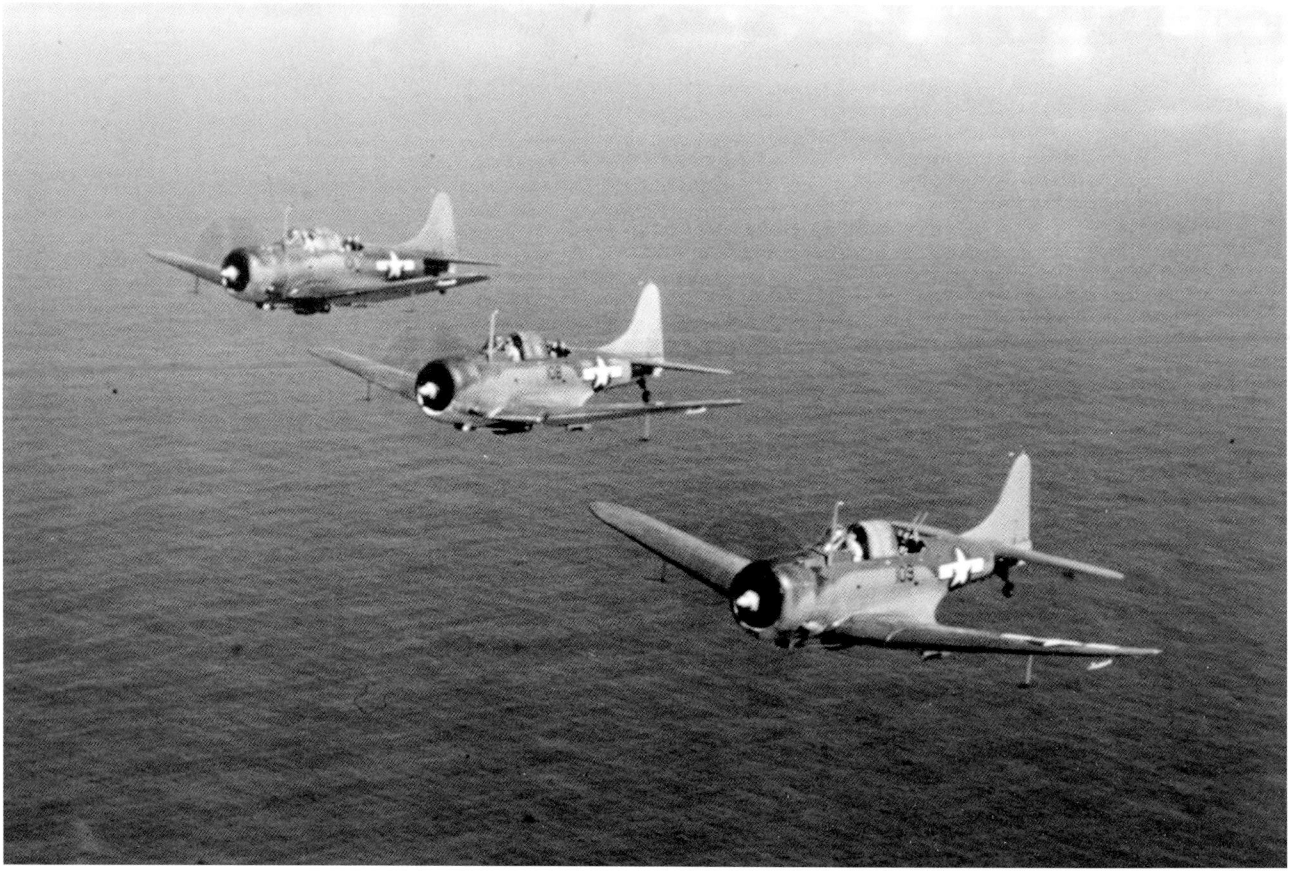

In spite of the inferiority of its M3 series light tanks when compared to the M4 series medium tanks, the Marine Corps retained gun-armed light tanks in service until June 1944. The replacement for the M3 series light tanks was the M5 series light tank seen here on Cape Gloucester. They had first showed up in Marine Corps service in the summer of 1943. (*USMC*)

(**Opposite, above**) Pictured on Cape Gloucester is a Marine Corps 0.25-ton 4 × 4 truck best known by its popular nickname of the 'Jeep'. It is towing a 37mm M3A1 anti-tank gun fitted with an improvised gun shield that is much larger than the factory-supplied version. In Marine Corps service the gun was found in both special weapon battalions and infantry regiments. It was manned by a crew of four. (*USMC*)

(**Opposite, below**) The near-constant attacks on Rabaul and the terrific losses taken by the Japanese in planes and pilots caused them to withdraw all their remaining aircraft from the base in February 1944. This left only ground targets for the many Marine aviation squadrons to attack. Pictured are SBD (Scout Bomber Douglas) aircraft as employed by the Marines to strike Rabaul. (*USMC*)

Chapter Two

Early Central Pacific Battles

A new theatre of operation to be led by the US Navy was opened up by the American Joint Chiefs of Staff in August 1943. Plans called for the Marine Corps and US Army to seize a number of enemy-occupied atolls and islands in the Central Pacific. These captured islands, like stepping-stones across the ocean, would provide airfields and naval bases from which American military air and sea power could advance to the Japanese home islands. The ultimate goal was the invasion of these islands.

The Battle for the Gilbert Islands

The initial Central Pacific objectives chosen by the US Navy for the Marine Corps and US Army were two Japanese-occupied atolls in the Gilbert Island chain: Makin and Tarawa. They formed part of the outer perimeter of the Japanese Empire. The capture of Makin was assigned to the US Army 27th Infantry Division and of Tarawa to the 2nd Marine Division. These invasions were assigned the overall name of Operation GALVANIC.

Atolls are composed of numerous islands of varying sizes. The Japanese typically built airfields on the largest islands in an atoll. The atoll's enclosed lagoon, if navigable, would provide ship anchorage. The largest island in each atoll often bore the name of the atoll to which it belonged.

In the Tarawa atoll, the island selected for assault by the 2nd Marine Division was named Betio. Initially the Japanese had discounted an American interest in the island and had left it almost undefended, but the Marine Raiders' Makin Island raid on 17 and 18 August 1942 had shown Tarawa's weakness and significance and inspired the Japanese to build up the defences. By the time the Marines arrived it had been extensively fortified with almost 500 interconnected fighting positions (pillboxes) by 2,200 men from two Japanese Navy construction units (the Japanese equivalent of the US Navy Seabees). Many of these units' personnel were impressed Korean labourers.

The actual defence of Betio was entrusted to 2,600 troops of the elite Imperial Japanese Navy's Special Naval Landing Force (the Japanese equivalent of the US Marine Corps). They had a wide range of weapons with which to engage the Marines when the time came, including tanks, coast artillery guns, anti-aircraft guns and a large number of machine guns.

From a Marine Corps historical monograph titled *The Battle for Tarawa* by Captain James R. Stockman comes this description of the Japanese beach defence system:

> The basic beach defense weapon was the 13mm machine gun, supplemented by the 7.7mm machine gun. These were sited to cover most likely approaches to the beach with frontal fire, and to cover the forward side of the diagonally placed barriers on the reef with flanking fires, these fires interlocking in front of, and protecting, other beach defense weapon installations. Carefully built rifle and light machine-gun emplacements were positioned in the log-beach barricade and immediately behind it to provide local protection for automatic-fire weapons.
>
> On the beach, the Japanese placed antipersonnel mines and out on the fringing reef there were anti-vehicle mines; these were to complement the basic weapons ashore. Out in the water from the beaches there were anti-boat obstacles, the purpose of which was twofold: (1) To slow down and otherwise impede the movements of landing craft; (2) to force approaching landing craft into prearranged fire lanes where concentrated fires from all types of weapons could be employed most advantageously.
>
> The obstacles were of several types. There was a double apron barbed wire fence, located 50 to 100 yards out, which virtually encircled the island. On the south side of Betio there was a coconut log barrier and scattered through the water were concrete tetrahedrons. On the beaches, proper, the Japanese built log barriers, which in effect were retaining walls, and these were constructed to contain positions for machine guns and anti-boat guns.

The Japanese commander of Betio who had overseen the construction of the island's defensive system was so confident that he boasted to his men: 'A million Americans couldn't take Tarawa in 100 years.' The over-confident US Navy – the later lessons of D-Day in Europe were yet to be learned – believed that pre-invasion aerial and naval bombardment would destroy the majority of these positions and kill the troops manning them. The Marines would pay the price for those mistaken assumptions.

The Attack Begins

The preliminary US Navy bombardment of Betio began on 16 November 1943. Four days later on the early morning of 20 November 1943, there was an intense air and naval bombardment that lasted approximately two and half hours during which the assault waves formed up as Marines disembarked from their troopships into the craft that would take them to shore. The pre-invasion bombardment continued right up until thirty minutes before the first three assault waves headed towards the island.

The initial assault waves were transported to the landing zones in amphibious tractors that were hastily armoured just before the invasion. The need for these specialized vehicles had to do with the fact that, like most coral islands, Betio was circled by barrier reefs that standard US Navy landing craft could only pass over at high tide.

Despite the air and naval bombardment of Betio, the bulk of the Japanese defensive system was intact, as well as most of the defenders. This unforeseen event led to the decimation of the three initial assault waves. The same would occur to the reinforcements sent in on subsequent assault waves later that day.

Of the fourteen M4A2 medium tanks intended to land on Betio on the first day, only four successfully made it ashore and survived the battle. The other ten were lost to Japanese gunfire ashore or swamped by falling into unseen water-filled craters created by the pre-invasion bombardment. None of the intended M3A1 light tanks made it ashore on the first day of the assault as their US Navy landing craft were all sunk before reaching shore.

Due to the courage of individual Marines, or small groups of Marines who refused to give up despite the unrelenting enemy fire, some small footholds had been established on the island that day. When Colonel Daniel M. Shoup, officer in command ashore on Betio, filed a situation report to his divisional command post offshore at 7.05pm on the first day, he reported 'Casualties, many; percentage dead not known. Combat efficiency: We are winning.' Shoup was later awarded the Medal of Honor for his bravery and leadership on Betio and eventually rose to become a commandant of the Marine Corps following the Korean War.

A strong Japanese counter-attack that evening could have forced the Marines off the island. However, the pre-invasion air and naval bombardment had severed most of the buried Japanese telephone lines. Japanese commanders were unable to use runners to communicate because of the heavy fire on the island between the combatants. Thus the defenders couldn't mass the troops needed to launch a heavy counter-attack on the first night.

The Fighting Continues

The 2nd Marine Division's leadership was under no illusions regarding the precarious nature of their positions on Betio on the early morning of 21 November. The surviving officers and non-commissioned officers (NCOs) on the island quickly set about reorganizing their men back into proper fighting units. This allowed them to consolidate their gains and be prepared for possible enemy counter-attacks. With the addition of fresh reinforcements and the landing of twelve M3A1 light tanks, the Marines managed to expand their positions on Day Two of the invasion.

On Day Three, the Marines continued on the offensive, managing to seize most of Betio with the assistance of naval gunfire. Under the cover of darkness, the majority

Marine Corps Divisions

During the Second World War the Marines formed six divisions. By contrast, the US Army formed eighty-nine divisions of which twenty-two served in the Pacific. Unlike the US Army that had three different types of divisions – infantry, armoured and airborne – the Marine Corps' six divisional-sized units were all infantry divisions. There was always a supporting artillery regiment and service and special troops in each division. The latter oversaw all the larger weapons in the division, including tanks.

The six divisions served under two corps. Each corps, referred to as an amphibious corps, was intended to oversee two or more divisions during operations as well as all assigned support units. Reflecting its much larger size, the US Army formed twenty-four corps, each of which typically included two or three infantry divisions and a single armoured division.

The six divisions and the two corps fell under the overall command of an umbrella organization known as the Fleet Marine Force (FMF), formed in 1933. Specialized battalion-size combat support and service units were assigned to the six divisions by the FMF based on mission requirements. Units not part of the FMF included shore-based commands and guard contingents aboard larger warships.

The six divisions were numbered in sequence of activation from one through to six. Prior to 1941, the largest formation was a brigade. Two permanent brigades were formed between 1935 and 1936, one based on the east coast of the United States and the other on the west coast. These pre-war brigades were the foundation (or cadre) for the formation in 1941 of the 1st and 2nd Marine divisions. There would also be five provisional brigades formed just prior to Pearl Harbor and shortly thereafter for specific missions. They would be disbanded after completion of their missions.

The heart and soul of the six divisions were the eighteen infantry regiments. Each division had three infantry regiments, with approximately 3,000 men. Each corresponding level down had the same triangular structure. Each infantry regiment was composed of three infantry battalions of between 900 and 1,000 men. Each battalion was made up of three rifle companies of between 180 and 240 men. Each company had three rifle platoons of approximately forty men each, which in turn were broken down into three rifle squads of nine men each.

During the course of the war the six divisions went through four different Tables of Organization and Equipment (TO&E) based on lessons learned from combat. The original division configuration had a manpower strength of 19,514, the second 19,965, the third 17,485 and the fourth 19,716. Despite these changes, the division's basic triangular structure, from regiments down to platoon level, remained the same, although the structure of infantry squads changed in the 1944 reorganization.

The number of personnel listed for each unit in a division was only in theory. The infantry regiments of the divisions took the highest losses and hence suffered the greatest fluctuations in numbers during the war years.

of the surviving Japanese troops on the Island launched three savage counter-attacks. These attacks were all broken up by Marine firepower, assisted by the close-range fire support of several US Navy destroyers. Marine losses were 45 killed and 128 wounded. A total of 325 enemy corpses were counted in the morning light of 23 November.

Losses

Betio was declared secure on 23 November, despite the fact that the last Japanese hold-outs were not eliminated until 28 November. The Marine Corps concluded that 4,690 Japanese troops and labourers were killed out of approximately 4,800 on the island when the invasion began. Only seventeen Japanese prisoners were taken. A total of 129 Korean labourers managed to surrender.

Total Marine casualties were 3,301 men. Of that number, 2,296 were wounded in action and 837 killed in action. The remainder either died of wounds after the fighting or were missing and presumed dead. One Marine's remains were found on Betio in 2013 and in 2015 a hastily-built cemetery containing the remains of thirty-six Marines was discovered. All remains were repatriated to the United States for reburial in a military cemetery.

There was a great deal of public outrage at the losses incurred in the capture of Betio. To offset this anger and place it in context of what was to come in the Pacific, a *New York Times* editorial on 27 December 1943 praised the corps for capturing Betio and warned the American public that future assaults in the Central Pacific might well result in even heavier losses, stating that 'We must steel ourselves now to pay that price.'

Not everybody had been convinced of the necessity of taking Betio, including Major General Julian C. Smith, the commander of the 2nd Marine Division. He stated in his post-war biography: 'Was Tarawa worth it? My answer is unqualified: No. From the very beginning the decision of the Joint Chiefs to seize Tarawa was a mistake and from their initial mistake grew the terrible drama of errors, errors of omission rather than commission, resulting in these needless casualties.'

Amphibious Tractors

Even before the Second World War, the US Navy had begun formulating a series of plans anticipating an eventual war with the Empire of Japan. These plans were formalized in the early 1920s. As the corps' portion of these plans called for them to invade and capture a number of Japanese-occupied islands in the Pacific, the navy searched for ways to quickly move Marines and their equipment from ship to shore.

One novel invention that piqued the corps' and US Navy's interest was a full-tracked, non-armoured amphibious tractor. Intended as a civilian rescue vehicle for the Florida Everglades, it first appeared in 1935. After testing a number of militarized prototypes, it was eventually ordered into production by the US Navy in August 1941 as the Landing Vehicle Tracked No. 1 (LVT-1).

By the time the assembly lines closed on the unarmoured LVT-1, a total of 1,225 units had been built. It was followed in the summer of 1942 by the construction of the progressively-improved unarmoured LVT-2 of which 2,963 were built. Both would be employed by the corps at Betio and hastily armed and armoured for the upcoming battle.

Unofficial nicknames for the LVT-1 and LVT-2 vehicles included 'Alligator', 'Amtracs' or just tractors. Those employed by the US Army were nicknamed 'Water Buffalos' and a number supplied to the British Army were known as 'Buffalos'.

Late-production units of the LVT-2 employed by the corps had an armoured cab and armoured engine intakes. There was also an all-around armoured version of the LVT-2 built only for the US Army and designated the LVT(A)-2. A total of 450 units were acquired by the US Army.

The next step in the evolution of the LVT for the corps was the LVT(A)-1. It had an armoured hull and was fitted with a light tank turret armed with a 37mm main gun. A total of 504 units were built. In Marine Corps service the LVT(A)-1 was referred to as an 'armoured amphibian' and in the US Army as an 'amphibian tank'. Its initial battlefield employment took place in January 1944 with the Marine landing at Roi-Namur.

A redesigned LVT-2 with a rear ramp became the LVT-4. It came off the factory floor unarmoured but could be fitted with an armour kit if required. It was the most numerous LVT built during the Second World War with a total of 8,348 constructed. Initial use of the LVT-4 by the corps took place during the Saipan campaign in June 1944. It was typically armed with at least two machine guns.

An armoured version of the LVT-4 armed with a turret-mounted short-barrelled low-velocity 75mm howitzer was designated the LVT(A)-4. Industry completed a total of 1,890 units of this variant. There were also 269 units of an improved version labelled the LVT(A)-5 assembled between 1944 and 1945.

Looking somewhat similar to the LVT-4 was the LVT-3, of which 2,962 were built between 1944 and the end of the Second World War. Like the LVT-4, the LVT-3 came off the factory floor unarmoured but had provision for the fitting of an add-on armour kit if required. Initial employment of the LVT-3 occurred during the Okinawa campaign in April 1945.

An end-of-war summary of the value of the LVT was provided to the corps during the Second World War by Lieutenant General Holland M. Smith: 'The development of the amphibian tractor, or LVT, which began in the middle 1930s provided the solution and was one of the most important modern technical contributions to ships-to-shore operations. Without these landing vehicles, our amphibious offensive in the Pacific would have been impossible.'

The Marshall Islands Campaign

Following the conquest of the Gilbert Islands, the American Joint Chiefs of Staff identified the Marshall Island chain – 32 atolls and approximately 1,000 islands of varying sizes – as the next step in the Central Pacific advance. The US Navy eventually selected three atolls in the Marshalls for initial seizure: Majuro, Kwajalein and Eniwetok. The plan for their capture was named Operation FLINTLOCK, which was itself broken down into a number of subsidiary operations.

The atolls provided excellent enclosed sheltered anchorages and had islands with airfields. The Kwajalein atoll, 60 miles long and 20 miles wide, is the largest in the world. Having broken the Japanese naval codes, the US Navy was also aware that it was lightly-defended compared to other atolls and their respective islands. The US Navy did not want a repeat of the heavy losses incurred at Betio.

The US Navy's plans targeted the larger islands in the Majuro and Kwajalein atolls. Once these were in American hands, the US Navy planned a three-month break to prepare for the invasion of the main islands in the Eniwetok atoll.

On 4 December 1943, the US Navy began a series of carrier raids on the Japanese-occupied islands. During December both US Navy and USAAF planes flying out of airfields in the Gilbert Islands took part in the aerial assaults. The Japanese had 110 aircraft with which to defend the Marshall Islands but 92 were destroyed in a US Navy carrier raid on 29 January 1944.

The Amphibious Assaults Begin

On 31 January 1944, 1,500 men landed on the island of Majuro. The attacking force consisted of a Marine Corps reconnaissance company from the 4th Marine Division and a US Army infantry battalion. Lightly defended, the island was declared secure on the same day it was assaulted, with no American casualties.

A much larger assault that day involved the 4th Marine Division, which was formed in August 1943. Its objective was the capture of Roi and Namur, two small islands in the Kwajalein atoll that were linked by a narrow causeway. In Marine Corps wartime documents and post-war historical publications, they are listed as 'Roi-Namur'.

Roi had an airfield and supporting facilities and Namur all the logistical support systems (fuel and ammunition) for both aircraft and ships. It was estimated that there were about 2,500 Japanese on the islands, with up to 600 Korean labourers.

The US Navy had steadily bombarded the islands both by air and sea during the previous two days. This was continued on the day of the invasion almost until the Marines' advance assault waves reached the islands. Before the actual Marine assaults on Roi-Namur, five smaller islands around them were seized and artillery emplaced to outflank the Japanese defensive positions on Roi-Namur. This had been something the corps had wanted to do before assaulting Betio, but that request had been denied by the US Navy.

Clearing the Islands

The Marine Corps assault on Roi-Namur was hampered by rough seas, high winds and the 4th Marine Division's inexperience. Compounding the problem was the breakdown of radio communications between the US Navy ships and the amphibious tractors that were tasked with bringing the Marines ashore. This can be attributed to the radios on the amphibious tractors not being waterproofed and thus soon soaked in the rough seas, rendering them inoperable.

In a Marine Corps historical monograph titled *Breaking the Outer Ring: Marine Landings in the Marshall Islands*, the author, John C. Chapin, then a second lieutenant, describes the confusion of the first assault waves as they headed towards Roi in their amphibious tractors:

> By now everything was mixed up, with our assault waves all entangled with the armored [amphibious] tractors ahead of us. I ordered my driver to maneuver around them. Slowly we inched past, as their 37mm guns and .50 caliber machine guns flamed. The beach lay right before us. However, it was shrouded in such a pall of dust and smoke from our bombardment that we could see very little of it. As a result, we were unable to tell what section we were approaching (after all our hours of careful planning, based on hitting the beach at one exact spot!). I turned to talk to my platoon sergeant, who was manning the machine gun right behind me. He was slumped over – the whole right side of his face disintegrated into a mass of gore. Up to now, the entire operation had seemed like a movie, or like one of the innumerable practice landings we'd made. Now one of my men lay in a welter of blood beside me, and the reality of it smashed into my consciousness.

Upon landing on Roi – essentially a flat surface with very little vegetation – the Marines met less resistance than expected. This was for two reasons: firstly, the number of Japanese defenders on the island had been overestimated; secondly, the air and naval bombardment had been so much more effective than that inflicted on Betio. Roi was declared secure on the same day it was invaded.

The Battle for Namur

The fighting on the connected island of Namur proved rather more difficult. It was covered by thick tangled vegetation and the rubble of destroyed buildings caused by the pre-invasion bombardment. This combination provided the defenders with more places to hide and proved tougher for the Marine tanks to manoeuvre through. The Marines also suffered a number of deaths and injuries when they unknowingly blew up a Japanese bunker that contained torpedo warheads.

Despite natural and man-made obstacles including anti-tank ditches, the Marine tanks and infantry began slowly eliminating all organized opposition on Namur on the first day of the invasion. With the fall of darkness and the Marines setting up defensive positions, the remaining Japanese troops took the opportunity to launch a counter-attack that was handily beaten back. By noon of the next day Namur was declared secure.

The Reasons for Success

One of the important factors that made the taking of Roi-Namur so much easier and less costly than Betio was the loss of the senior Japanese officers on the islands before and during the corps' assault. This is explained in an extract from a Marine Corps historical publication titled *The Marshalls: Increasing the Tempo* written by Marine Corps Lieutenant Colonels Heinl and Crown:

> Although unknown to the Marines at the time, the lack of positive Japanese command also played an important part in preventing the enemy from organizing an effective resistance. Preliminary bombardment of Namur had virtually destroyed the administration building housing the communication and intelligence facilities for both Namur and Roi. Thus, at one swoop the means of effective command were lost. Moreover, the enemy was early deprived of the very source of command-experienced high-echelon officers. Many of the ranking officers of Roi-Namur, including Vice Admiral Yamada, air commander for the Marshalls, perished in the destruction of the administration building. And on D-plus 1 the seven surviving senior officers were killed almost simultaneously while seeking sanctuary in a bomb shelter. The few prisoners taken during the operation reported that from then on it was a matter of every man for himself and no attempt was made to organize resistance.

Other factors that made the capture of Roi-Namur less difficult than expected were the fact that the Japanese defensive fortifications were incomplete. Those that were completed were of sub-standard construction. Unlike Betio, there were no underwater obstacles to hamper the corps' amphibious tractors and the US Navy's landing craft. In addition, the islands' Japanese defenders were not the elite troops encountered on Betio.

The Next Step

The Marine 22nd (Infantry) Regiment, a non-divisional assigned unit, had been tasked with assisting the US Army in the seizure of the island of Kwajalein. However, it was not called on. By 8 February 1944, all the surrounding islands in the Kwajalein atoll were in American hands.

At the same time as the Marines' assault on Roi-Namur on 31 January 1944, elements of the US Army 7th Infantry Division landed on three small islands surrounding the Japanese-occupied island of Kwajalein, which was part of the Kwajalein atoll. On the islands the US Army emplaced artillery pieces to outflank the Japanese defensive positions on Kwajalein, which was to be assaulted the next day.

The US Army's fight for the island of Kwajalein proved much tougher than that of the Marines on Roi-Namur. It took until 3 February 1944 for the US Army to declare the island secure. Of the 4,000 Japanese troops on the island, approximately 100 survived the fighting, surrendering along with 165 Korean labourers. US Army losses were 142 killed and 845 wounded.

Stepping up the Timetable

As Operation FLINTLOCK had proceeded more quickly than originally anticipated and the US Navy still had 10,000 uncommitted reserve troops in both the US Army and Marine Corps, US Navy commanders decided to begin Operation CATCHPOLE in February 1944 rather than in May 1944 as originally planned.

Operation CATCHPOLE was a subsidiary activity of Operation FLINTLOCK. It involved the seizure of three of the larger islands in the Eniwetok atoll, which formed part of the Marshall Island chain. They were Engebi, Parry and Eniwetok. The Marines were to take the first two islands and the US Army the third, with Marine Corps' tanks and one infantry battalion of the 22nd Marine Regiment in support.

From a Marine Corps Historical Branch publication titled *Central Pacific Drive* by Shaw, Nalty and Turnbladh appears the following extract. In it there is a description of how the senior Japanese officer in charge of the Eniwetok atoll islands intended to defend his positions:

> General Nishida clung to the Japanese tactical doctrine of destroying the invader at the beaches. 'If the enemy lands, make use of the positions you are occupying during the daytime,' he directed. 'Endeavor to reduce losses, and at night strike terror into the enemy's heart by charges and destroy his will to fight.'

Despite the presence of between 700 to 800 Japanese defenders on Engebi, it was declared secure the next day for the loss of 85 Marines killed and another 166 wounded. On 19 February 1944, the Marines were called in to assist the US Army in the capture of Eniwetok Island, which was held by 908 Japanese troops. It was secured on the following day.

The 22nd Marine Regiment landed on Parry Island on 22 February 1944 to do battle with 1,115 Japanese troops. Like Engebi and Eniwetok, it fell relatively quickly after initial heavy fighting. Marine Second Lieutenant Cord Meyer Jr, who fought on both Engebi and Parry islands, wrote home about his experiences on the latter:

> We were hard hit there, and with terrible clarity the reality of the event came home to me. I had crawled forward to ask a Marine where the Japs were, pretty excited really and enjoying it almost like a game. I crawled up beside him but he

wouldn't answer. Then I saw the ever widening pool of dark blood by his head and knew that he was dying or dead. So, it came over me what this war was, and after that it wasn't fun or exciting, but something that had to be done.

Fortune smiled on me that day, or the hand of a Divine Providence was over me, or I was just plain lucky. We killed many of them in fighting that lasted to nightfall. We cornered fifty or so Imperial [Japanese] Marines on the end of the island, where they attempted a banzai charge, but we cut them down like over-ripe wheat, and they lay like tired children with their faces in the sand.

That night was unbelievably terrible. There were many of them left and they all had one fanatical notion, and that was to take one of us with them. We dug

Marine Corps Tanks

Prior to the Second World War, the corps was very aware that once ashore on an enemy-occupied island or country, a landing force had to be able to defend itself against the possibility of an enemy armoured counter-attack.

In 1934, the corps planned for having two tank companies of 5-ton light tanks for its two brigades proposed for duty in the Atlantic and Pacific fleets. The vehicle selected was the two-man Marmon-Herrington CTL-3. The corps bought a total of thirty-five Marmon-Herrington tanks, but the coming of the Second World War required adoption of US Army light tanks for a variety of reasons. The tanks were purchased by the US Navy, for the corps, through US Army procurement channels.

The first Marine Corps tanks to see combat were the M2A4 and M3 series in August 1942 during the Guadalcanal Islands campaign. These light tanks were eventually replaced in service by the M5A1 light tank beginning in late 1942. The M5A1 light tank was armed with the same turret-mounted 37mm gun and several machine guns as the M3 series light tanks.

By the autumn of 1942, it had become clear that the 37mm gun-armed light tanks lacked the firepower and armour protection to be decisive on the Pacific island battlefields. This resulted in the corps in October 1942 ordering from the US Army the first M4 series medium tanks, popularly known in US media as the 'Sherman'.

Called by the Marines 'the medium' or the 'M4', the Sherman was armed with a 75mm main gun that could destroy many Japanese bunkers that the 37mm main gun of light tanks could not. The first combat employment of the Sherman medium tanks occurred on Betio Island in November 1942.

Sherman tanks would continue to see productive employment with the Marine Corps until the end of the war. The Sherman's replacement was the heavier and better-armed and armoured M26 heavy tank named the 'Pershing' post-war.

in with orders to kill anything that moved. I kept watch in a foxhole with my sergeant, and we both stayed awake all night with a knife in one hand and a grenade in the other. They crept in among us, and every bush or rock took on sinister proportions. They got some of us, but in the morning, they all lay about, some with their riddled bodies actually inside our foxholes. With daylight, it was easy for us and we finished them off. Never have I been so glad to see the blessed sun.

Marshall Islands Clean-Up

Between 7 March and 6 April 1944, the 22nd Marine Regiment performed a final mopping-up operation in the Marshall Islands. The regiment would establish an American presence on twelve additional Marshall Island atolls and three separate islands. In the process, a small number of Japanese troops were found and eliminated, with the loss of an occasional Marine. By the time the Marshall Islands campaign concluded, 636 Marines had been killed and 1,232 wounded.

A few atolls in the Marshall Islands with larger contingents of Japanese troops were not invaded. As these troops were cut off from re-supply (either food or ammunition), they soon became impotent from a military standpoint. They were continuously bombed and strafed by Marine aircraft until the end of the war to make sure they could not leave the atolls.

From this picture taken in September 1943 by an American aircraft we see the Tawara atoll with the approximately 2-acre island of Betio in the foreground. The Tawara atoll formed part of the Gilbert Island chain in the Central Pacific. Clearly visible in the picture is the airfield that dominates the very small island. The landing beaches for the invasion of Betio were all concentrated on the left side of the airfield. (*National Archives*)

Pictured on a troopship bound for Betio are the men of the 2nd Marine Division and the LVT-1s of the 2nd Amphibian Tractor Battalion. Despite the US Navy's belief that its pre-invasion bombardment of Betio would eliminate all the Japanese defensive works on the island, the Marines were not taking any chances and scraped together some 9mm steel plates to weld onto their LVT-1s for added protection. *(USMC)*

Marines are being shown a relief map of Betio while on a troopship sailing towards the island. The seizure of Betio was the first large-scale amphibious operation by the Marine Corps in the Central Pacific that involved crossing a barrier reef. It was the reef line that made the Marines insist on the employment of the LVT-1 and LVT-2 for the initial landings on Betio, despite the US Navy's insistence that they were not needed. (USMC)

Commander of the 2nd Marine Division for the invasion of Betio was Major General Julian C. Smith seen here. His contemporaries had a very high regard for him. Unassuming and self-effacing, 'there was nothing wrong with his fighting heart.' Lieutenant Colonel Ray Murray, one of his battalion commanders, described Smith as 'a fine old gentleman of high moral fiber; you'd fight for him.' Smith's troops perceived that their commanding general had a genuine love for them. (USMC)

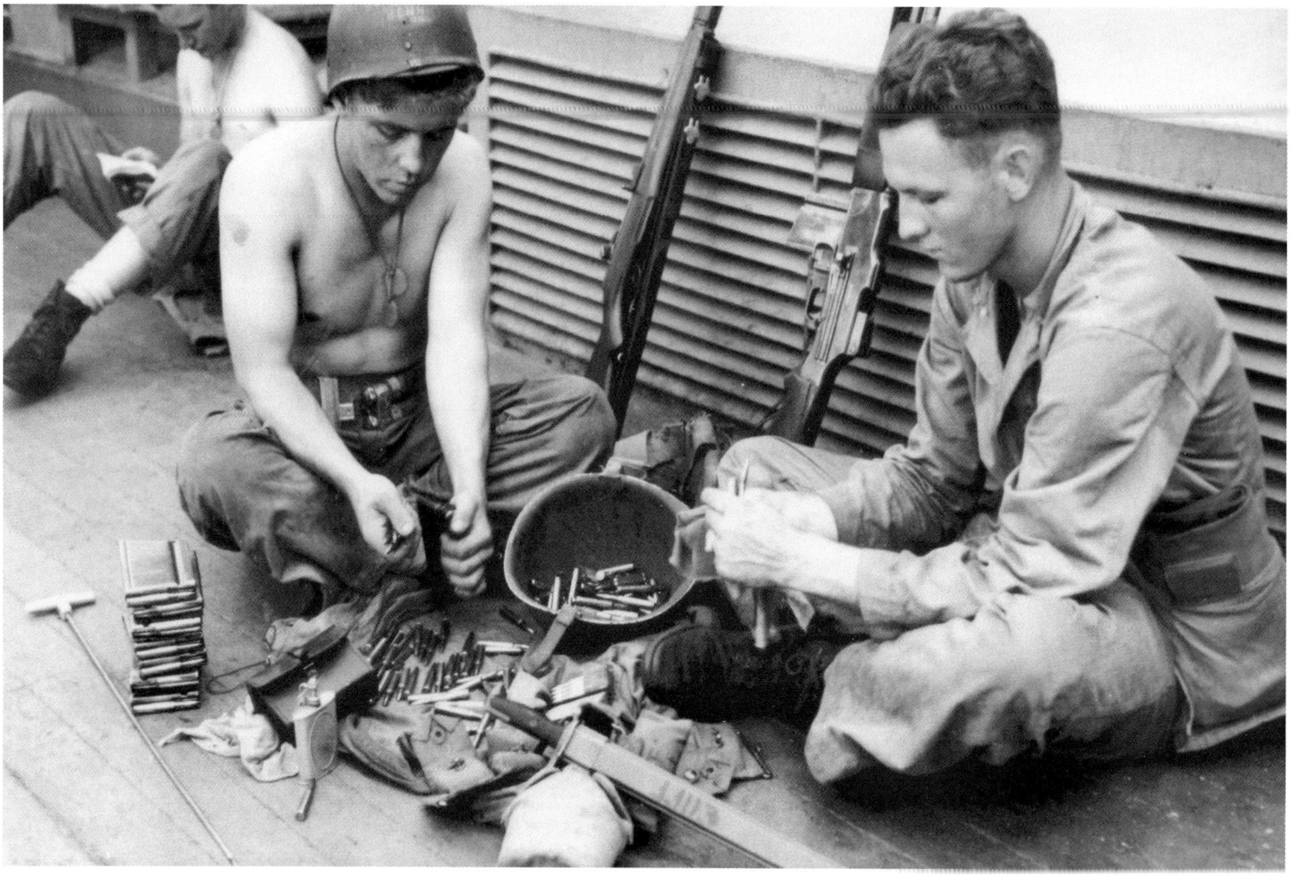

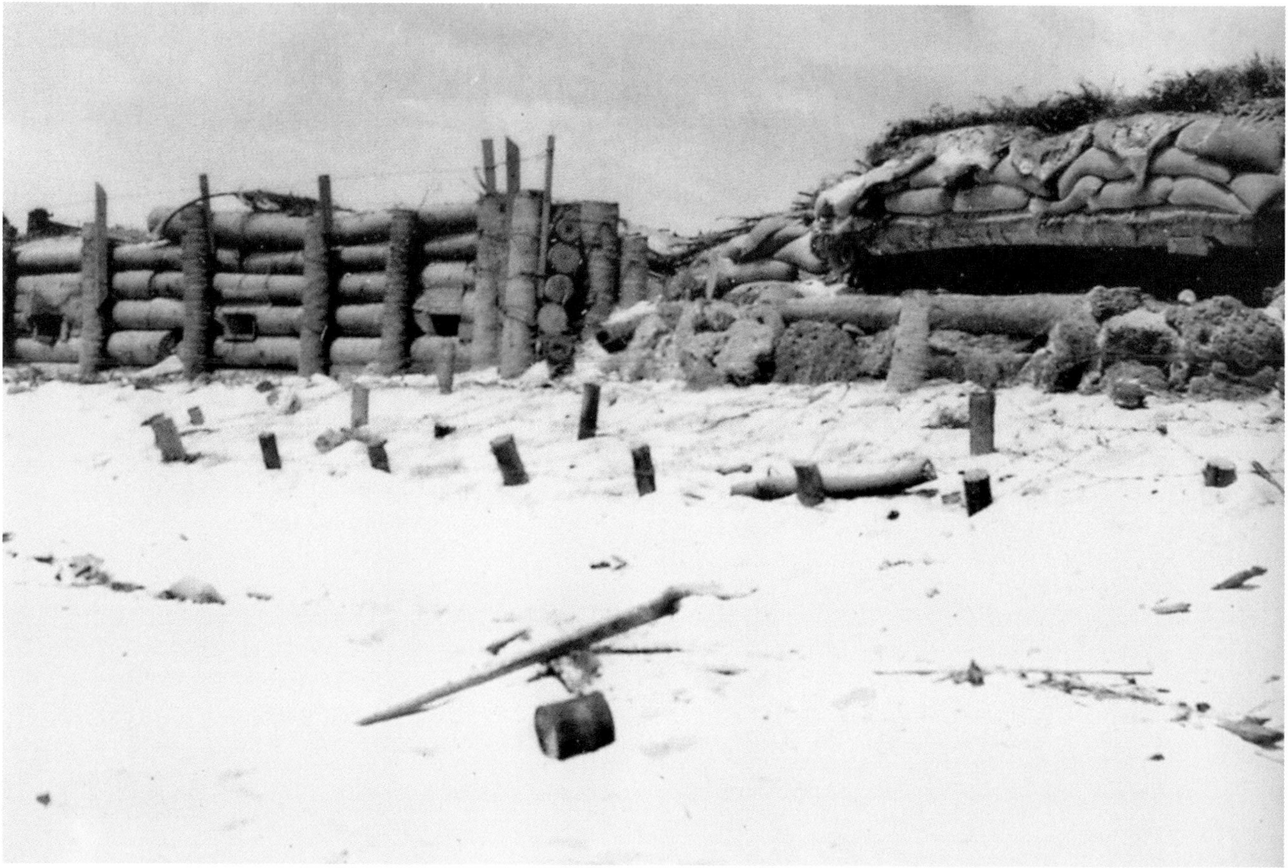

(**Opposite, above**) Marines on a troopship heading towards Betio are shown cleaning individual rounds for both the .30 calibre M1918A1 Browning Automatic Rifle (BAR) and the .30 calibre M1 rifle leaning against the ship's superstructure. Loaded twenty-round box magazines for the BAR are seen in front of the knee of the Marine on the left-hand side of the image. In the foreground is an M1 bayonet and scabbard for the .30 calibre M1 rifle. (*USMC*)

(**Above**) Among the defensive works emplaced on Betio by the Japanese prior to the Marine assault were four 8in coast artillery guns with an example seen here in this post-invasion picture. They were British-designed and built by the firm of Vickers and bought by the Japanese military for use during the Russo-Japanese War (1904–1905). The US Navy pre-invasion bombardment of Betio destroyed these guns before the Marines landed. (*USMC*)

(**Opposite, below**) Reflecting the fact that Betio was only 3 miles long and 800 yards at its widest point and 10ft above sea level at its highest point, its major defensive works were located on the beaches. The coconut log sea wall that surrounded the majority of the island was its first defensive line and had spaced firing embrasures along its length, with intervening pillboxes made of coconut log and sandbags as shown in this post-invasion picture. (*USMC*)

(**Above**) A post-invasion picture of one of the spaced firing embrasures that were located along the length of the coconut log sea wall that surrounded much of Betio. The island's impressive defences were designed by its original commanding officer Rear Admiral Tomanari Saichiro who was known as a superb engineer. He was replaced in August 1943 by another rear admiral better known as a fighter than an engineer. (*USMC*)

(**Opposite, above**) In this post-invasion picture taken on Betio we see the destroyed remains of a Japanese air-defence radar. They were first encountered in the Central Pacific campaign in early 1943. The Japanese air-defence early-warning system for Betio would have also depended on personnel based on outlying atolls to radio in the approach of American aircraft or warships. (*USMC*)

(**Opposite, below**) Encountered by the Marines on Betio were small reinforced concrete pillboxes as seen here in this post-invasion picture. These would have just enough room for the crew of a Japanese 7mm light machine gun referred to as the Type 99. The weapon was fed by a detachable thirty-round box magazine and had a maximum effective range of 875 yards. There would be an opening in the coconut log sea wall for the crew to access or exit the pillbox. (*USMC*)

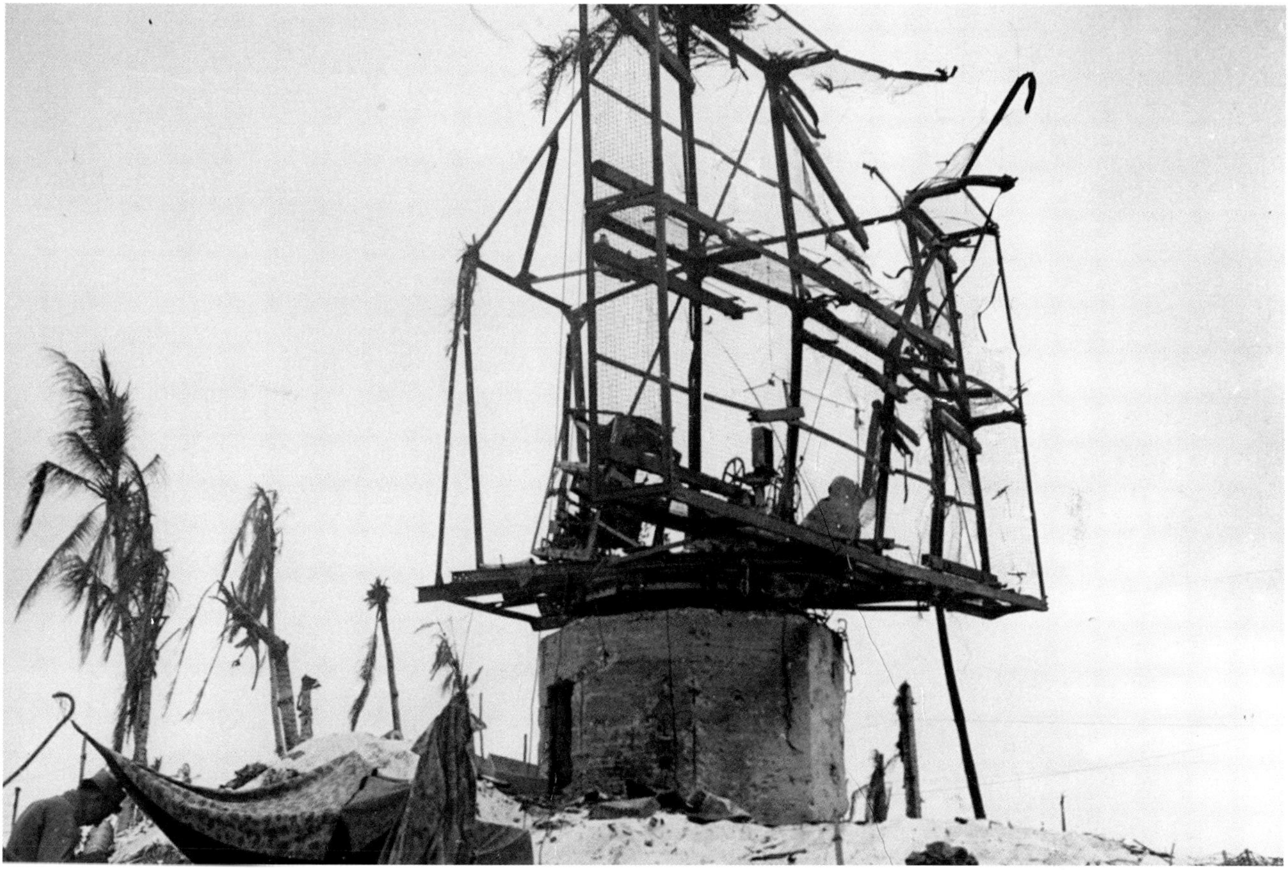

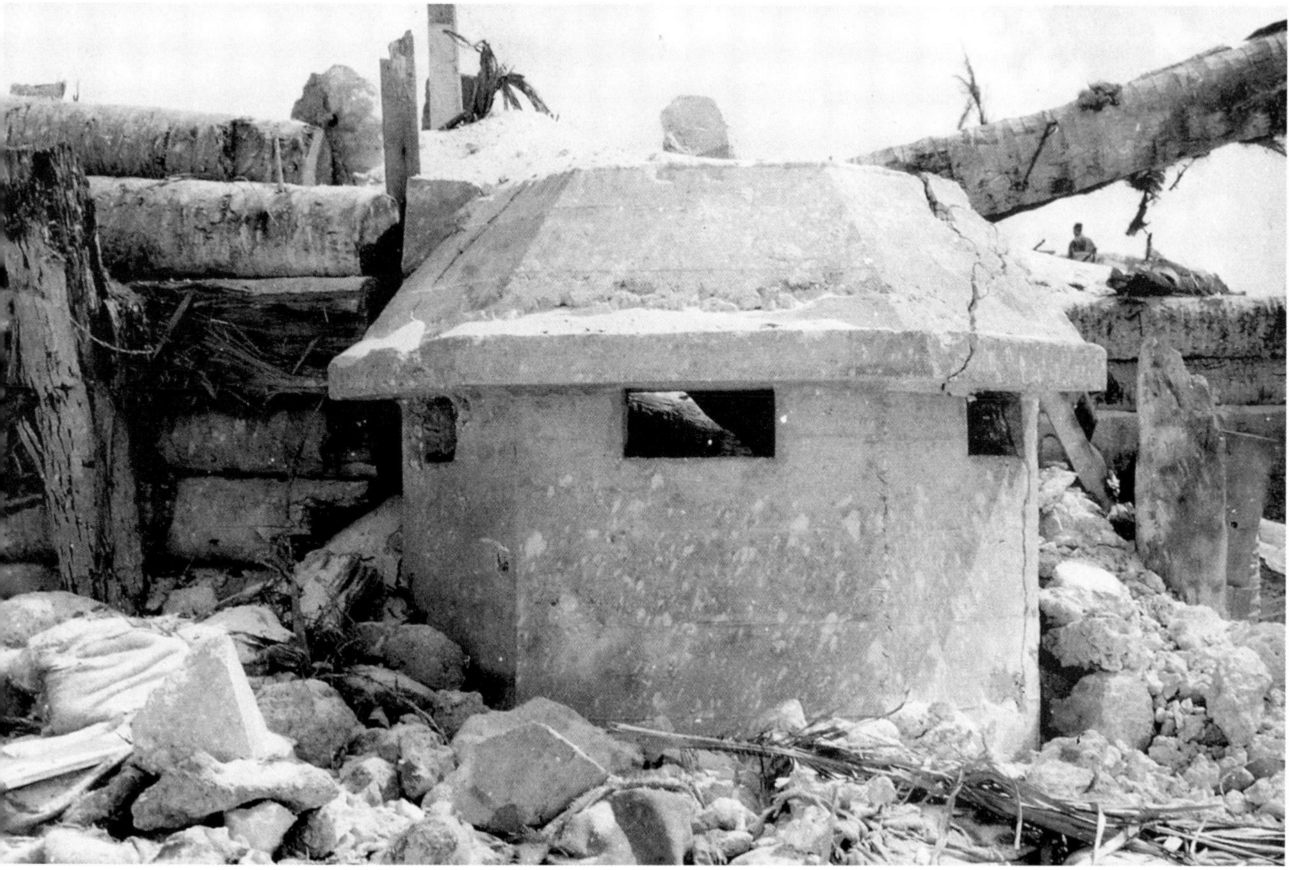

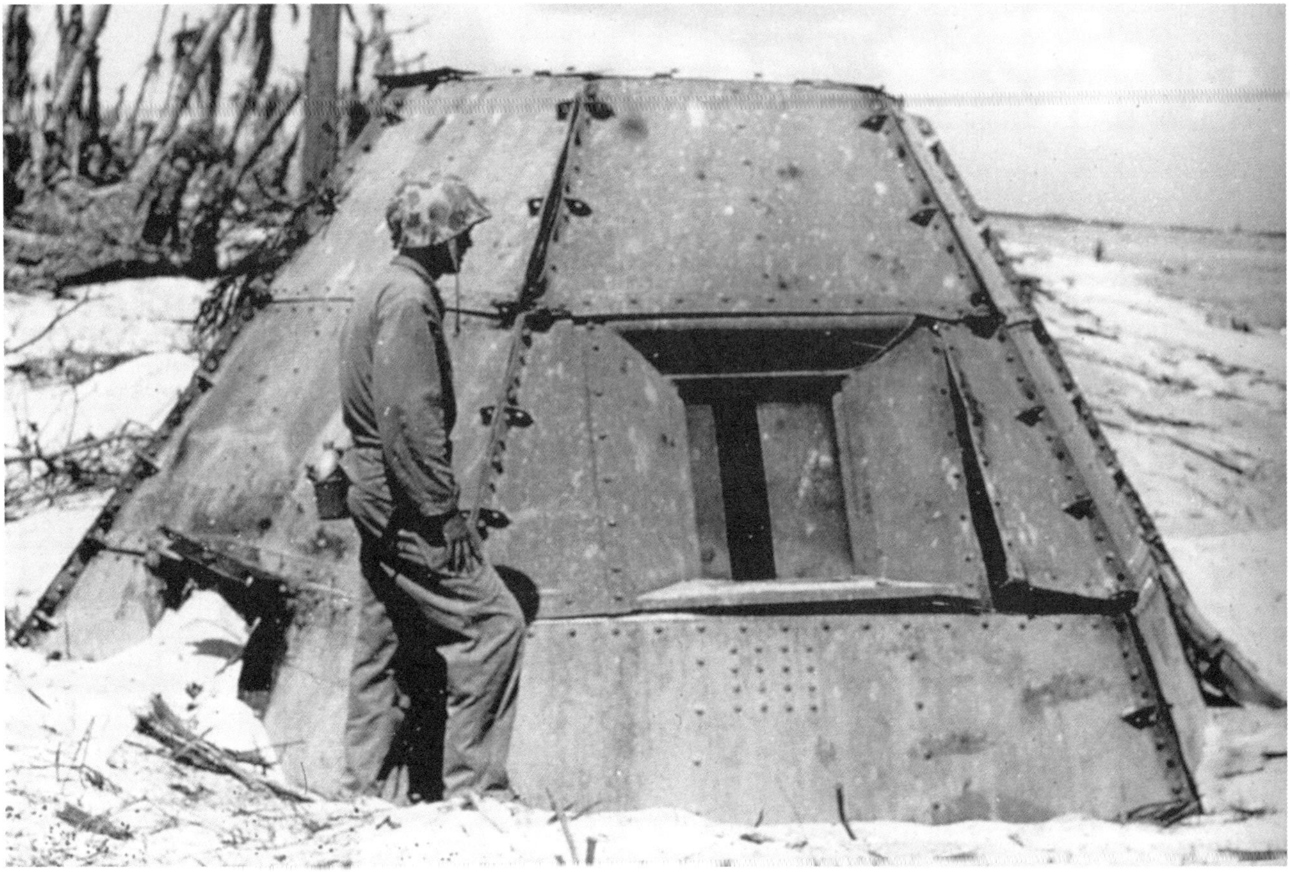

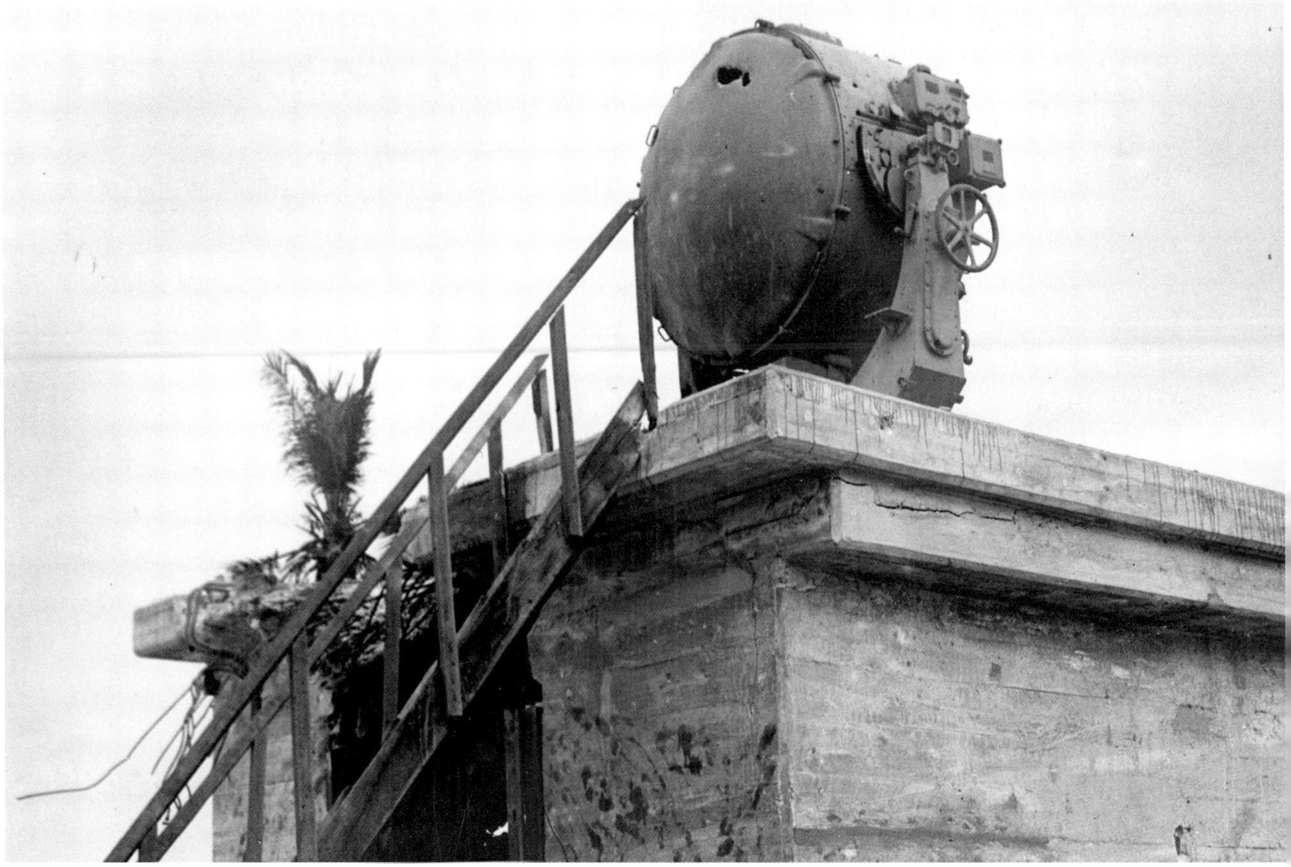

(**Opposite, above**) An interesting piece of defensive work found on Betio beaches was the prefabricated hexagonal-shaped steel pillbox seen here. The Marines deduced that they were command and observation posts that were to be encased in concrete, but only two had been completed when the Marines attacked the island. (*USMC*)

(**Opposite, below**) A part of Betio's naval-defence system was this searchlight seen here in a post-invasion picture. The largest anti-aircraft gun on Betio was designated the Type 89 and consisted of a mount armed with two 127mm guns. The guns and mounts were originally designed and built for Japanese warships in the early 1930s and were considered a dual-purpose gun for engaging enemy aircraft and ships. (*USMC*)

(**Above**) Descending the scramble net of a troopship off Betio on 20 November 1943 are Marines of the 2nd Division. The infantry regiments of the division that were the spearhead of the island's invasion were the 2nd, 6th and 8th Marines; the artillery regiment was the 10th Marines; and the engineers, pioneers and Naval Construction Battalion ('Seabees') were consolidated into the 18th Marines. (*USMC*)

In this post-invasion picture, we see an immobilized LVT-1 on the coconut log sea wall that surrounded most of Betio. The employment of LVTs was not considered necessary by the US Navy leadership for the invasion of Betio, despite the island's encircling barrier reef that was of undetermined depth. The Marine Corps leadership thought otherwise and bluntly informed the US Navy leadership that if there were no LVTs present for the assault on Betio there would be no Marines on site. (USMC)

The US Navy pre-invasion bombardment of Betio was of relatively short duration due to the desire to maintain the element of surprise over the Japanese senior leadership in the Pacific. This was achieved but resulted in the bulk of the Japanese defences on the island surviving intact. The result was the decimation of the first day's assault forces on Betio, as is illustrated by the bodies of two dead Marines on one of the island's beaches. (USMC)

A derelict LVT-1 is in the foreground of this post-invasion picture taken on Betio with an LVT-2 behind it. The 2nd Amphibian Tractor Battalion assigned to the assault on Betio had in its inventory seventy-five worn-out LVT-1s employed during the Guadalcanal campaign and fifty brand-new LVT-2s. The latter was a big improvement over its predecessor with a new suspension system and a more powerful engine and superior powertrain of the M3A1 light tank. (USMC)

Colonel David M. Shoup was the 2nd Marine Regiment's commanding officer for the assault on Betio. He went ashore on Day 1 of the invasion with his staff and what turned out to be the only working radio. For his actions over the two days he spent on Betio in turning possible defeat for the Marines into victory he received the Medal of Honor. He is seen here post-invasion resting his weight on a bicycle because he had badly wrenched a knee on arrival at the island. *(USMC)*

Of the approximately 5,000 Marines that were landed on Betio on 20 November 1943, it was estimated that 1,500 had been killed or wounded. The wounded were floated out on rafts as pictured through the island's shallow lagoon to the surrounding barrier reef by Day 2 of the invasion. At that point, they would be picked up by US Navy landing craft and transported to the troop transports for further treatment. *(USMC)*

On Day 1 of the invasion of Betio the bulk of the Marine survivors on the island were huddled behind the coconut log sea wall as seen here for protection from the relentless Japanese fire. Behind the Marines pictured is an LVT-1. Of the 125 LVTs employed for the assault on Betio, only thirty-five were still operational when the island was finally declared secure. Fifty-two of the LVT-1s and thirty LVT-2s were lost to direct enemy action. *(USMC)*

Slated for delivery to the shores of Betio on Day 1 of the invasion were fourteen Marine M4A2 medium tanks and a number of Marine M3A1 light tanks. Due to the heavy Japanese fire and various obstacles, not all the medium tanks made it ashore. One of the medium tanks that made it ashore is shown here. None of the M3A1 light tanks made it ashore on Day 1 of the Betio assault. *(USMC)*

This Marine Corps M4A2 medium tank on Betio has been riddled with Japanese anti-tank gunfire. By the end of Day 2 of the invasion the Marines had four of their medium tanks operating on the island. The first of the M3A1 light tanks made it ashore on Day 2. They were employed to protect the medium tanks from attack by enemy tank-hunting teams armed with magnetic mines. *(USMC)*

As there were only enough LVTs for the first three assault waves on Betio on Day 1 of the invasion, subsequent assault waves were brought in by shallow-draft US Navy unarmoured landing craft. These consisted of Landing Craft, Vehicle, Personnel (LCVP) as seen here heading towards Betio, and the larger Landing Craft, Medium (LCM). *(USMC)*

As the Marine leadership had predicted but the US Navy leadership would not take into consideration, the landing craft that were tasked with bringing in the follow-on assault waves to Betio on Day 1 all grounded on the island's barrier reef. This forced the Marines to disembark and wade through the island's lagoon, exposing themselves to murderous enemy fire. Out of desperation, some Marines sought the cover of a Japanese-built pier to reach shore but failed, as attested to in this photograph. (USMC)

(**Above**) Slowly but surely, some of the Marines pinned behind the coconut log sea wall on Day 1 of the Betio invasion managed to organize themselves and head inland as pictured. Aiding them was a single M3 Gun Motor Carriage (GMC), five 75mm towed howitzers and a few towed 37mm anti-tank guns. Despite this additional firepower, none of the planned objectives were secured by the Marines on the first day of their invasion. (*USMC*)

(**Opposite, above**) The Japanese defenders had anticipated the use of tanks if and when the Americans invaded and as seen in this post-invasion picture had dug an anti-tank ditch. A War Department publication dated October 1944 describes Japanese anti-tank ditches as ranging from 4ft to 8ft in depth and 10ft to 20ft in width and typically protected by minefields. The Japanese defenders on Betio had received land mines but they did not have time to emplace them before the Marines attacked. (*USMC*)

(**Opposite, below**) In this post-invasion photograph taken on Betio, Marines are inspecting a knocked-out Japanese Navy Type 95 light tank. The three-man tank had a 37mm main gun and two 7mm machine guns. The maximum armour thickness on the tank was 12mm. It weighed approximately 20,000lb and had a height of 7ft. (*USMC*)

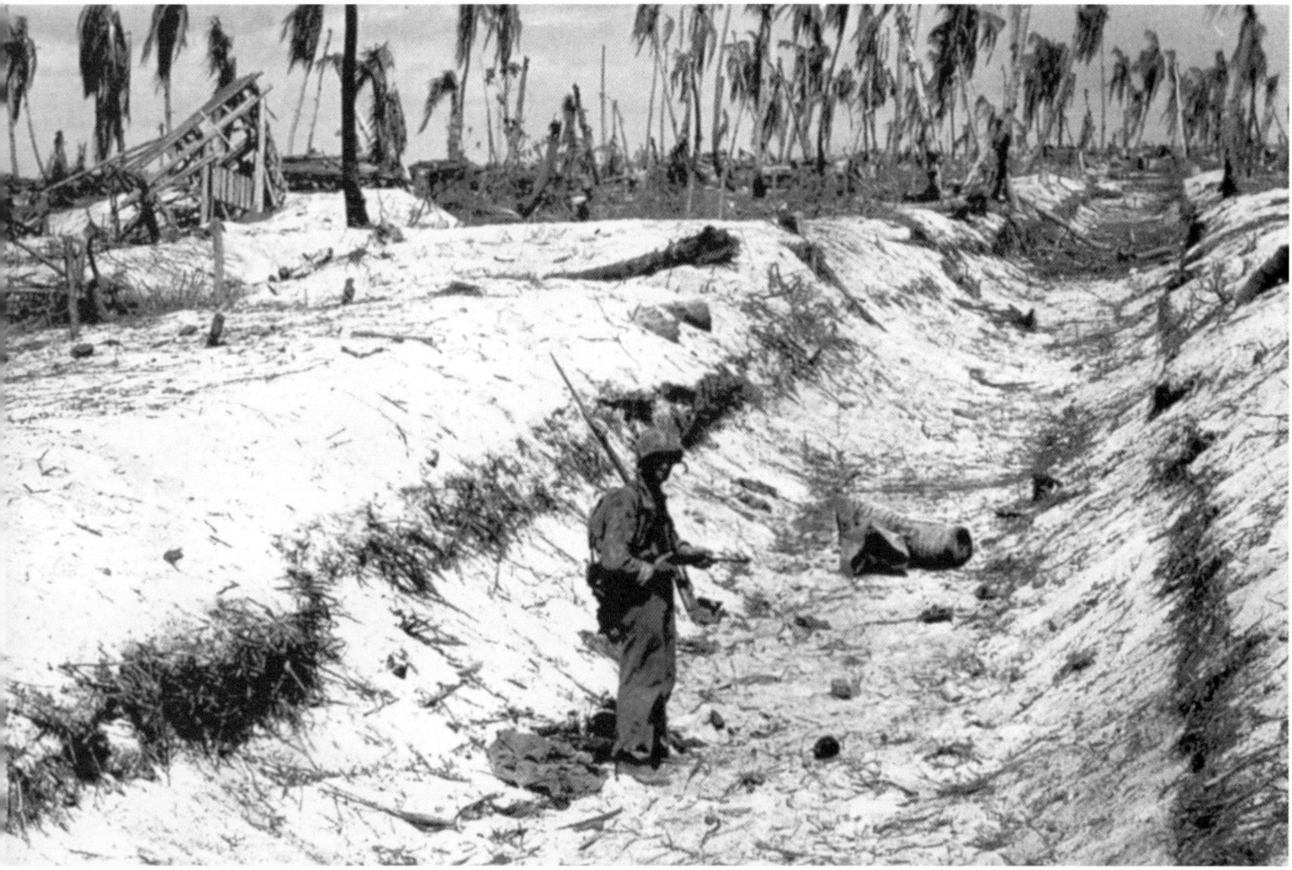

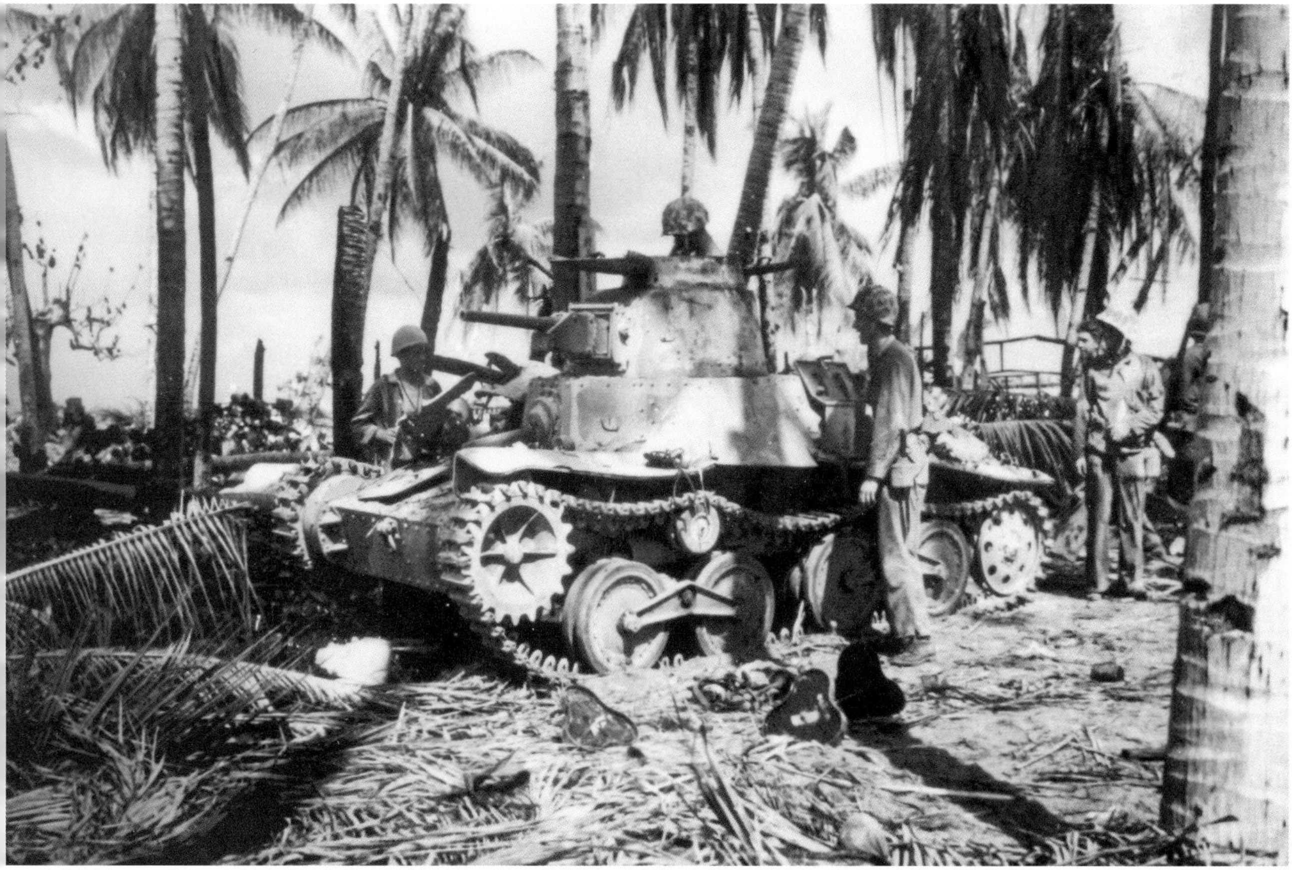

(**Above**) The Marines continued to pour more men and equipment into Betio to secure the island as quickly as possible. By Day 2 of the invasion Marine numbers and firepower, assisted by US Navy destroyer gunfire, had turned the tide of battle against the Japanese. Pictured here are Marines wading through the island's lagoon to reach shore on Day 3 of the assault. By this time, all the Japanese defensive positions that had taken such a toll of the Marines on Day 1 and 2 had been destroyed. (USMC)

(**Opposite, above**) By the end of Day 3 of the invasion of Betio the Marines searching out the Japanese defenders began finding many who had committed suicide rather than suffer the shame of surrender, as seen in this picture. The island of Betio was finally declared secure by the Marines on 23 November 1943 at 3.30pm. It took the Marines until 28 November 1943 to clear the other small islands in the Tarawa atoll of Japanese military personnel. (USMC)

(**Opposite, below**) Pictured in this post-invasion photograph is the Japanese command bunker on Betio. Its thick reinforced concrete walls managed to withstand all the US Navy's large-calibre projectile strikes. As a command bunker, it lacked any gun ports. It finally fell to the Marines when somebody with a flame-thrower managed to douse the interior through a partially-opened steel armour door. (USMC)

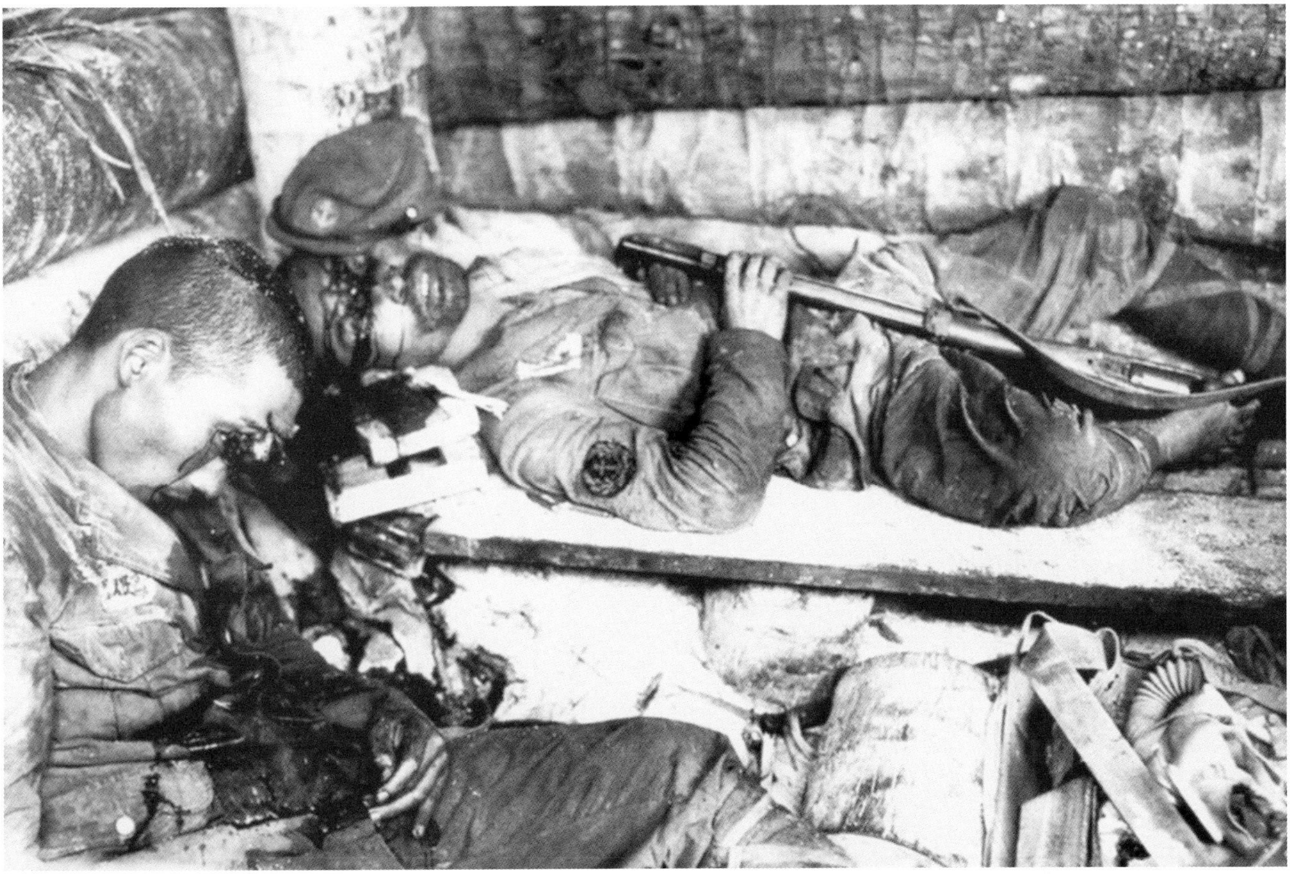

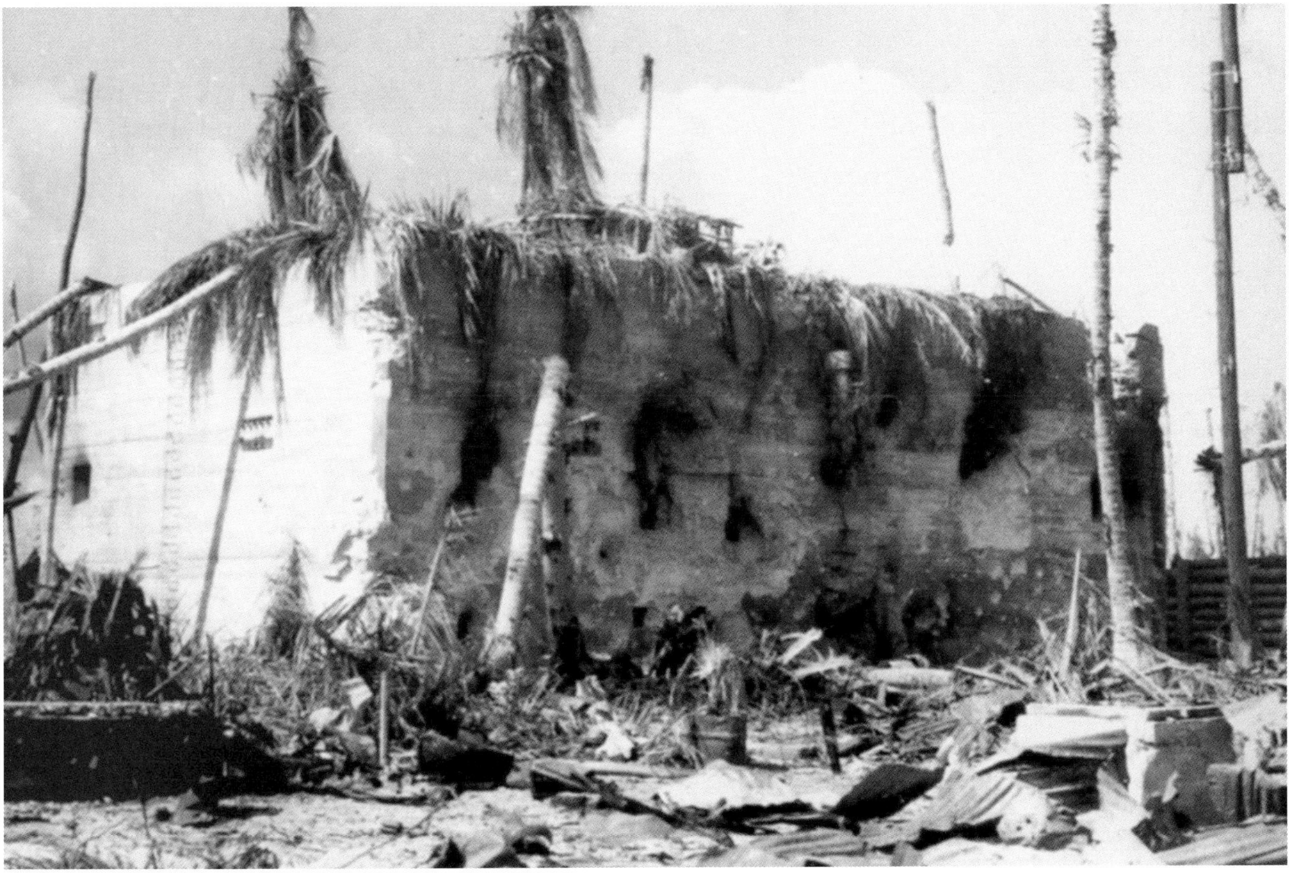

Lieutenant General Holland M. Smith, pictured here, was commissioned a second lieutenant in the Marine Corps in 1905. Beginning in the early 1930s, he became increasingly interested in the development of amphibious warfare concepts. He was the commander of the V Amphibious Corps, which oversaw the capture of Betio. His well-known ferocious temper earned him the nickname 'Howling Mad Smith'. *(USMC)*

The Japanese airfield on Roi Island in the Kwajalein atoll is shown here during an attack by US Navy aircraft on 29 January 1944. Note the smoke from bombs, fragmentation devices, burning aircraft and facilities, plus a bright explosion bottom-left centre. Marines landed on Roi three days later. The Kwajalein atoll is a part of the Marshall Islands chain in the Central Pacific. (*US Navy*)

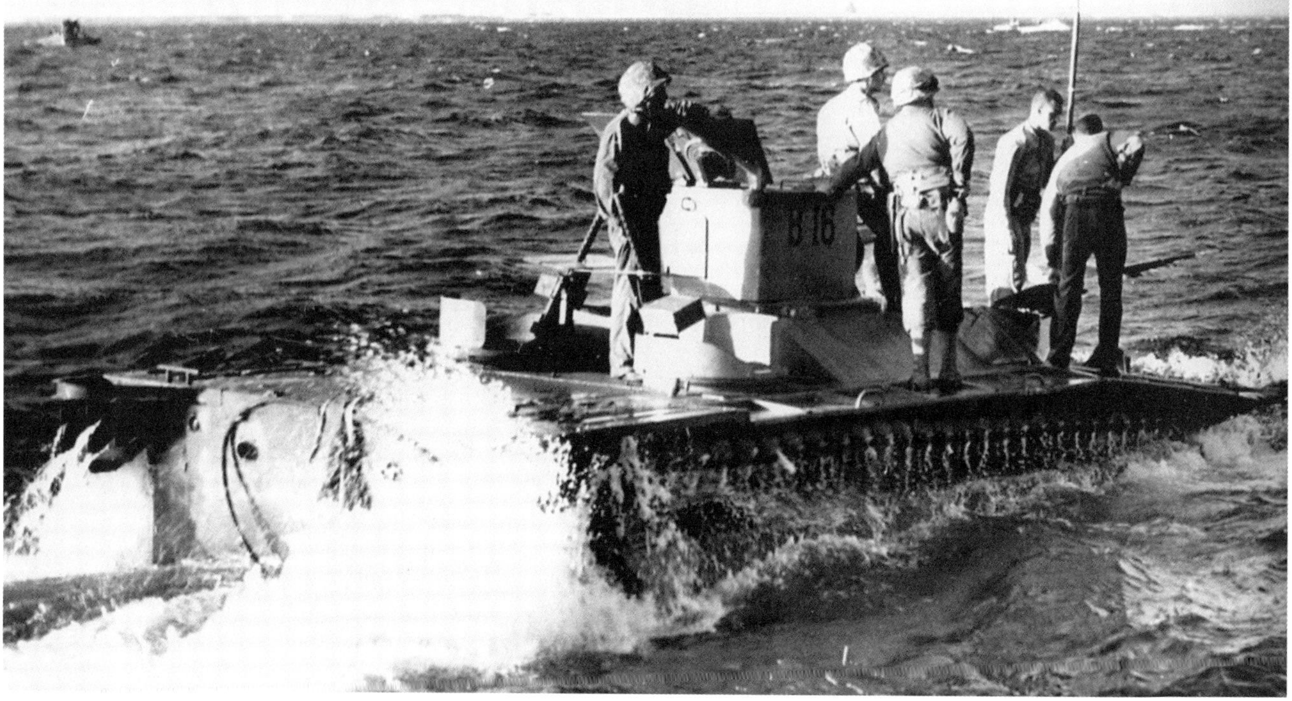
B 16

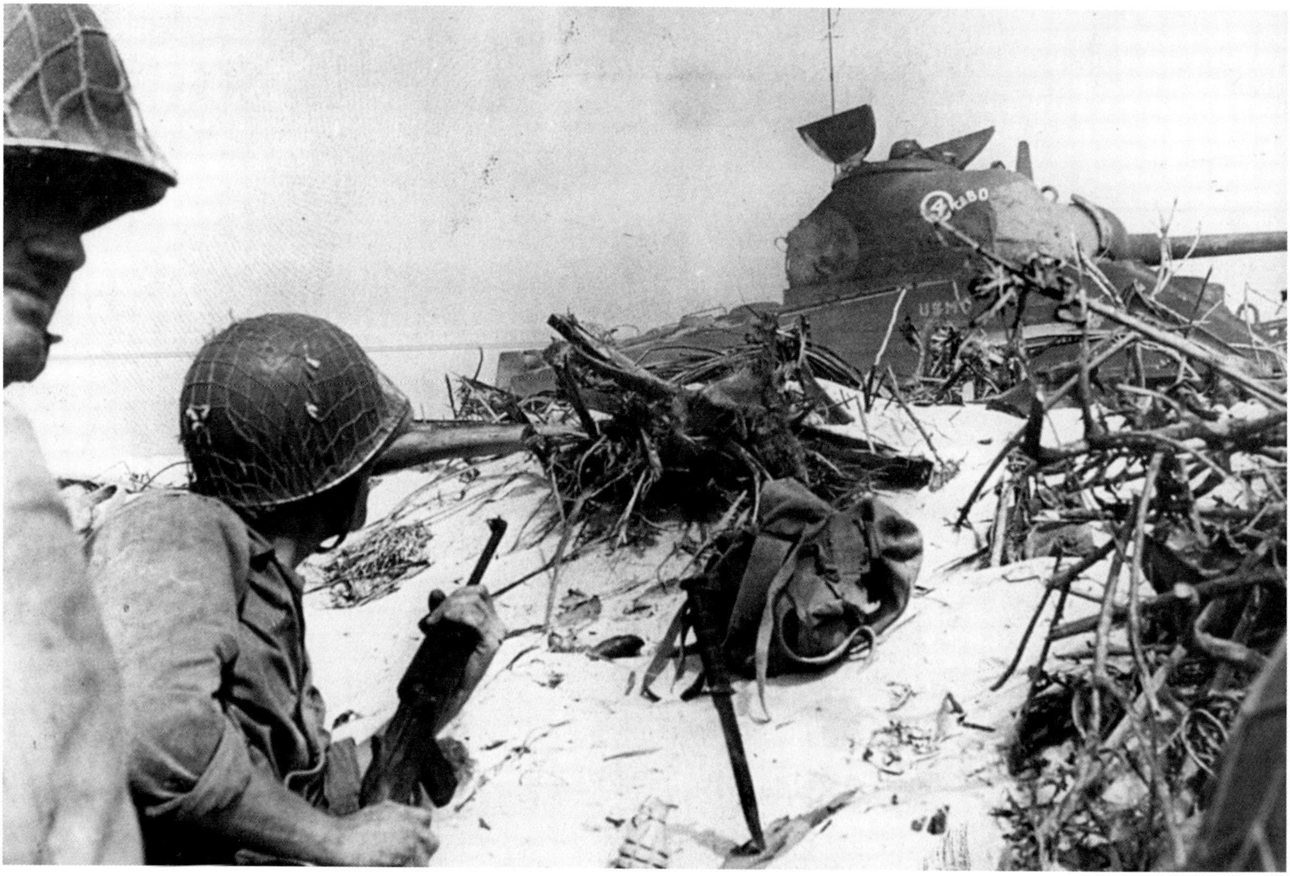
USMC

(**Opposite, above**) A Marine Corps LVT(A)-1 churns through the water on its way to Roi Island. The crew is not taking any chances and except for the driver all are standing on top of the vehicle in case it starts to sink. The LVT(A)-1 was an armoured version of the unarmoured LVT-2 that in addition had an armoured roof surmounted by a 37mm gun-armed turret adapted from the M3A1 light tank. (*USMC*)

(**Above**) A group of Marines are shown on one of the landing beaches on Roi on 29 January 1944, the first day of the invasion. An LVT(A)-1 is seen in the background. Having learned valuable lessons from the near disaster on Betio, the US Navy subjected Roi and the connected island of Namur to a much more intense and longer bombardment, although the rubble created by destroyed buildings on Namur created countless hiding places for the enemy. (*USMC*)

(**Opposite, below**) Pictured is one of the Marine Corps M4A2 medium tanks that took part in the initial assault on Roi Island. The reason the Marines took the twin diesel-engine-powered M4A2 into service was the fact that it was available in the required numbers when the corps decided to form its first two medium tank battalions in early 1943. The bulk of the M4A2 medium tanks constructed was committed to Lend-Lease and went primarily to the British and Russian armies. (*USMC*)

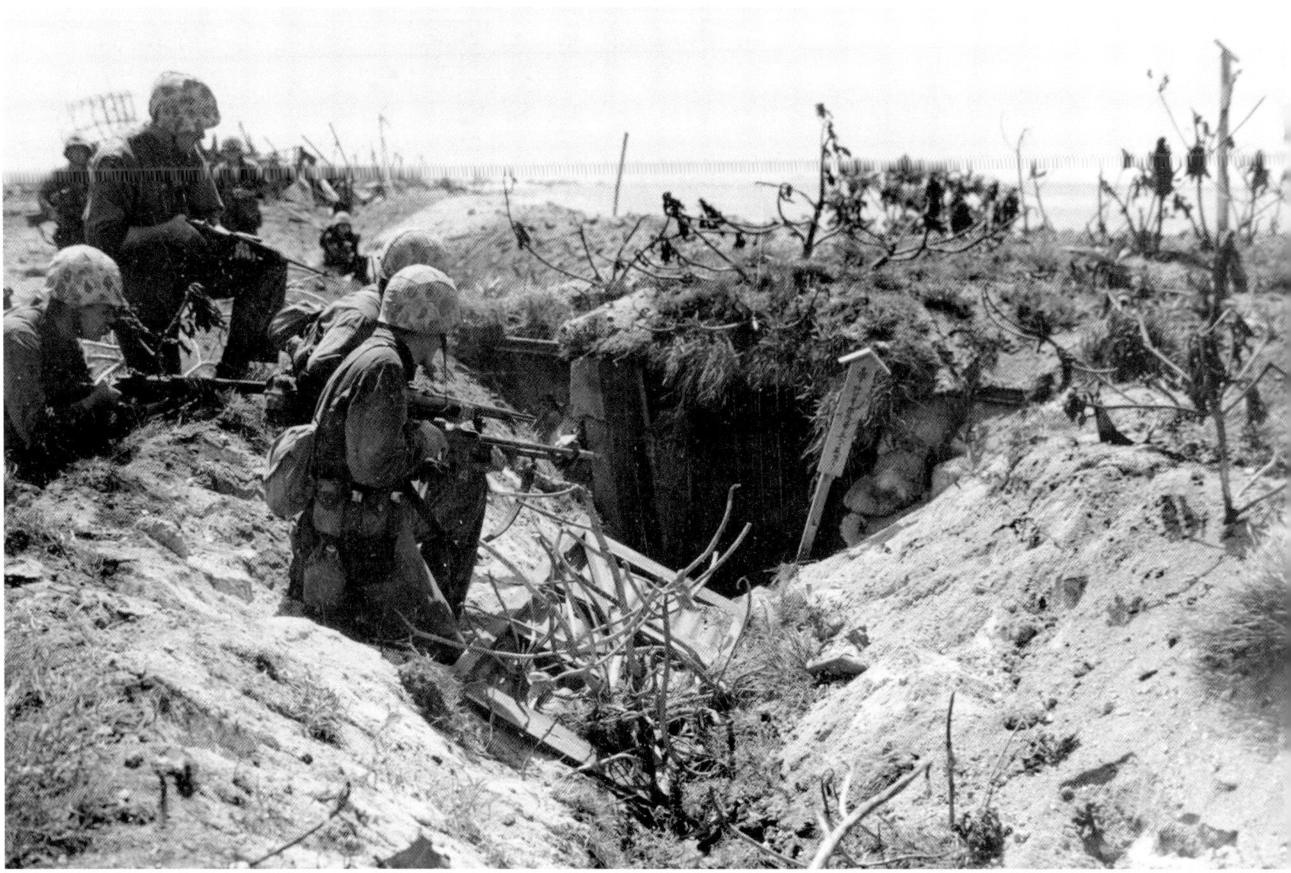

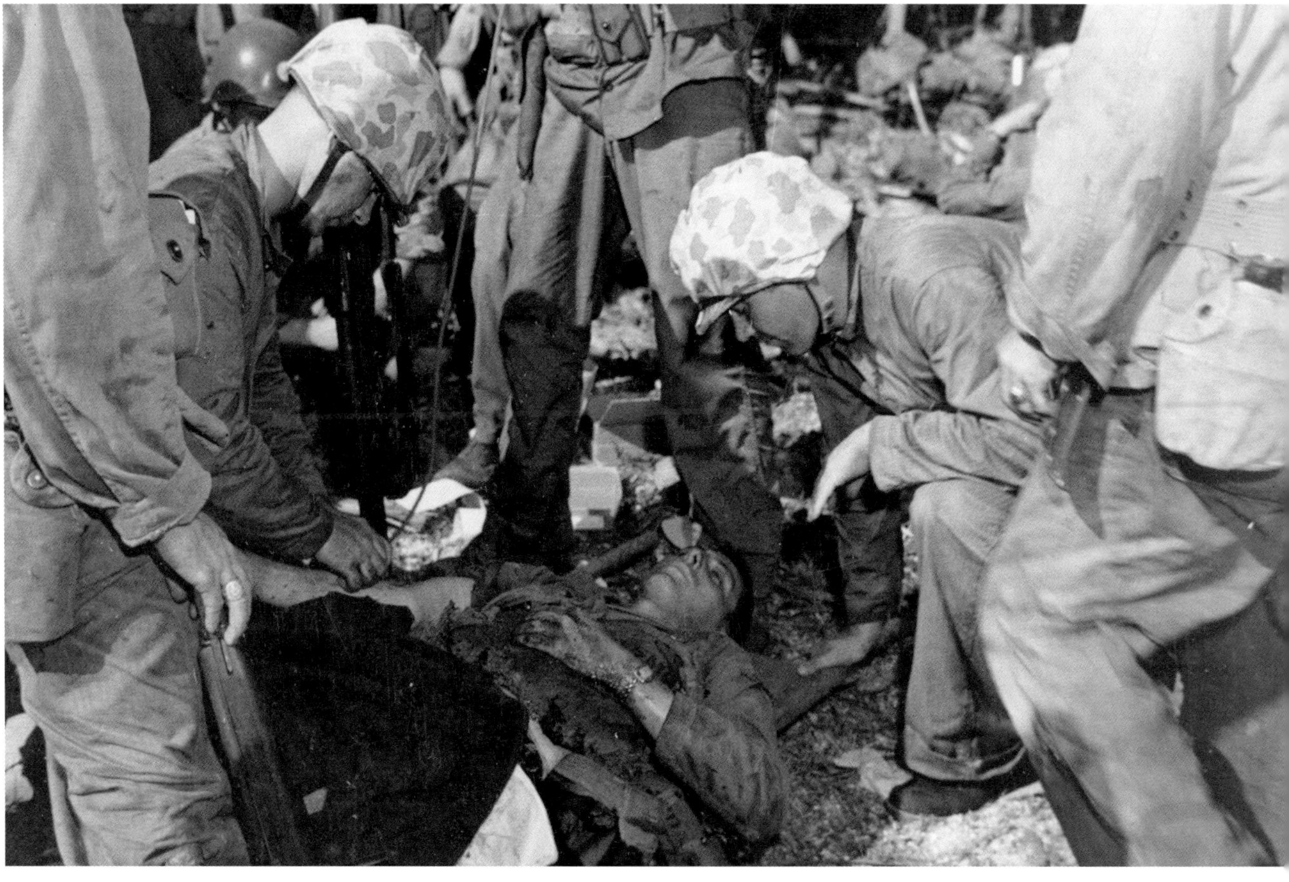

(**Opposite, above**) In this obviously posed picture, Marines are seen at the entrance to a Japanese dugout on Roi Island following its capture. Note the Japanese signpost by the entrance. The Marine in the foreground holds a Browning Automatic Rifle (BAR). The other Marines shown are armed with the M-1 rifle, also referred to by many as the 'Garand', and the M1 carbine adopted by the corps in 1942. (USMC)

(**Opposite, below**) A navy chaplain is shown possibly administering the last rites to a wounded Marine on Roi. The Marines learned in combat, once wounded, not to call out for a corpsman as this would alert the enemy to their arrival. Instead, a wounded Marine or his buddies would call out 'Sailor, Sailor' or 'gizmo' as the corpsmen were US Navy personnel and not Marines. (USMC)

(**Above**) Although the typical young Marine infantryman never thought he would be one of those killed in combat, fighting a fearless and tough foe like the Japanese always led to losses as is illustrated by this Marine killed on Roi. Those killed in combat were quickly buried, often on the spot where they died, until such time as their bodies could be moved to a suitable cemetery on site. (USMC)

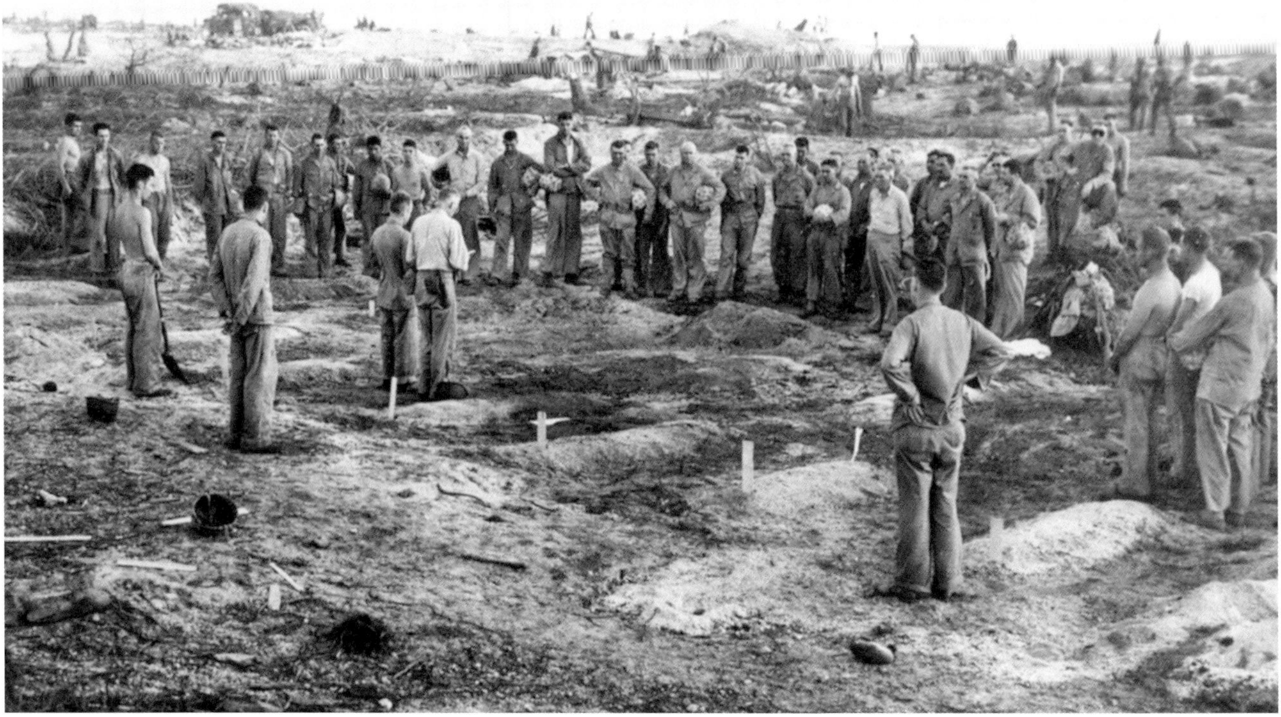

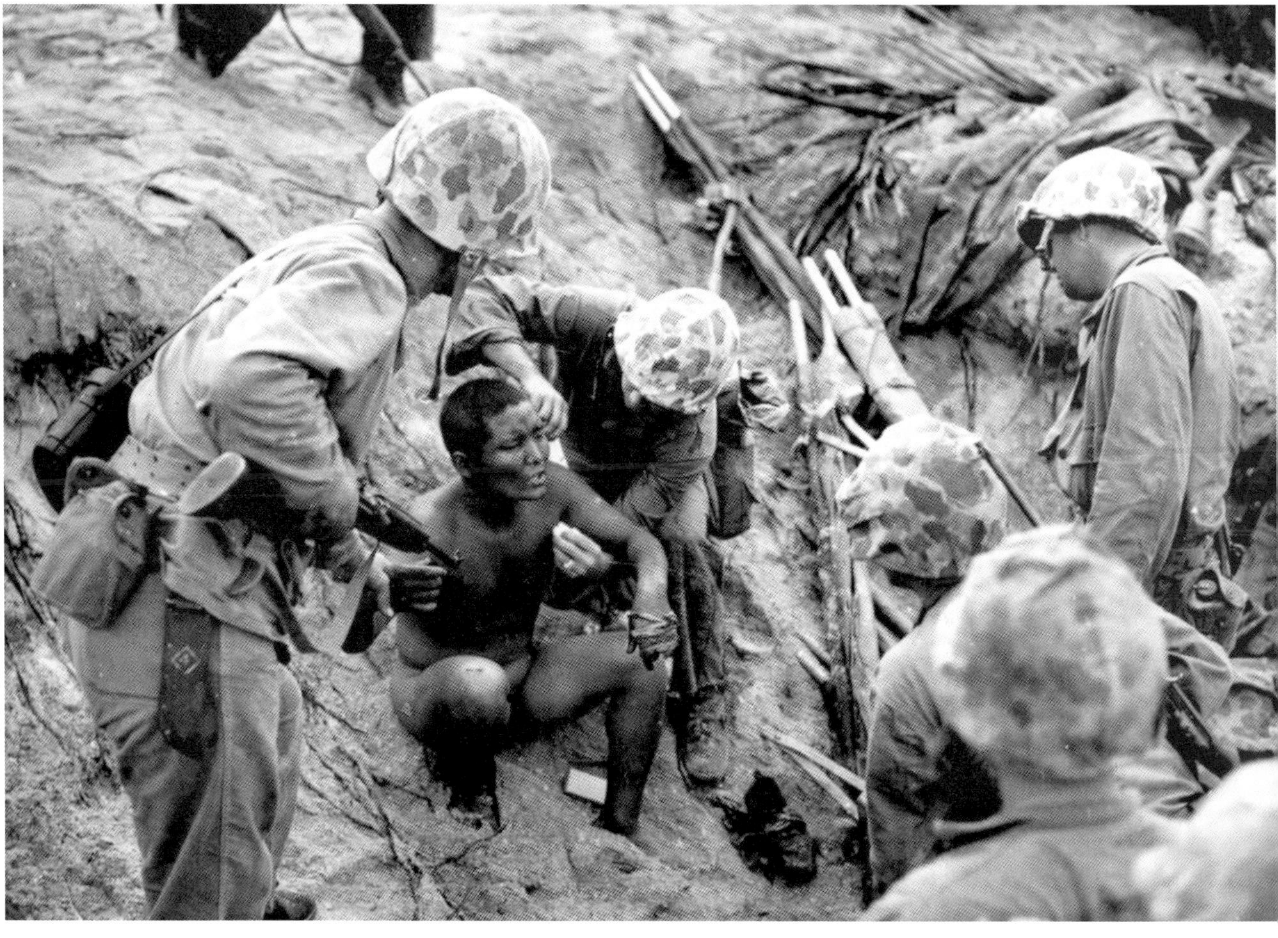

(**Opposite, above**) At a cemetery on Roi, Marines are shown paying their last respects to buddies killed in taking the island. When the identity of a deceased Marine had been confirmed, his family was sent a Killed In Action (KIA) certificate as well as any awards he might have been given. After the war, families of the deceased were offered the option of leaving them in these overseas military cemeteries or brought home for burial at a Veterans' Administration Cemetery. (USMC)

(**Opposite, below**) Seen here on Roi is possibly a Japanese prisoner, which tended to be very rare during most of the war in the Central Pacific. Very often the prisoners taken were Korean labourers employed by the Japanese in the construction units to build airfields and island defences. When prisoners were captured, they were almost always motioned to strip to their underwear for fear of hidden grenades. (USMC)

(**Above**) The Marine landings on the island of Namur did not go as planned. The LVT crews, such as those pictured here, became confused as the intense pre-invasion bombardment had destroyed the landmarks they had been taught to use for navigation. In addition, billowing black smoke from burning oil tanks, aviation fuel and structures covered a great deal of the island. (USMC)

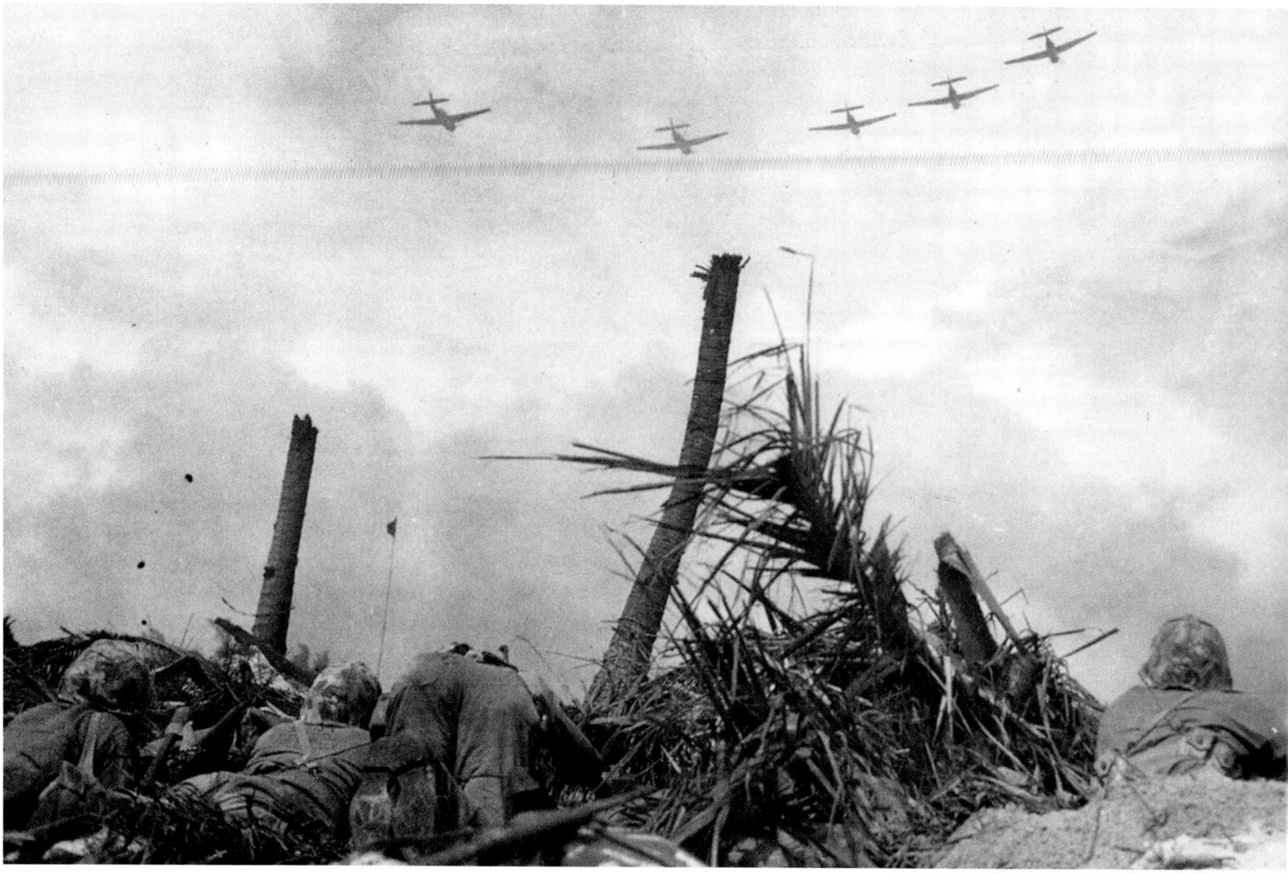

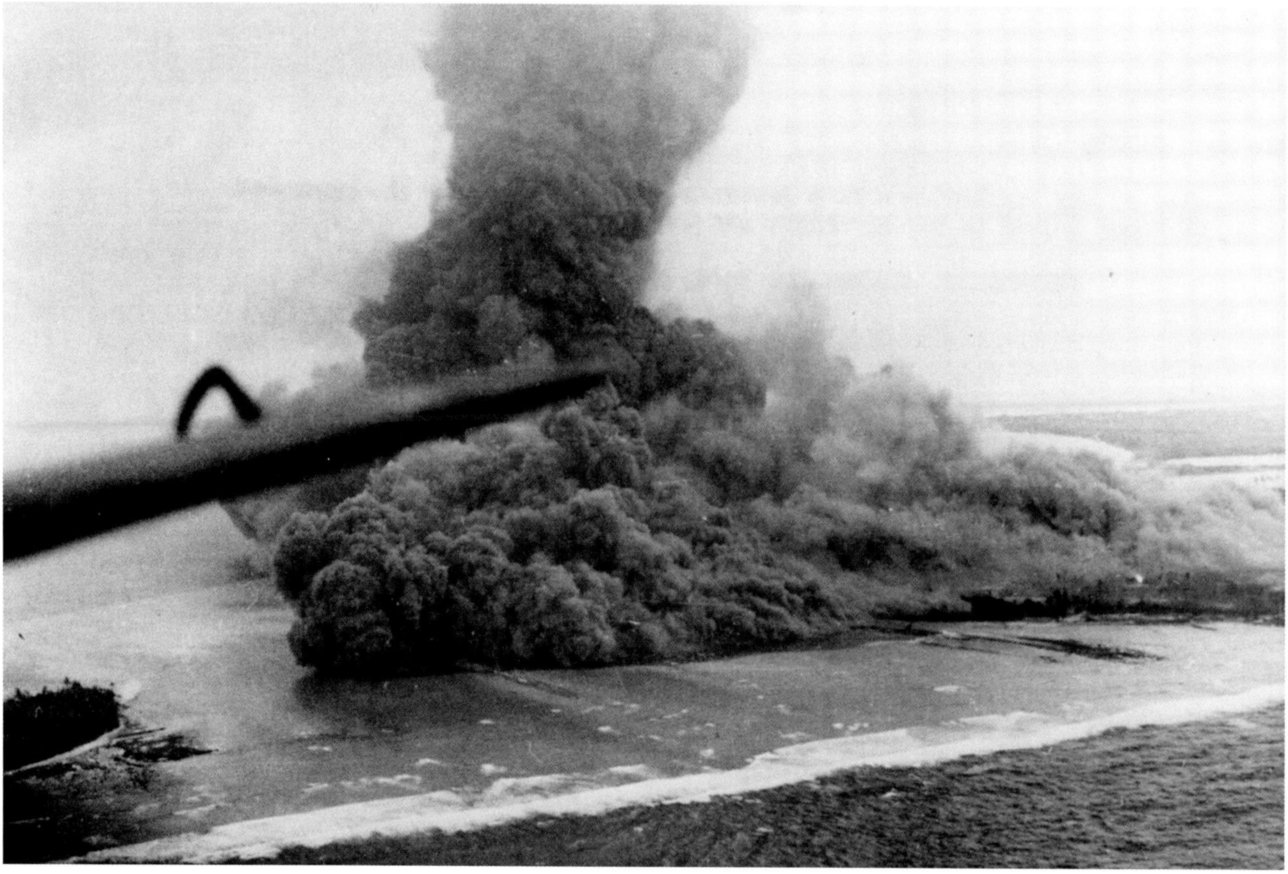

(**Opposite, above**) In this picture taken on Namur Island on 31 January 1944 we see Marines taking cover in the island's thick scrub vegetation. In some places the undergrowth was 6ft high and made it impossible to see more than a few feet. It also provided handy concealment for the enemy. Overhead is a formation of US Navy planes attacking the other side of the island. *(USMC)*

(**Above**) A Marine Corps M4A2 medium tank is crushing a Japanese coconut log bunker on Namur. Attacked by Japanese infantry tank-hunting teams armed with magnetic anti-tank mines on New Georgia and Betio, the Marine tankers began adding wooden planks to the hull sides as pictured here. Concrete reinforced with rebar was poured between the planks and hull for the same reason. *(USMC)*

(**Opposite, below**) Namur was the administrative centre and weapon storage site for the airfield on Roi and had a number of reinforced concrete buildings. As Marine assault teams began rooting out the Japanese defenders from these buildings with explosive charges, they unknowingly blew up a building containing a large number of torpedo warheads. The resulting chain explosion is seen here. More than 100 Marines were wounded and a further twenty killed. *(US Navy)*

(**Above**) US Navy corpsmen are attending to a wounded Marine on Namur. The corpsmen would apply sulphur powder to wounds to prevent infection and also provide morphine shots for pain. Once stabilized at a battalion aid station, a patient would be transported to a troop transport ship. These vessels had medical staff with operating rooms. The more seriously wounded would be transferred to a hospital ship and finally to a land-based hospital. (*USMC*)

(**Opposite, above**) The Marines on Namur were supported by M5A1 light tanks such as the one pictured here, in addition to larger M4A2 medium tanks. The device on the tank's rear hull is the lower portion of a deep-water wading kit. Also available for medium tanks, these were to address the serious losses of tanks in water-filled craters on Betio. (*USMC*)

(**Opposite, below**) Seen here on Namur are two Marines operating a light air-cooled .30 calibre M1919A4 machine gun. This weapon was found in Marine rifle company weapons platoons. The Marines in the photograph are wearing the reversible helmet camouflage covers first issued in late 1942. Helmet covers are typically a distinguishing feature of Marines as US Army soldiers normally did not cover their helmets. (*USMC*)

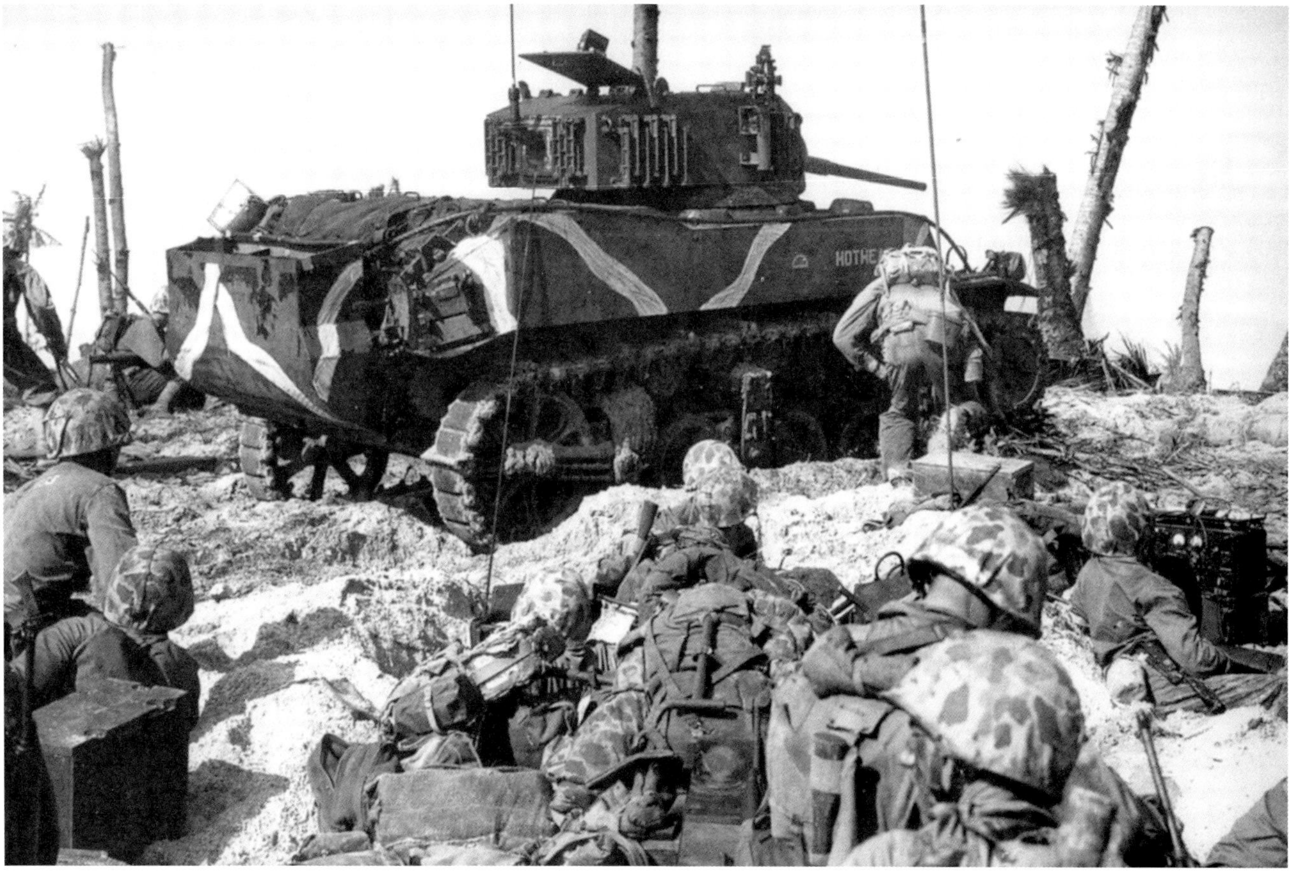

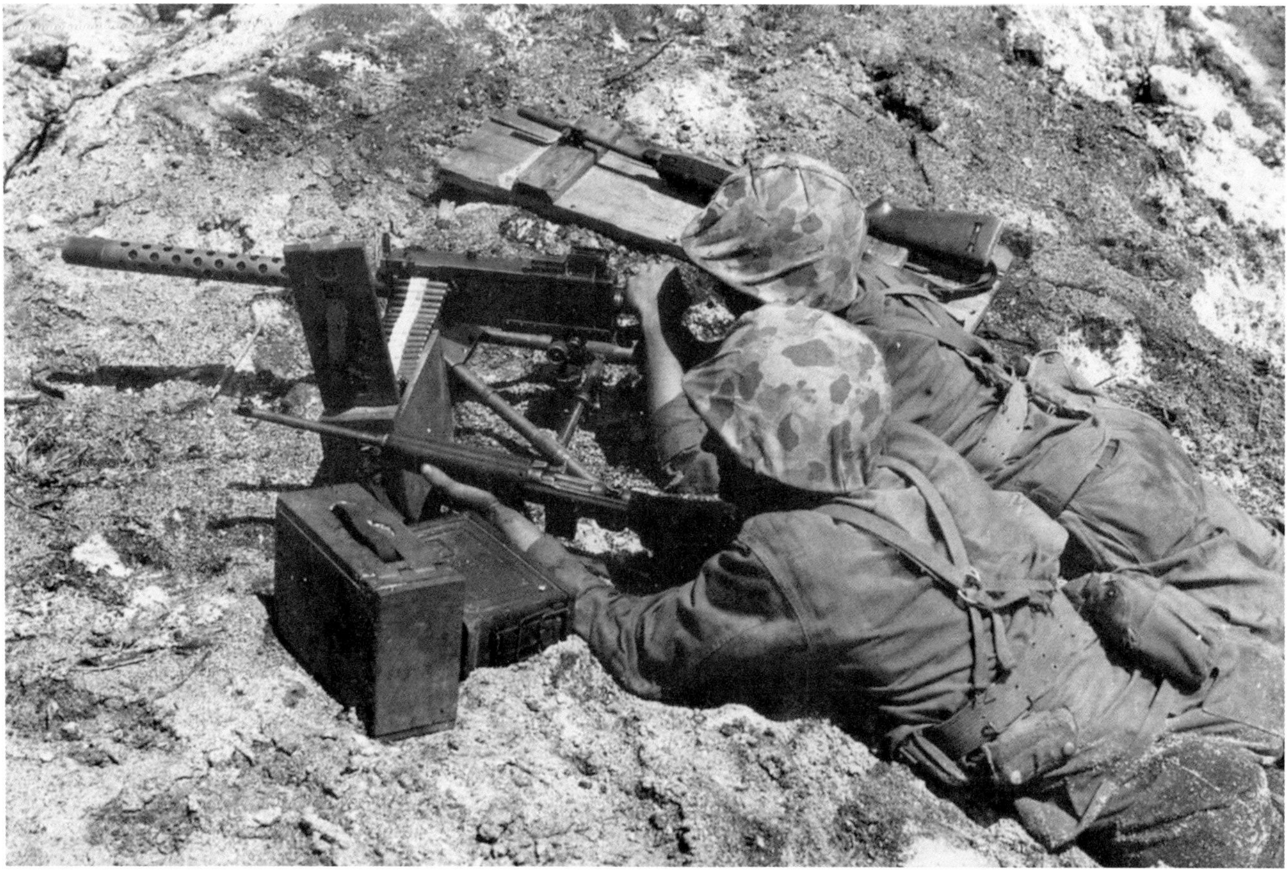

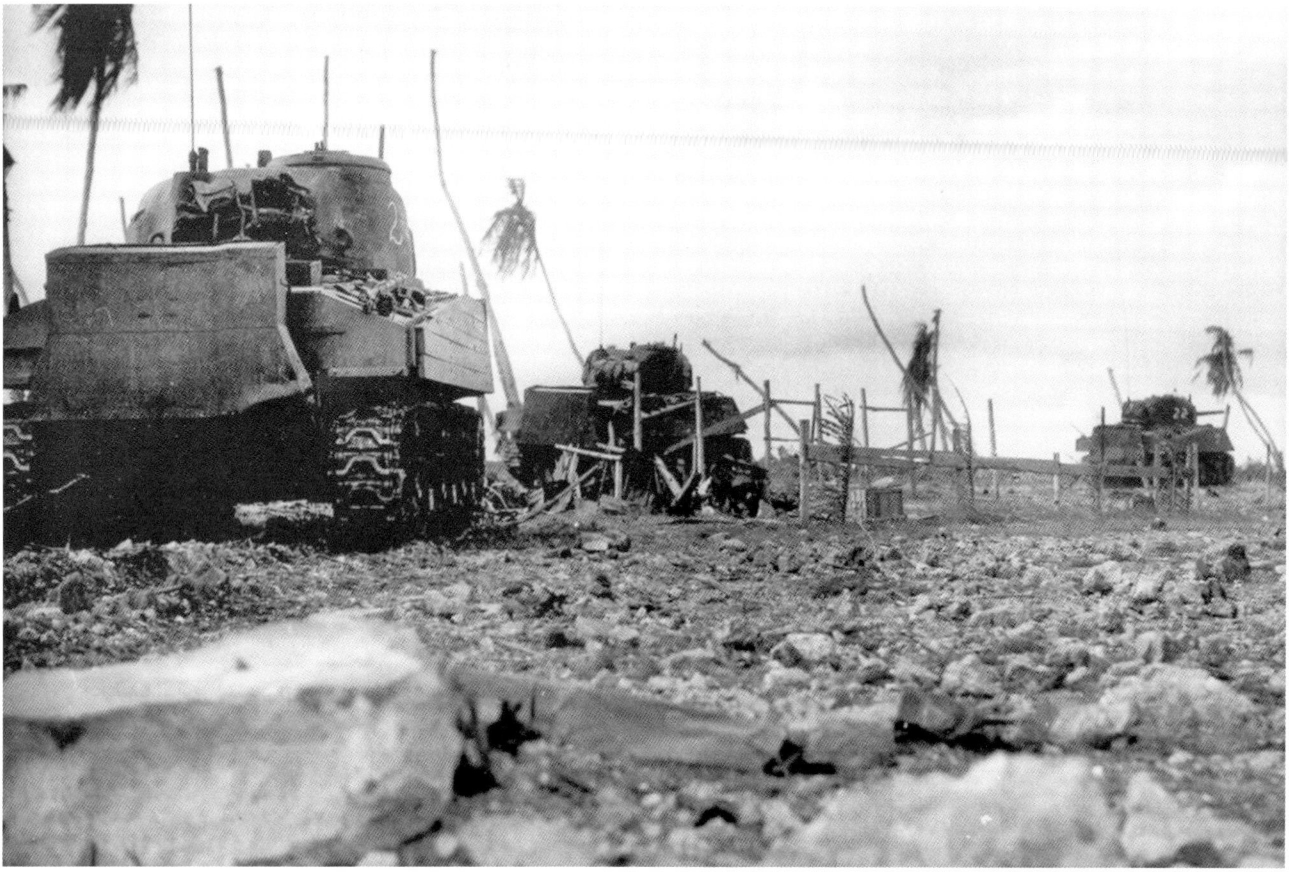

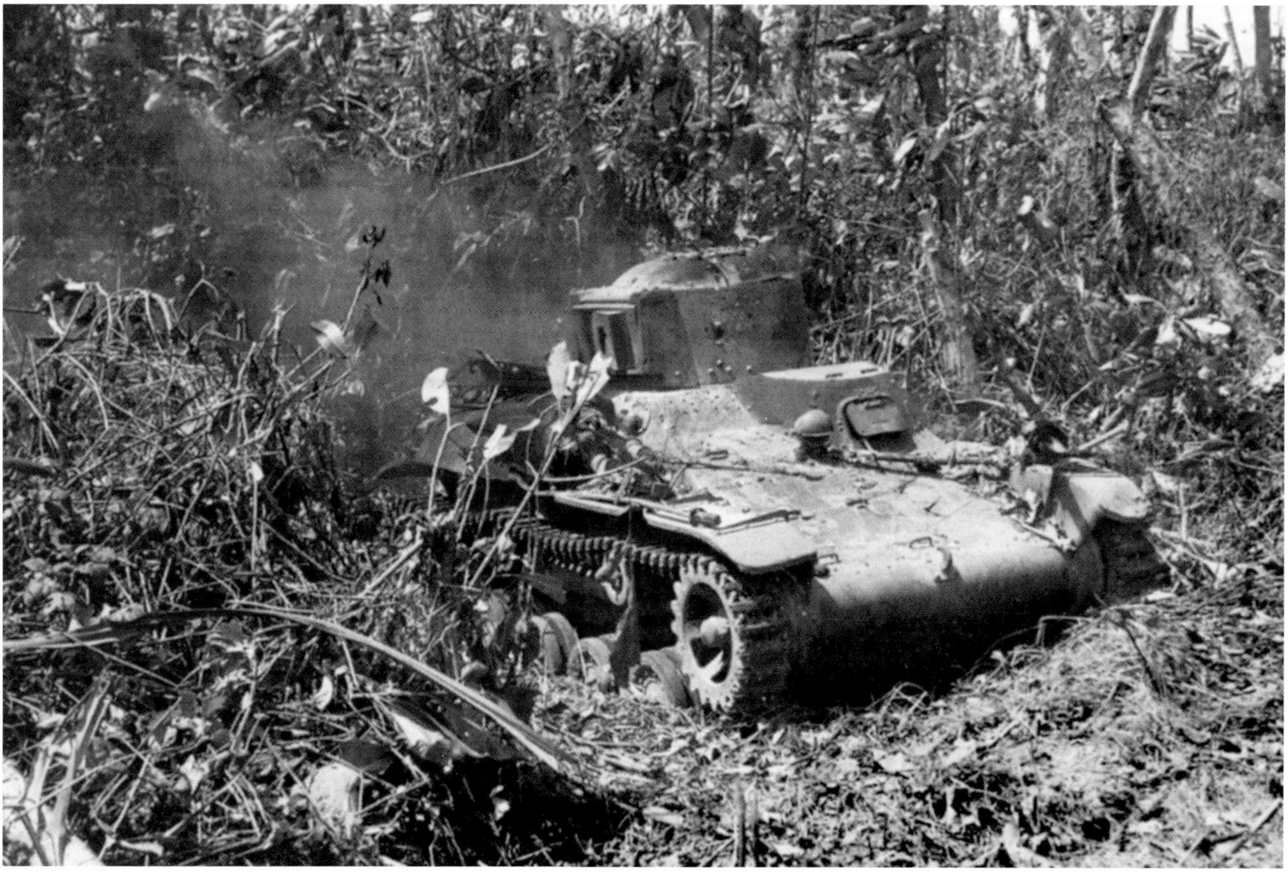

(**Opposite, above**) Such was Japanese resistance on Namur that four M4A2 medium tanks landed on Roi were driven over the causeway connecting the islands to aid in taking the island. Pictured here are three M4A2 medium tanks on Namur, all with the bottom portion of the wading trunk fitted. After landing, the upper portion was typically removed so it would not block the traverse of the tank's 75mm main gun. (*USMC*)

(**Above**) Two Marines are shown gingerly walking through the ruins of a reinforced concrete building on Namur that was employed as a storage site for what appear to be aerial bombs. Prior to March 1944, a Marine rifle squad normally consisted of a squad leader (sergeant), an assistant squad leader (corporal), two scouts, three riflemen, a grenadier and an automatic rifleman armed with a .30 calibre Browning Automatic Rifle (BAR). (*USMC*)

(**Opposite, below**) The Marines quickly dispatched this Japanese machine-gun-armed Type 94 light tank on Namur. During the first night on the island, the Marines took serious casualties from well-camouflaged Japanese soldiers who so spooked many Marines in rear areas that friendly fire became a dangerous issue. (*USMC*)

The 4th Division Marines on Roi Island salute as the flag is raised to mark the capture of Roi and Namur. The Marines' final thankless task was the policing and burial of dead Japanese soldiers. The stench of bodies putrefying in the blazing tropical sun was overpowering. Health conditions were so bad that 1,500 men of the division were suffering from dysentery when the Marines finally re-boarded their troop transports. (USMC)

The initial waves of US landing craft (seen at the top of this picture) are approaching Engebi Island, part of Eniwetok atoll, on 19 February 1944. The island, still smoking from the pre-invasion US Navy bombardment, was heavily cratered. As was now somewhat standard practice, Marine artillery units were deployed on islands around Engebi prior to its actual invasion to provide supporting fire. (USMC)

Marine Corporal Anthony P. Damato was posthumously awarded the Medal of Honor for his courage during the battle against the Japanese on Engebi Island. When an undetected enemy soldier approached Damato's fox-hole and threw in a grenade, he covered it with his body to absorb the blast, sacrificing himself to save his comrades. (USMC)

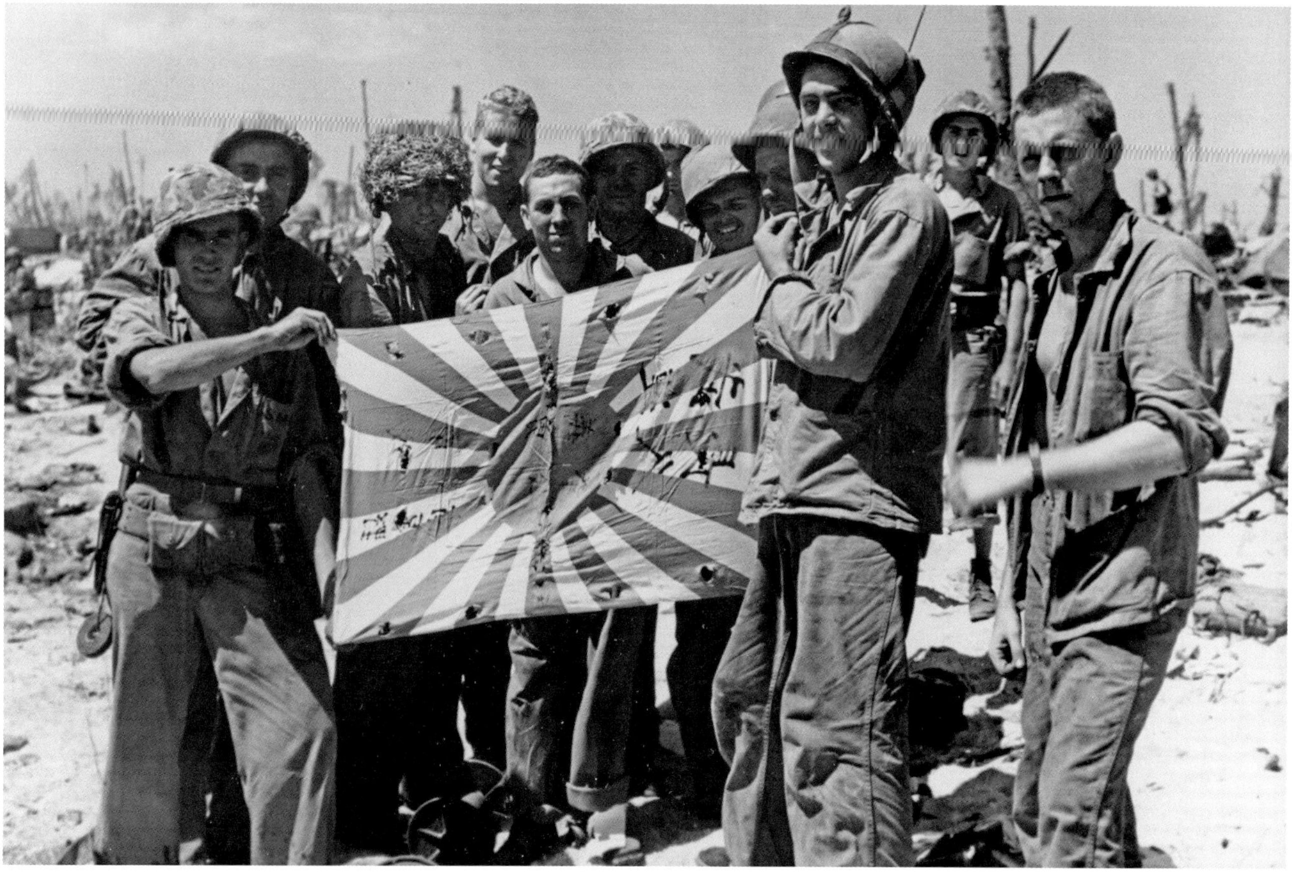

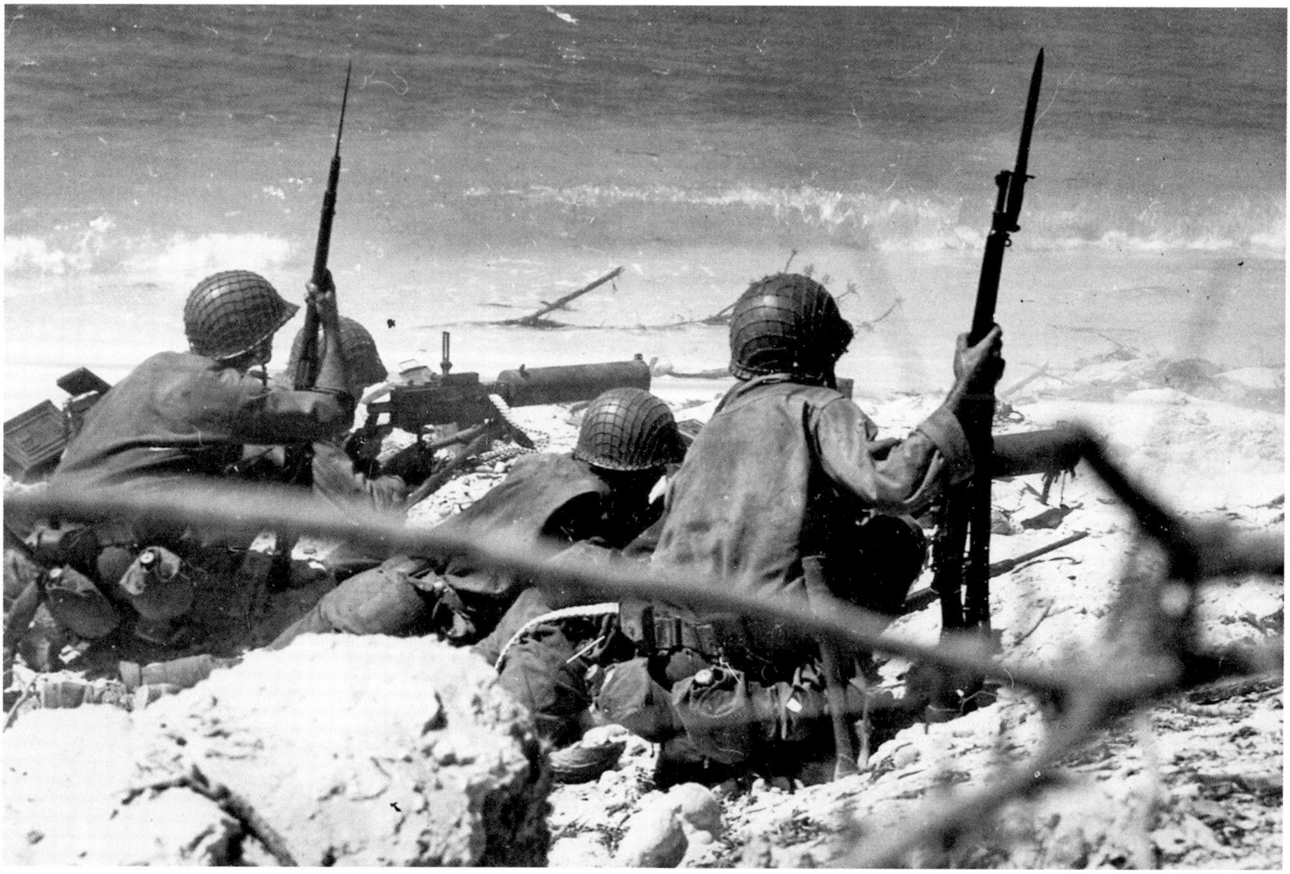

(**Opposite, above**) Marines and coast guardsmen proudly display a Japanese flag picked up by one of them during the capture of Engebi Island. Note the bullet holes in the enemy flag, and the strange helmet camouflage on one of the Marines pictured. The coast guardsmen in the picture are there because they operated many of the landing craft. (*US Coast Guard*)

(**Opposite, below**) Marines are seen here on an Eniwetok Island beach engaging a nearby Japanese machine-gun position with a heavy water-cooled .30 calibre M1917A1 machine gun. The weapon with tripod weighed approximately 94lb. They were initially found in infantry battalion weapons companies moved into rifle company weapons platoons. (*USMC*)

(**Above**) An M1 rifle stuck into the sand of a beach on Parry Island marks one of the fallen Marines. The island was one of three in the Eniwetok atoll, located at the western edge of the Marshall Islands, that was selected for capture by both Marine Corps and US Army units. The Marines' 22 February 1944 landings on Parry Island involved a lot of confusion including US Navy shelling of Marines on the island. (*USMC*)

The Marines in this picture have taken cover behind the corpse of an enemy soldier while fighting on Parry Island. The Japanese defenders had three tanks, which they hid near the landing beaches. These did not engage the Marines until Marine M4A2 medium tanks came ashore in the fourth assault wave. It was at this point that the Japanese tanks sallied forth from their concealed positions and were promptly blown apart by the 75mm main guns on the Marine tanks. *(USMC)*

The main reason for seizing some of the many Japanese-occupied Central Pacific atolls and their islands was their airfields. Rebuilt and enlarged, these former Japanese airfields supported basing of United States Army Air Forces (USAAF) four-engine bomber squadrons tasked with attacking the Japanese home islands. Here we see a B-24 Liberator taking off from Eniwetok Island airfield on 13 April 1944. *(US Navy)*

Chapter Three

Getting Ever Closer

With the seizure of the important islands of the Eniwetok atoll, American Joint Chiefs of Staff decided that the Mariana Islands would be the next Central Pacific objective. Unlike the Gilbert and Marshall islands chains that were part of the Japanese Empire's outer defensive perimeter in the Pacific, the Mariana Islands were considered part of the inner defensive perimeter. Once captured, USAAF four-engine bombers would be able to reach the Japanese home islands.

The US Navy, with the support of the corps and US Army, was tasked with the capture of the three largest of the Mariana Islands: Saipan, Tinian and Guam. The invasion date for Saipan was set for 15 June 1944 and that of Guam for 18 June 1944. The invasion of Tinian depended on the progress made in the conquest of Saipan and Guam as some of the same troops would be involved. To take these islands the US Navy had at its disposal three Marine divisions – the 2nd, 3rd and 4th – and the US Army 27th and 77th Infantry divisions; a total of approximately 130,000 men.

The Battle for Saipan

Capturing the island of Saipan was going to be a much bigger endeavour for the corps than that encountered in the Gilbert and Marshall Island chains. Rather than a small flat coral island in a large atoll composed of many islands, Saipan was an ancient volcanic island of 72 square miles with a wide variety of terrain ranging from swamps to flat cane fields. Dominating the island was a volcanic dome 1,554ft high that offered the defenders an unsurpassed artillery observation post.

Pre-invasion training was based on a new 1944 Table of Organization and Equipment for the Marine divisions involved. Their size was reduced by 2,500 men to 17,465. The single artillery regiment in each division lost one of their 75mm howitzer battalions, but the three infantry regiments in each division retained their previous general structure. Rifle squads, however, were reorganized to comprise thirteen men each instead of the previous nine men each.

The new thirteen-man rifle squads were composed of three 'fire teams' of four men each. The centrepiece of each fire team was a .30 calibre Browning Automatic Rifle (BAR), which effectively doubled the number of such weapons in the division. The number of 60mm mortars in the division TO&E was similarly increased, while the number of flame-throwers grew tenfold. In addition, the tank battalions were able to replace all their M3A1 or M5A1 light tanks with M4A2 medium tanks.

The Invasion Begins

The US Navy launched a series of carrier air strikes on the Mariana Islands on 11 June 1944 and began pre-invasion gunfire bombardment of Saipan on 13 June 1944. On the morning of 15 June 1944 the first assault wave, comprising units of the 2nd and 4th Marine divisions, headed for the assigned beaches on the island's west coast. Riding in a fleet of 300 LVTs (Landing Vehicle, Tracked), the Marines met heavy enemy fire as they crossed Saipan's reef line onto their respective landing beaches.

In spite of the heavy barrage of enemy fire, more than 8,000 Marines made it ashore on Saipan in the first twenty minutes of the invasion. By that afternoon, there were approximately 20,000 men with both tanks and artillery pieces on the island. Despite this success, the Marines knew that they had a gruelling struggle ahead to take the island from its roughly 30,000 defenders. Most of the defenders were soldiers of the Japanese Army, while the rest were from Japanese Navy ground forces.

As in the Solomons, the Marines faced being cut off and isolated if the US Navy lost control of the surrounding waters. Thus the US Navy's primary mission was holding the sea lanes. In a two-day (19 to 20 June) engagement, the US Navy eliminated any significant threat to the invasion fleet in what came to be called the 'Marianas Turkey Shoot'. During the extremely one-sided engagement fought by American aircraft and submarines, the Japanese lost over 600 planes, 3 aircraft carriers and 3,000 men against the American losses of 123 carrier planes and 109 air crew. Many of the aircraft lost had to ditch during a counter-attack beyond the planes' combat radius, a calculated risk that the US Navy was prepared to take.

Tanks in Battle

On the first night ashore, a raiding party of Japanese naval infantry supported by tanks attacked a flank of the corps' landing beaches on Saipan. The Japanese attackers were robbed of the cover of darkness by illumining star shells fired by the supporting US Navy warships and were quickly disposed of by the now-alerted defenders.

On the morning of the second day of the invasion of Saipan (16 June 1944), the Japanese launched another tank-led infantry assault. It was quickly decimated by the fire of M4A2 medium tanks. That evening the Japanese began preparing for what would be their largest tank attack of the war in the Pacific. It involved the forty-four tanks of the 9th Tank Regiment led by Colonel Hideki Goto. That event is described in the previously mentioned Marine Corps Historical Branch publication titled *Central Pacific Drive* by authors Shaw, Nalty and Turnbladh:

> Before darkness, American aerial observers had spotted several enemy tanks in the area inland of the 2nd Marine Division beachhead, so the troops were alert

> **Marine Divisional Artillery**
>
> Every Marine division of the Second World War had a single artillery regiment of between 2,207 and 2,661 men. The number of men depended on which of four different Tables of Organization and Equipment (TO&E) was in effect at the time. The TO&E also defined the number of artillery battalions and the types of artillery pieces employed in a Marine divisional artillery regiment.
>
> In the original 1942 TO&E, a division had three battalions equipped with 75mm howitzers and a single battalion armed with 105mm howitzers. This was further broken down with the 75mm howitzer battalions each having three batteries of four guns. The single 105mm artillery was subdivided into three batteries of five guns. The 75mm howitzer had a maximum effective range of 9,160 yards and the 105mm howitzer a maximum effective range of 12,330 yards.
>
> By the time the 1945 TO&E came into effect, the three 75mm howitzer battalions were gone, replaced by three 105mm battalions. Within each battalion there were three four-gun batteries. In addition, a single 155mm howitzer-equipped battalion had been added consisting of three batteries of four howitzers each. The 155mm howitzer had a maximum effective range of 16,355 yards.

to the possibility of an armored attack. At 0330 on the morning of 17 June, the Marines of 1/6 heard the roaring of tank motors. Star shells illuminated the darkened valley from which the noise seemed to be coming, a company of Sherman medium tanks was alerted, and supporting weapons began delivering their planned fires. Within 15 minutes, the hostile tanks, with Ogawa's [Japanese infantry commander] infantrymen clinging to them, began rumbling into the battalion sector.

'The battle,' wrote Major James A. Donovan, Jr, executive officer of 1/6, 'evolved itself into a madhouse of noise, tracers, and flashing lights. As tanks were hit and set afire, they silhouetted other tanks coming out of the flickering shadows to the front or already on top of the squads.' Marine 2.36-inch rocket launchers, grenade launchers, 37mm antitank guns, medium tanks, and self-propelled 75mm guns shattered the enemy armor, while rifle and machine gun fire joined mortar and artillery rounds in cutting down the accompanying foot soldiers.

A total of thirty-two tanks of Colonel Hideki Goto's 9th Tank Regiment were lost during the morning of 17 June 1944. Of the twelve surviving tanks, some were destroyed in an encounter with Marine Corps tanks on 24 June 1944. Marine Corps tanks would also suffer serious losses during the Saipan campaign. However, rather than being lost to enemy tanks or anti-tank guns, many were destroyed by enemy artillery fire or Japanese infantry tank hunter teams often armed with magnetic mines.

Good Timing

As the Marines continued to fight their way across Saipan in an endless series of bloody engagements, it would have been difficult to convince them that they were in fact a bit fortunate that the invasion of Saipan had occurred when it did. This was because the Japanese defences on the island were not what they could have been.

The incomplete nature of the Japanese defensive positions on Saipan and the number of defenders encountered was due to a couple of factors: first, US Navy submarines had choked off the supply of construction materials (such as concrete) to the island, as well as reinforcements; second, the quick success of the Marshall Islands campaign and the US Navy's advancing the date of the Mariana Islands campaign by three months threw off the Japanese timetable for finishing the fortifications on Saipan. One Japanese prisoner stated that had the American assault taken place three months later the island of Saipan would have been impregnable.

Cave-Fighting

Joined by the US Army 27th Infantry Division on 23 June, the two Marine divisions pushed the surviving Japanese troops into the northern half of Saipan. The terrain turned mountainous, with the Japanese defenders taking refuge in an endless series of caves. They would often hide in them during the day and venture out under cover of darkness to attack both Marine and US Army positions.

In addition to man-portable flame-throwers, the Marine tank units on Saipan had been issued with twenty-four flame-thrower tanks based on the M3A1 light tank. The latter were known as 'Satan Flame Tanks' and were escorted into battle by Marine M5A1 light tanks providing covering fire against enemy infantry tank-hunting teams.

Unfortunately, the flame guns on the Satan flame tanks proved both unreliable and with too short a range to be truly effective. Another factor limiting their battlefield usefulness was the cramped interior space of the M3A1 light tanks that made it extremely difficult for the crews to operate the onboard flame gun.

Banzai Attack

Hounded by both Marine and army units, the desperate Japanese defenders of Saipan launched a massive last-ditch counter-attack, often referred to as a 'banzai attack', on the night of 7 July 1944. It was aimed primarily at army units but also encompassed some Marine Corps units. In a Marine Corps historical publication is this passage from a Marine infantryman describing being caught up in that attack:

> Suddenly there is what sounded like a thousand people screaming all at once, as a horde of 'mad men' broke out of the darkness before us. Screams of 'Banzai' fill the air, Japanese officers leading the 'devils from hell', their swords drawn and swishing in circles over their heads. Jap soldiers were following their leaders, firing their weapons at us and screaming 'Banzai' as they charged toward us.

Our weapons opened up, our mortars and machine guns fired continually. No longer do they fire in bursts of three or five. Belt after belt of ammunition goes through that gun, the gunner swinging the barrel left and right. Even though Jap bodies build up in front of us, they still charged us, running over their comrades' fallen bodies. The mortar tubes became so hot from the rapid fire, as did the machine gun barrels, that they could no longer be used.

Although each [attack] had taken its toll, still they came in droves. Haunting memories can still visualize the enemy only a few feet away, bayonet aimed at our body as we empty a clip into him. The momentum carries him into our foxhole, right on top of us. Then pushing him off, we reload and repeat the procedure. Bullets whiz around us, screams are deafening, the area reeks with death, and the smell of Japs and gunpowder permeate the air. Full of fear and hate, with the desire to kill … [Our enemy seems to us now to be] a savage animal, a beast, a devil, not a human at all, and the only thought is to kill, kill, kill … Finally it ends.

Banzai attacks were greatly feared by Marine infantrymen, but they also provided a sense of relief as upon their conclusion they knew that the enemy had spent itself in the one last futile gesture demanded by their military code of honour. On the morning of 8 July 1944 the surviving Marines and army soldiers counted approximately 4,000 Japanese corpses littering the ground. Army losses were 918 dead with the Marines losing 127 dead.

Losses

Following the banzai attack of 7 July 1944, organized Japanese resistance came to an end and the island was declared secure on 9 July 1944. In spite of that, fighting persisted for months thereafter as Japanese stragglers were hunted down. Out of the estimated 30,000 Japanese defenders on Saipan, fewer than 1,000 made it into captivity. Many of those who had survived the fighting committed suicide rather than admit defeat.

The American dead on Saipan, both Marine and army, are recorded at 3,426, with another 10,346 wounded. Among the wounded Marines was the well-known American actor Lee Marvin, who died in 1987 at the age of 63. As an enlisted man serving with the 4th Marine Division, he was struck twice by Japanese fire on 18 June 1944. He was hospitalized for more than a year to recover from his wounds and was medically discharged from the Marine Corps in 1945.

The Battle for Tinian

Located 3.5 miles from Saipan was the Japanese-occupied island of Tinian. With 39 square miles of terrain, its seizure was the Marines' next objective after the conquest of Saipan. Reasons for its capture included the need to stop the Japanese defenders on the island reporting to Tokyo what the Americans were doing on Saipan. Secondly, unlike the more mountainous terrain of Saipan, a large portion of Tinian was flat and open. This made it ideal for building large airfields that could support USAAF four-engine bombers capable of bombing the Japanese home islands.

The US Navy began a preparatory bombardment of Tinian on 11 June 1944. This intensified on 22 July 1944. Joining in on the bombardment were Marine Corps and US Army artillery units firing from Saipan. The 4th Marine Division landed on Tinian on 24 July 1944, with attached units from the 2nd Marine Division. By the end of the first day there were more than 15,600 Marines ashore out of an eventual total of 40,000. Besides artillery, they brought forty-eight M4A2 medium tanks and fifteen Satan flame tanks.

The Enemy Reaction

Enemy resistance to the actual landing sites was far less severe than that experienced on Saipan. This was due to a successful feint landing by the US Navy and Marine Corps on another part of the island and resulted in the Japanese island commander holding a portion of his forces in reserve until he confirmed the locations of all the Marine landings.

The Japanese commander of Tinian waited until the evening of 24 July 1944 to mount a series of counter-attacks on the Marines' positions. With the assistance of the US Navy, all assaults were beaten back with the attackers suffering heavy losses. At first light on 25 July 1944, the Marines counted 1,241 Japanese corpses in front of their positions.

One of the Japanese counter-attacks on the first night of the Marine landings on Tinian included tanks. What happened to some of those tanks is described in this passage from a Marine Corps historical publication titled *The Seizure of Tinian* by Major Carl W. Hoffman:

> The three lead tanks broke through our wall of fire. One began to glow blood-red, turned crazily on its tracks, and careened into a ditch. A second, mortally wounded, turned its machine guns on its tormentors, firing into the ditches in a last desperate effort to fight its way free. One hundred yards more and it stopped dead in its tracks. The third tried frantically to turn and then retreat, but our men closed in, literally blasting it apart ... Bazookas knocked out the fourth tank with a direct hit which killed the driver. The rest of the crew piled out of the turret, screaming. The fifth tank, completely surrounded, attempted to flee. Bazookas made short work of it. Another hit set it afire, and its crew was cremated.

During the 1930s, Japanese tanks were on a par with what other major armies were fielding at the time. However, with the outbreak of the Second World War Japan's finances and industrial infrastructure were hard-pressed to meet all the demands placed upon them. Their tank development lagged as its priority fell, whereas American equipment progressed due to requirements in the European Theatre of Operations and the much larger American industrial base. Thus by 1944 Japanese tanks, in both firepower and armour protection, were markedly inferior to American tanks.

The Push Across the Island

Between 25 and 26 July 1944, the remainder of the 2nd Marine Division landed on Tinian. The plans called for the two divisions to begin pushing forward together and sweep across the island's long axis. All the Marine units involved in this capture of Tinian were understrength as there had not been time to bring in reinforcements following the fall of Saipan. That being said, the combat experience gained by the Marines in fighting on Saipan stood them in good stead as they dealt with Tinian's fanatical Japanese defenders.

By 31 July 1944, the two Marine divisions had seized all the Japanese-built airfields on Tinian and were heading towards the small portion of the island that was more rugged. At this point, the fighting became much tougher as all the Japanese defenders were now concentrated in one area. Their elimination by the Marines was made more difficult for two reasons. One was the terrain and the other that the Japanese defenders had herded most of the island's Japanese settlers, Korean labourers and indigenous population along with them. This prompted the Marines to make an extra effort to entice all concerned to surrender. Their efforts were more successful than on Saipan and more than 8,000 civilians entered into temporary American captivity.

Mopping-Up

On 1 August 1944, the island of Tinian was declared secure. Marine Corps losses for the campaign were officially recorded as 317 dead and 1,550 wounded, with another 27 missing in action. A single US Army regiment also took part in the capture of Tinian and also had men killed and wounded.

Of the estimated pre-invasion Japanese garrison of 9,000 men on Tinian, approximately 5,000 were documented as killed in action. A total of 252 surrendered. Despite the island being declared secure on 1 August, somebody did not inform the Japanese defenders and on the following day the Marines faced another large counter-attack.

This counter-attack of 2 August 1944 was the largest mounted by the Japanese following the island being declared secure. Subsequent counter-attacks were smaller in size and all ended with the majority of the attackers being killed. Between 2 August 1944 and 1 January 1945, the Marines on Tinian killed a total of approximately 500 Japanese troops, in the process losing 38 Marines killed and 125 wounded.

The Battle for Guam

Guam was the third island to be seized in the Marianas. Some 32 miles in length and varying between 4 and 12 miles in width, it was the largest in the island chain. Its terrain was more akin to Saipan's rugged topography, with the addition of jungles. Guam had been a United States possession since 1898, until it was occupied by the Japanese on 10 December 1941 after a brief struggle with a small understrength Marine Corps detachment.

The recapture of Guam would offer the US Navy a large anchorage for its ships and the space for more airfields from which USAAF four-engine bombers could reach the Japanese home islands. The original plans had called for the invasion of Guam on 15 June 1944. However, the Battle of the Philippine Sea on 19 and 20 June 1944 pushed the invasion back to mid-July 1944.

The preparatory aerial bombardment of Guam began on 11 June and lasted until 13 June 1944. It involved both US Navy carrier aircraft as well as land-based USAAF four-engine bombers. On 27 June 1944 US Navy battleships began bombarding the island. They were joined by US Navy carrier-based aircraft which repeatedly attacked Japanese positions. US Navy Underwater Demolition Teams (UDTs) destroyed beach-landing obstacles between 14 and 17 July 1944.

The Invasion Begins

As the 2nd and 4th Marine divisions were still involved with the fighting on the island of Tinian, the capture of Guam was assigned to the 3rd Marine Division, the 1st Provisional Marine Brigade and the US Army's 77th Infantry Division.

The two Marine units landed on 21 June 1944 in the face of heavy enemy resistance. The US Army 77th Infantry Division landed on Guam between 23 and 24 June 1944, encountering even fiercer resistance upon landing than the Marines. It was estimated that Guam was defended by 18,500 Japanese troops.

With the support of tanks and artillery landed on the first day, the Marines slowly overcame Japanese shoreline defenders and pushed slightly inland. As darkness approached, the Marines began to build up their defensive positions for the expected Japanese counter-attack, which was not long in coming.

As at Tarawa, as on most islands subjected to heavy American aerial and naval bombardment, Guam's defenders' underground phone line communications were disrupted. Lacking the ability to quickly assess the situation and mass forces effectively, the defenders' counter-attacks on the corps' landing sites were disorganized and beaten back with high losses.

The Closing Act

By 29 June 1944 the 3rd Marine Division had linked up with the US Army 77th Infantry Division and seized the bulk of the island. The Japanese were running out of both food and ammunition at that point and knew they no longer had any chance of stopping the Americans taking over Guam. They therefore withdrew to the most rugged and heavily-wooded portion of the island to set up a defensive line. The intention was to hold the island as long as possible.

The Marines and army soldiers continued to push forward and on 4 August 1944 the main Japanese defensive positions were broken. The last Japanese mountain strongpoint was captured on 8 August 1944. On 10 August 1944, the island was declared secure with supposedly the last organized Japanese resistance crushed.

Approximately 11,000 Japanese troops were killed with another 1,250 surrendering during the capture of Guam. Survivors existed in small isolated groups that were hunted down by the American military until the end of the Second World War. The combined total of Marines and army soldiers killed during the taking of Guam is listed as 1,370 with a further 7,800 wounded.

The crews on a number of 5in guns on a US Navy battleship prepare to begin the pre-invasion bombardment of Saipan on 13 June 1944. The island was part of the Marianas Island chain located in the Central Pacific. The seizure of Saipan was something new for the Marine Corps. Instead of a small, flat coral island in an atoll, it was a very large island of 72 square miles, with terrain varying from flat cane fields to swamps to steep cliffs leading to the commanding 1,554ft high Mount Tapotchau. (USMC)

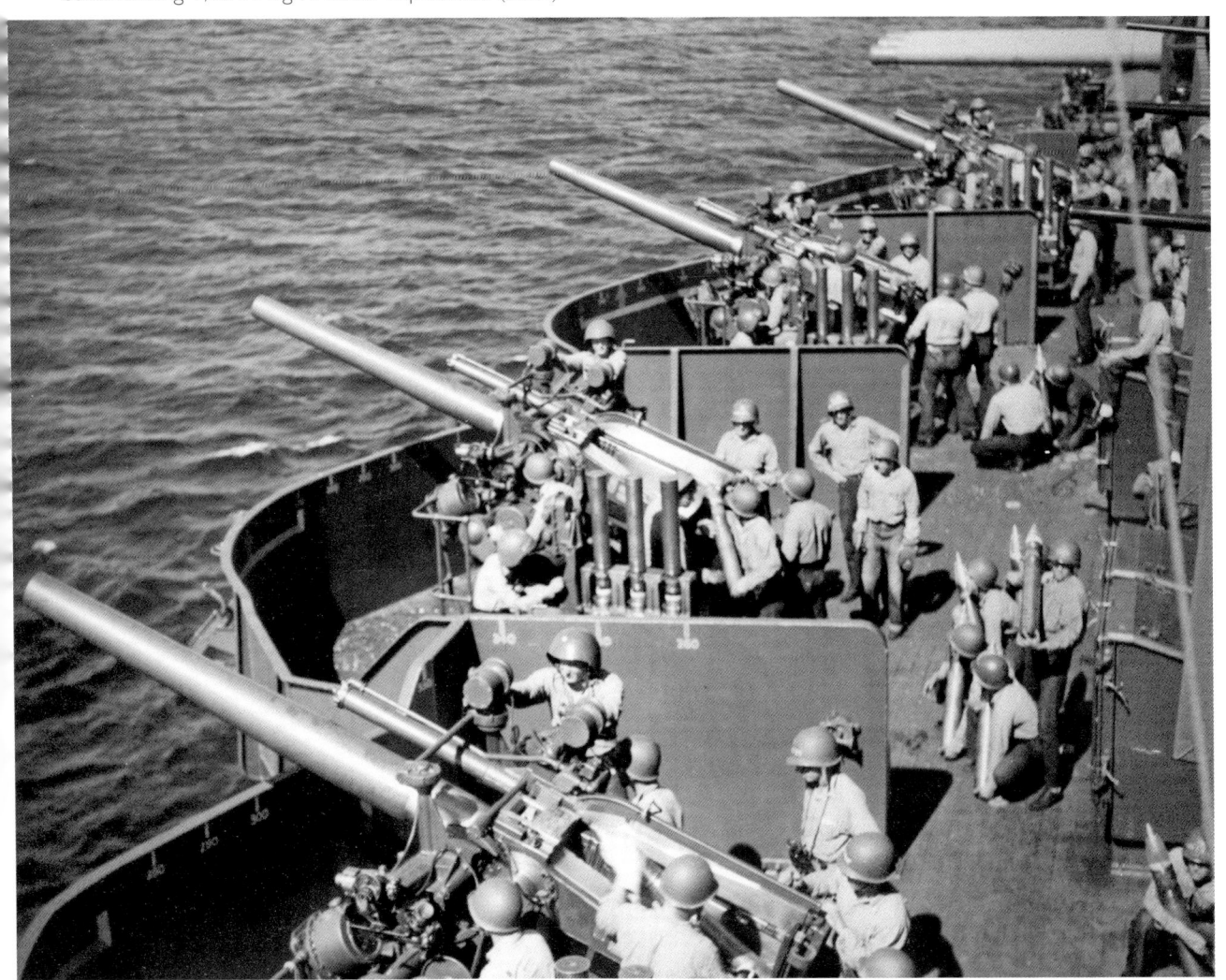

Fires rage at a fuel dump (left centre) and a sugar refinery (right) during the US Navy pre-invasion bombardment of Saipan. The capture of Saipan and other islands in the Marianas was important for a couple of reasons. First, American forces would cut Japanese lines of communication and provide bases from which the US Navy could control the Western Pacific. Second, they would provide bases from which the USAAF's new long-range four-engine B-29 'Super Fortress' bomber could reach the home islands of Japan. *(USMC)*

The operation plan for Saipan called for an assault on the western side of the island as seen in this map, with the 2nd Marine Division on the left and the 4th Marine Division on the right. The army's 27th Infantry Division was in reserve. While each of the two Marine divisions had previously fought as complete units, the army division had experienced only two minor landings. Its regiments and battalions were not sufficiently experienced at manoeuvring as a division. *(USMC)*

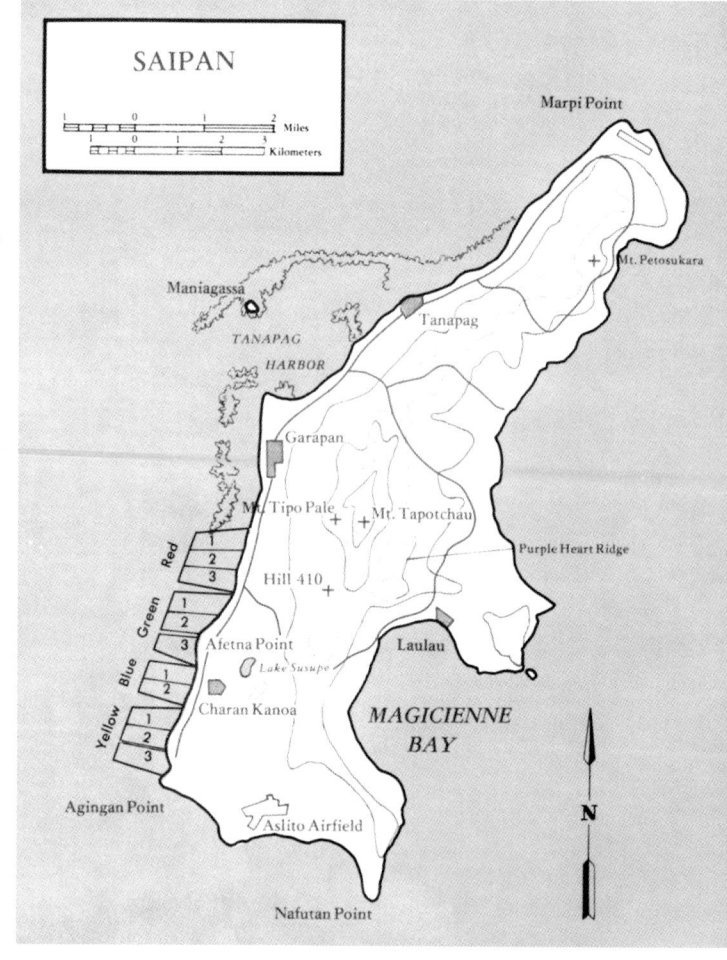

This classic photograph of Marines on a Saipan beach crawling around on all fours was due to the heavy volume of enemy fire. Marine Colonel Robert E. Hogaboom commented in an historical monograph: 'The opposition consisted primarily of artillery and mortar fire from weapons placed in well-deployed positions and previously registered to cover the beach areas, as well as fire from small arms, automatic weapons, and anti-boat guns sited to cover the approaches to and the immediate landing beaches.' (USMC)

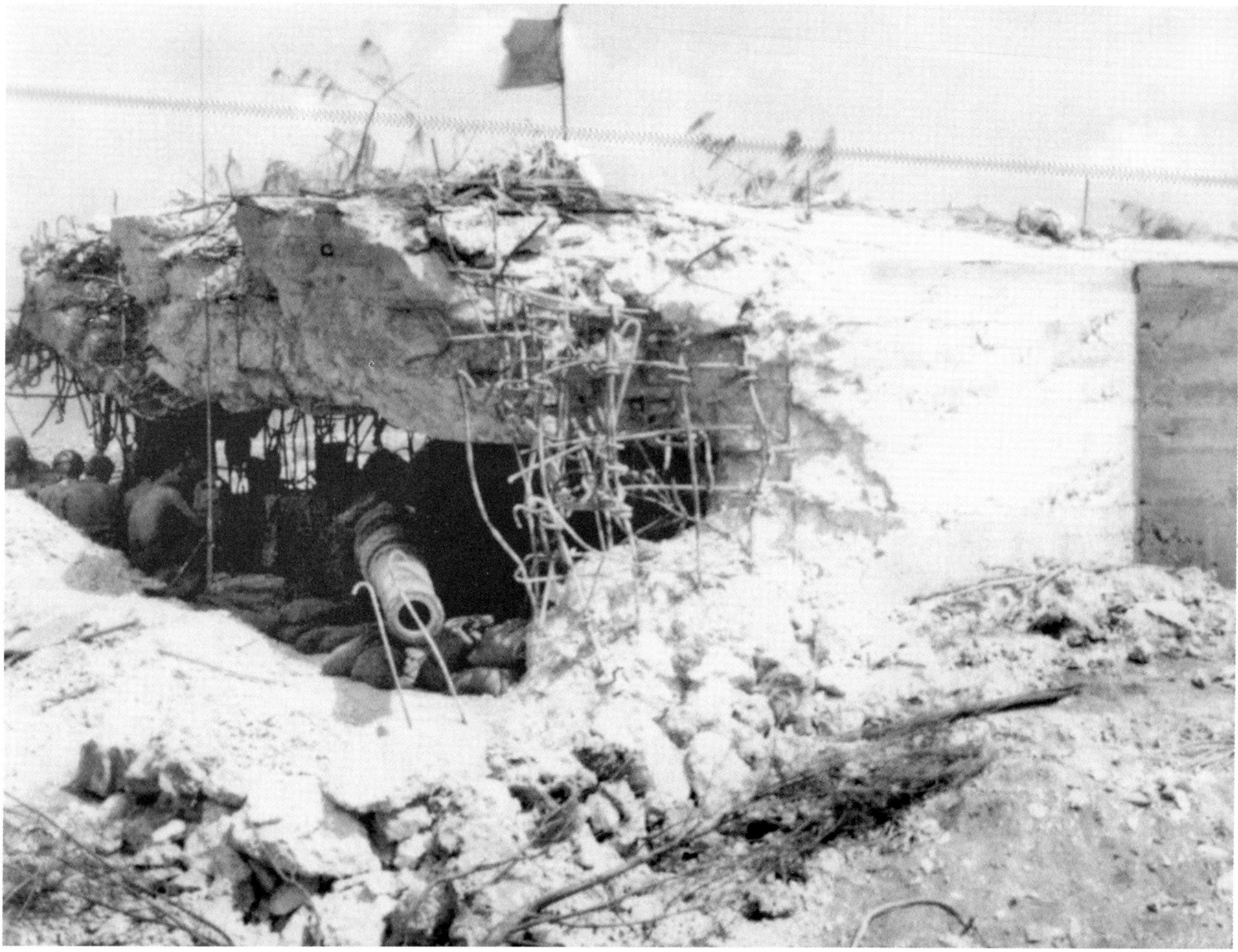

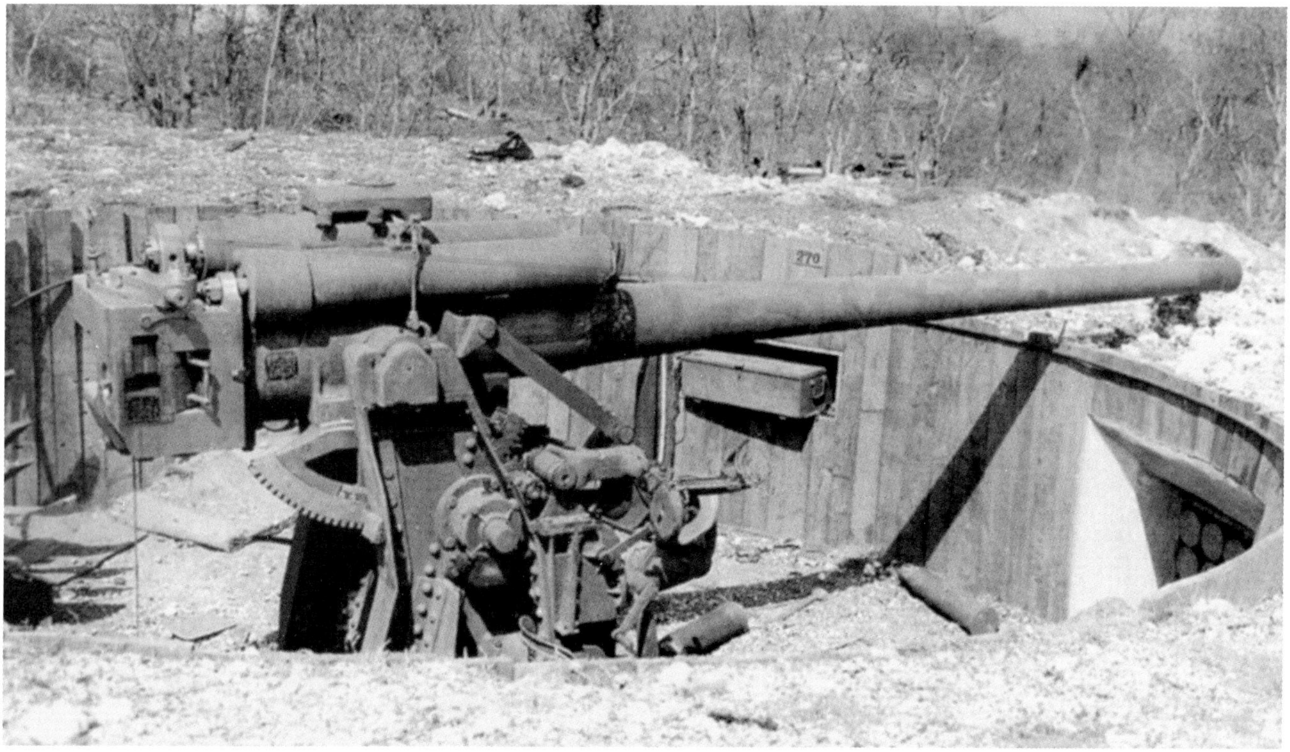
270

(**Opposite, above**) A Japanese coast artillery/anti-aircraft gun position took a direct hit from a large-calibre US Navy gun. In the grand scheme of things, the naval bombardment of Saipan was not quite what it should have been. The US Navy battleships had been stationed outside the range of enemy shore batteries and possible mined areas. These factors had limited the effectiveness of their fire due to the ranges being in excess of 10,000 yards. (USMC)

(**Opposite, below**) Captured intact by the Marines on Saipan was this dual-purpose gun intended as both a coast artillery and anti-aircraft weapon. An American wartime manual stated that Japanese anti-aircraft companies observed were typically situated within a 1-mile radius around the area to be defended, with the greatest concentration of guns between the defended areas and sea approaches to their location. (USMC)

(**Above**) Prior to Saipan the Japanese had put all their defensive efforts into stopping amphibious assaults on the beaches, only to see American naval gunfire demolish them. On Saipan, the Japanese attempted a more elastic defensive strategy at first, which involved launching a series of combined arms on the landing sites. As had happened before, Marine firepower, along with naval gunfire support, decimated the Japanese efforts as seen here. (USMC)

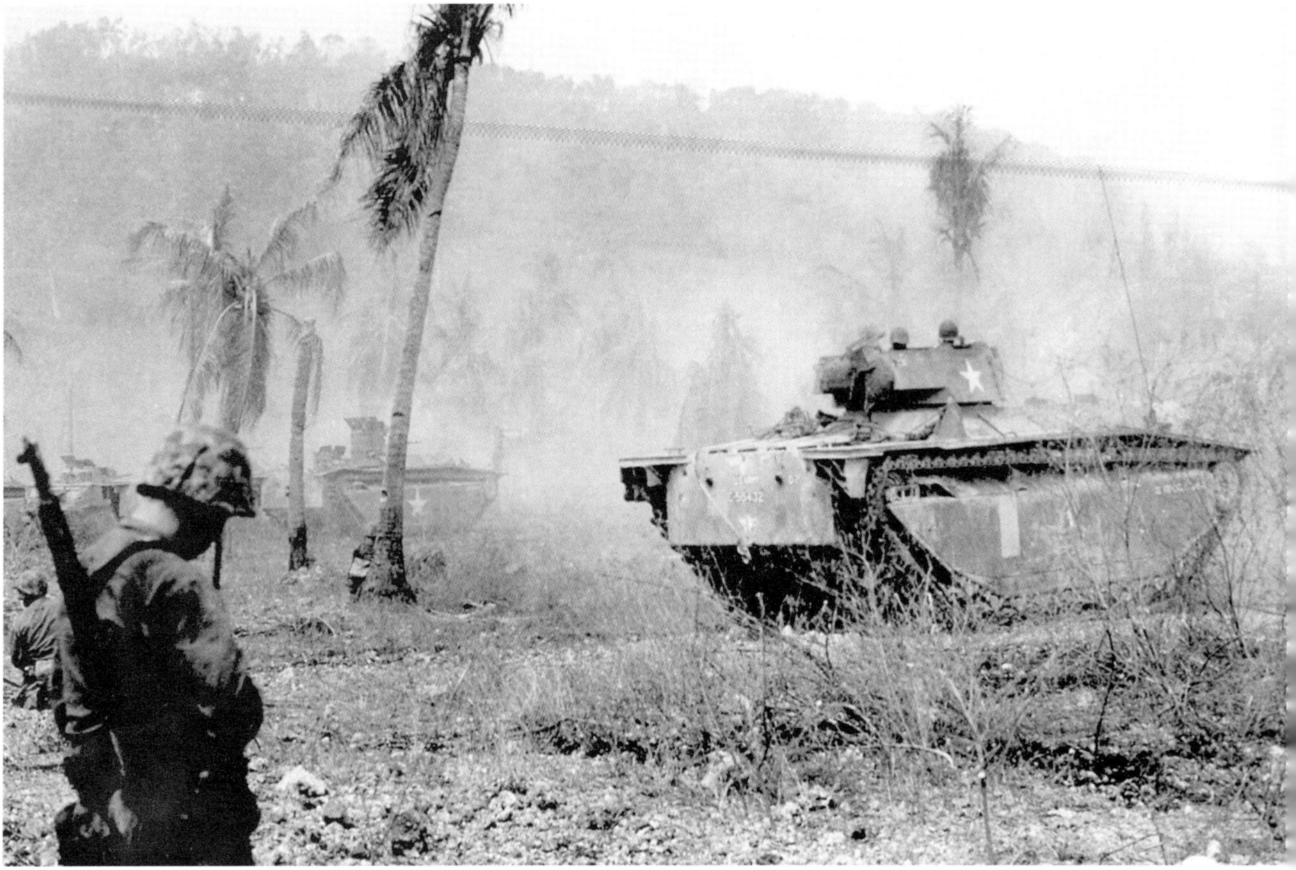

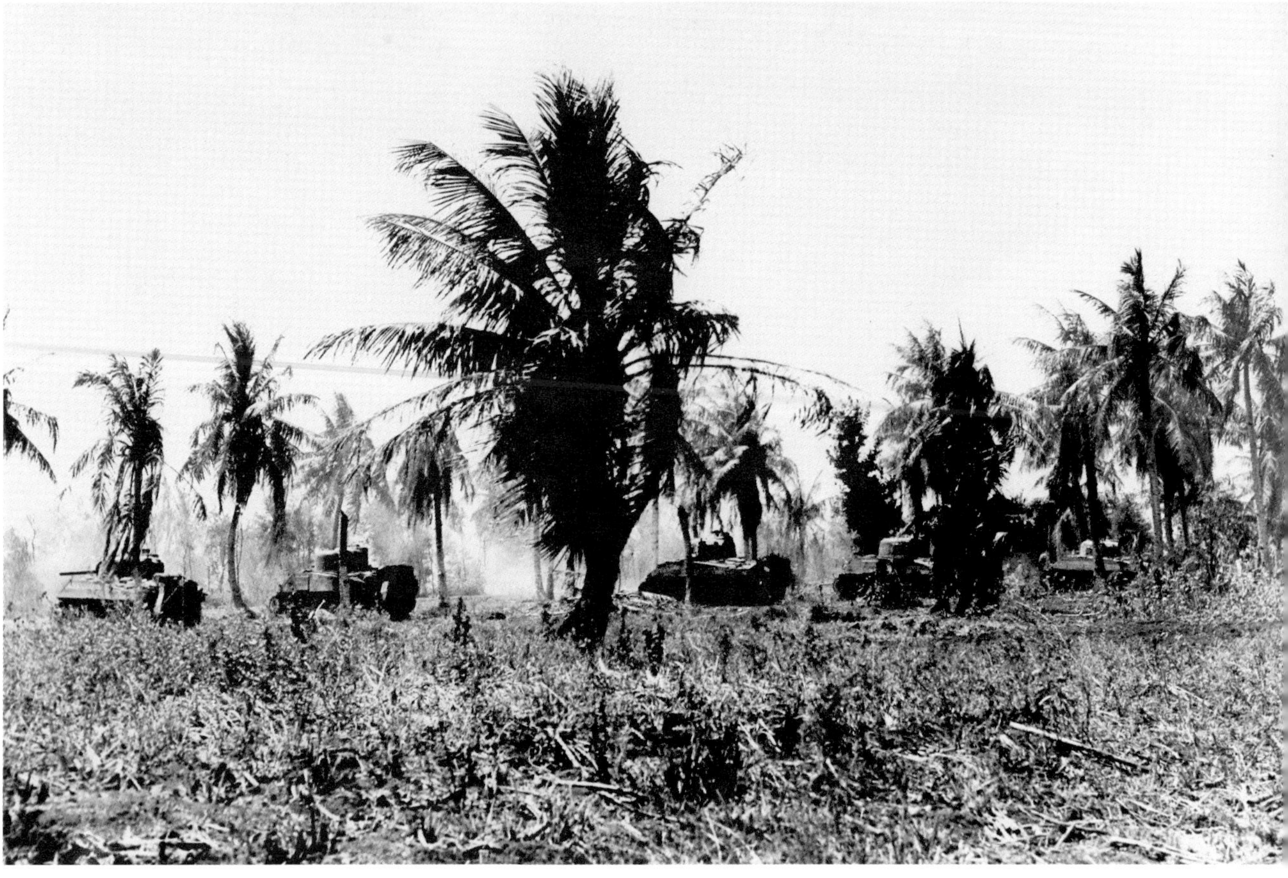

(**Opposite, above**) In this picture, we see two armed and armoured LVTs moving inland off the Saipan invasion beaches. In the foreground is an LVT(A)-4 and in the background an LVTA-1. The LVT(A)-4 was the replacement for the LVTA-1 and had an open-topped turret armed with the same 75mm howitzer used in the M8 Howitzer Motor Carriage (HMC). (*USMC*)

(**Opposite, below**) By the time of the invasion of Saipan, the Marine Corps was well aware of the combat limitations of the thinly-armoured LVT(A)-1 and LVT(A)-4 armoured amphibians. Therefore, they would land the more thickly-armoured M4 series medium tanks as quickly as possible to take over in the combat support role, as seen here. Saipan saw the first large-scale employment of a new towed anti-tank gun by the Japanese. (*USMC*)

(**Above**) This destroyed Japanese 47mm towed anti-tank gun was labelled the Model 1. It first appeared in service in early 1942 and was a replacement for their early-war 37mm towed anti-tank gun designated the Model 1934. Whereas the earlier anti-tank gun had great difficulty in penetrating the front and sides of the M4 series medium tank, the 47mm anti-tank gun could penetrate the armour on the sides of the American medium tank from any range and the frontal armour at close range. (*USMC*)

On Saipan is a Marine 60mm mortar team. The mortar was designated the M2 and was of French design. It was modified and built in the United States under licence. It was fired from the Mount M2 which consisted of a baseplate and bipod with a traversing and elevating mechanism. Together, the mortar tube and mount weighed approximately 29lb. The weapon's rate of fire could be up to eighteen rounds per minute. (USMC)

This Japanese soldier killed on Saipan was armed with the 7.7mm Type 99 light machine gun. It weighed 20lb and was fed by curved thirty-round box magazines. Based on a Czech design, it had a quick-change barrel. It was an upgraded replacement for the Type 96, which fired a 6.5mm round. However, hard-pressed Japanese industry could never build enough of the Type 99 to replace the older-generation Type 96. (USMC)

In this picture taken on Saipan we see the crew of a Marine Corps M3A1 37mm anti-tank gun in action. Note the addition of an extra piece of armour applied to the top of the factory-supplied armour shield to increase protection for the gun crew. The number of holes in the add-on armour indicates that a great deal of enemy fire has been directed at the weapon. The breech mechanism on the gun was manually-operated and not semi-automatic as were the 37mm main guns on the Marine Corps light tanks. (*USMC*)

(**Above**) Marine infantrymen on Saipan are shown taking cover behind an M4A2 medium tank. By this time Marine tank battalions had been reorganized to reflect a new Table of Organization and Equipment (TO&E). In lieu of the previous one medium and two light tank companies of eighteen tanks each, the new 1944 TO&E called for three medium tank companies of fifteen M4A2 medium tanks each and a single M4A2 medium tank in the headquarters and service company. (USMC)

(**Opposite, above**) The man-portable M1A1 flame-thrower could be a very effective weapon against Japanese bunkers. The down side was that they were heavy, short-ranged and extremely hazardous for the operator. Attempts by the Marine Corps and US Army to mount the M1A1 flame-thrower in the bow machine-gun position of the M3A1 light tank as seen here were a failure. The M3A1 series tank's vibration in normal operation damaged the flame gun's components, rendering it inoperative. (USMC)

(**Opposite, below**) Initially the Marines settled for modifying twenty-four M3A1 light tanks with a British-designed and built flame-thrower gun. Rather than firing the flame gun out of the bow gun position, they instead replaced the 37mm main gun in the tank's turret. These converted flame-thrower tanks were nicknamed the 'Satan', such as the one seen here in use on Saipan. (USMC)

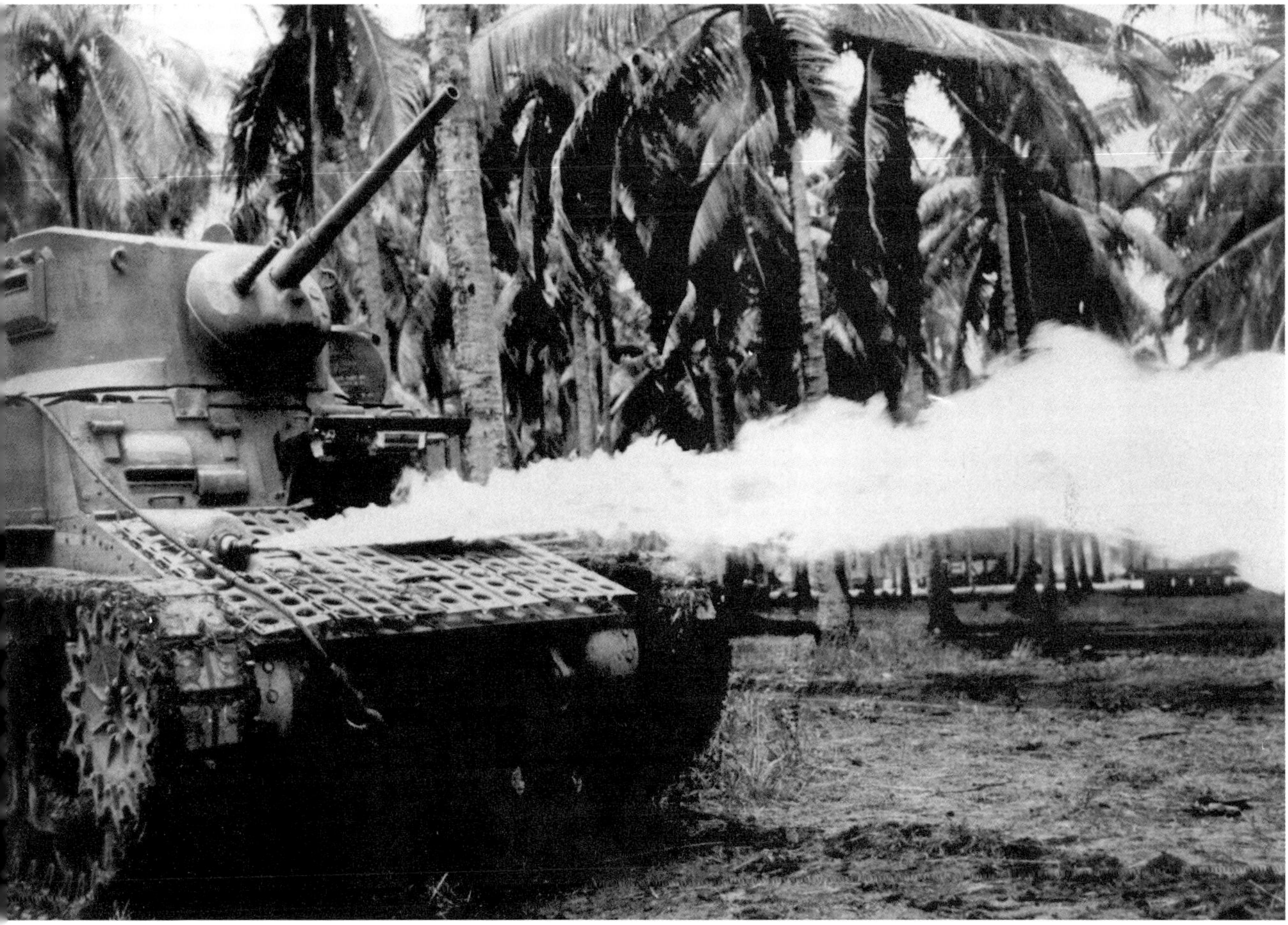

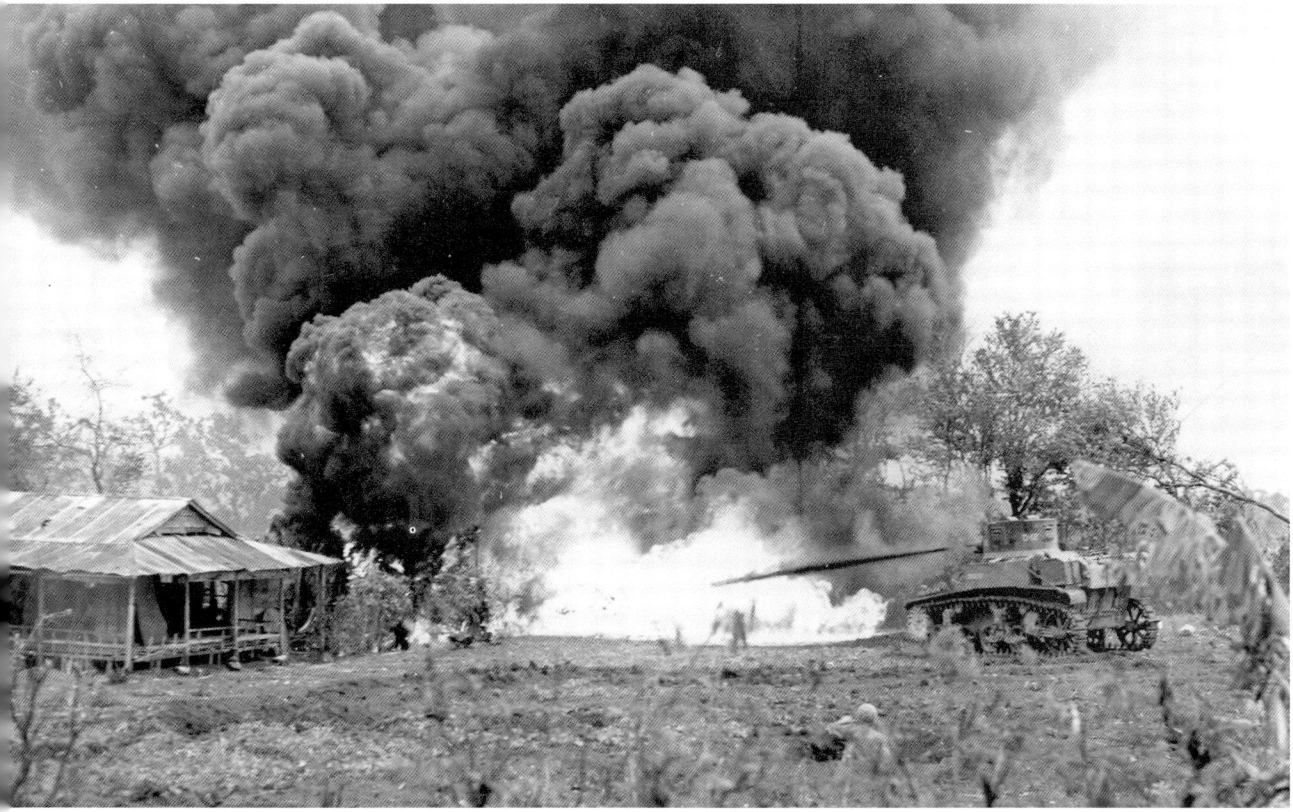

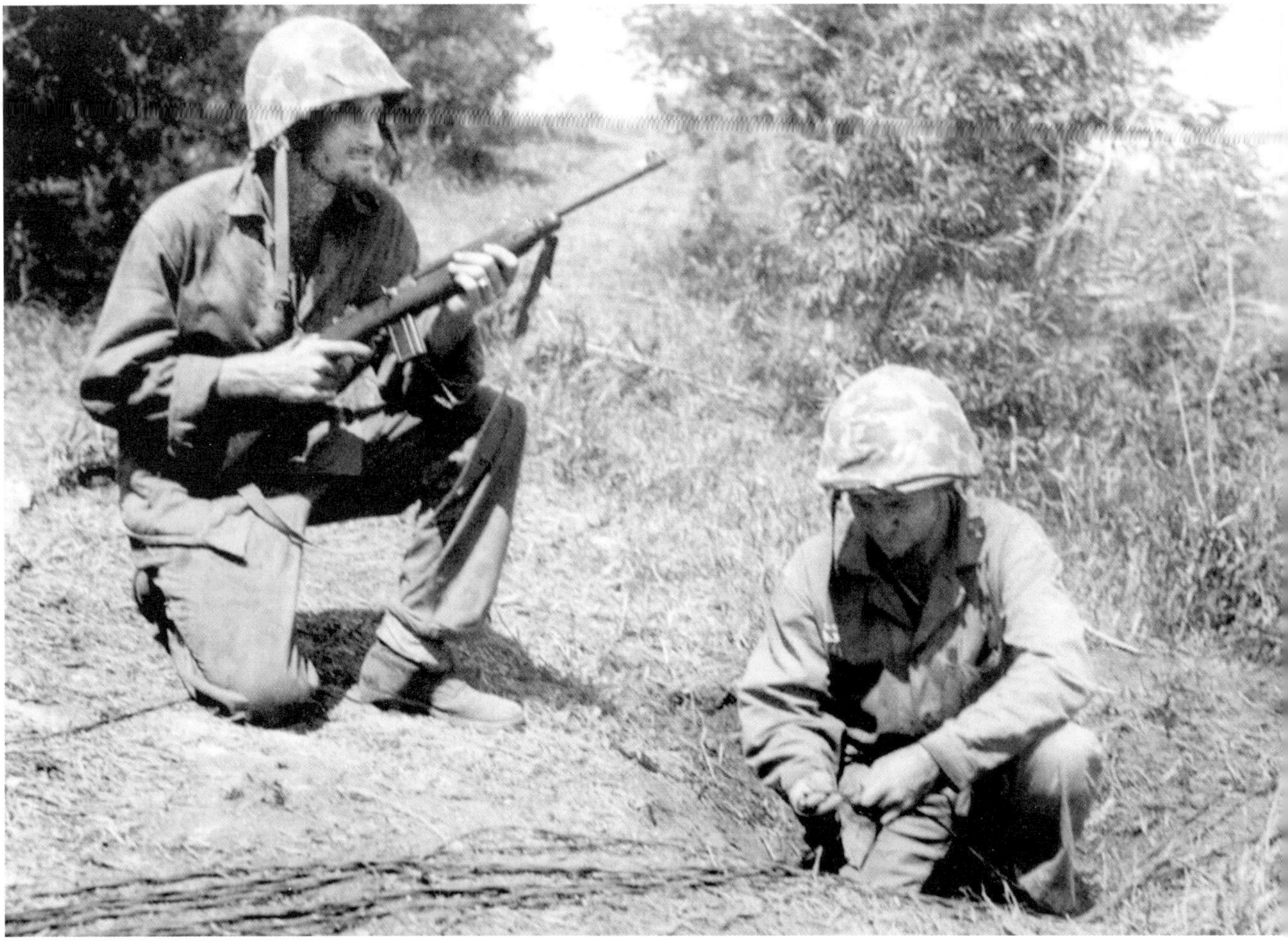

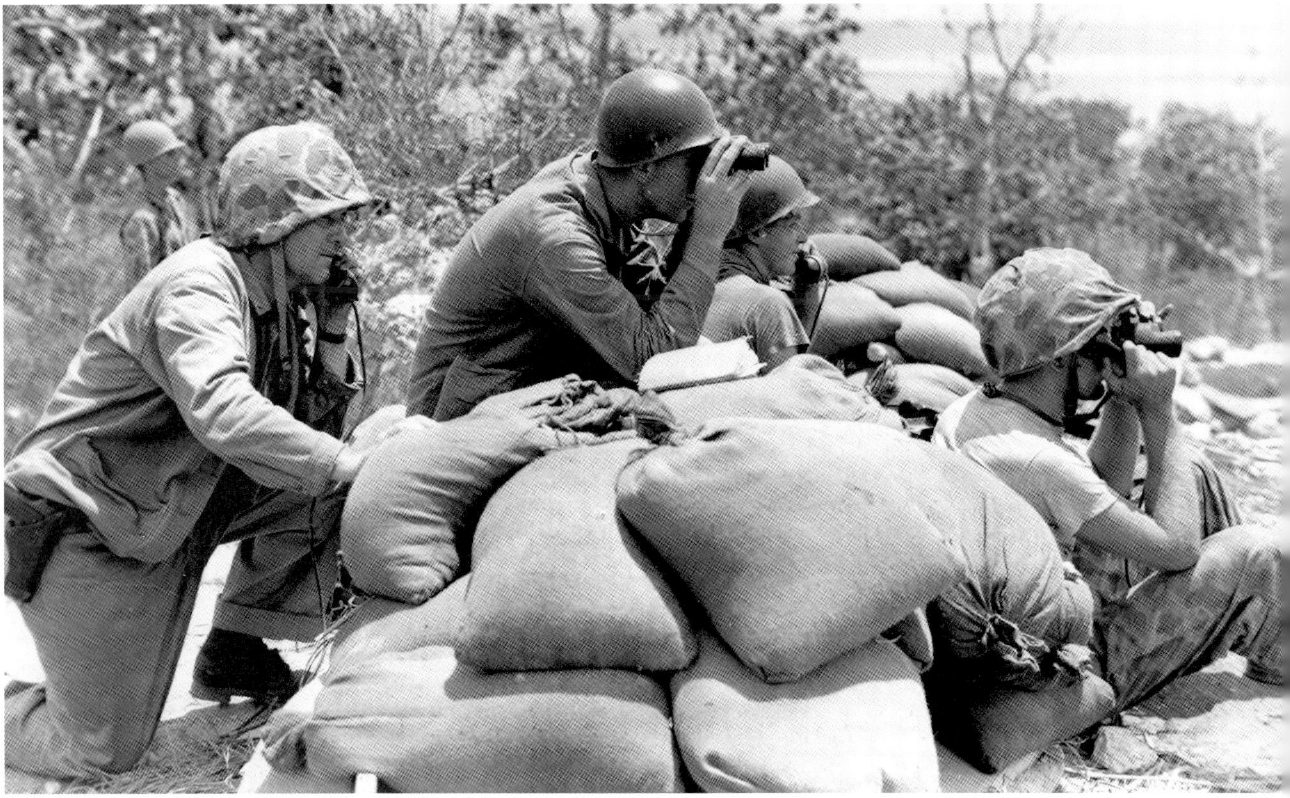

(**Opposite, above**) Two Marine Corps wire repairmen are shown at work on Saipan. Despite the fact that wires were cut for many reasons, all armies were forced to use them despite the availability of radios because of their limited range and reliability in that time period. (*USMC*)

(**Above**) Unlike the minimally-inhabited islands previously assaulted by the Marines, Saipan had a significant civilian population and built-up areas. Saipan had two towns along its western shore that had to be secured by the Marines without incurring too many civilian deaths. In these urban areas were some well-constructed buildings providing excellent defensive positions which Marines like the two pictured here had to destroy. (*USMC*)

(**Opposite, below**) Pictured are Marine and US Army Forward Observers (FOs) on Saipan. They provided the eyes of the artillery and in their quest for the best observation positions often placed themselves in the most exposed positions. The information gathered by the FOs would be radioed or telephoned back to an artillery battalion liaison who would pass it on to a Fire Direction Centre (FDC) for a fire mission. (*USMC*)

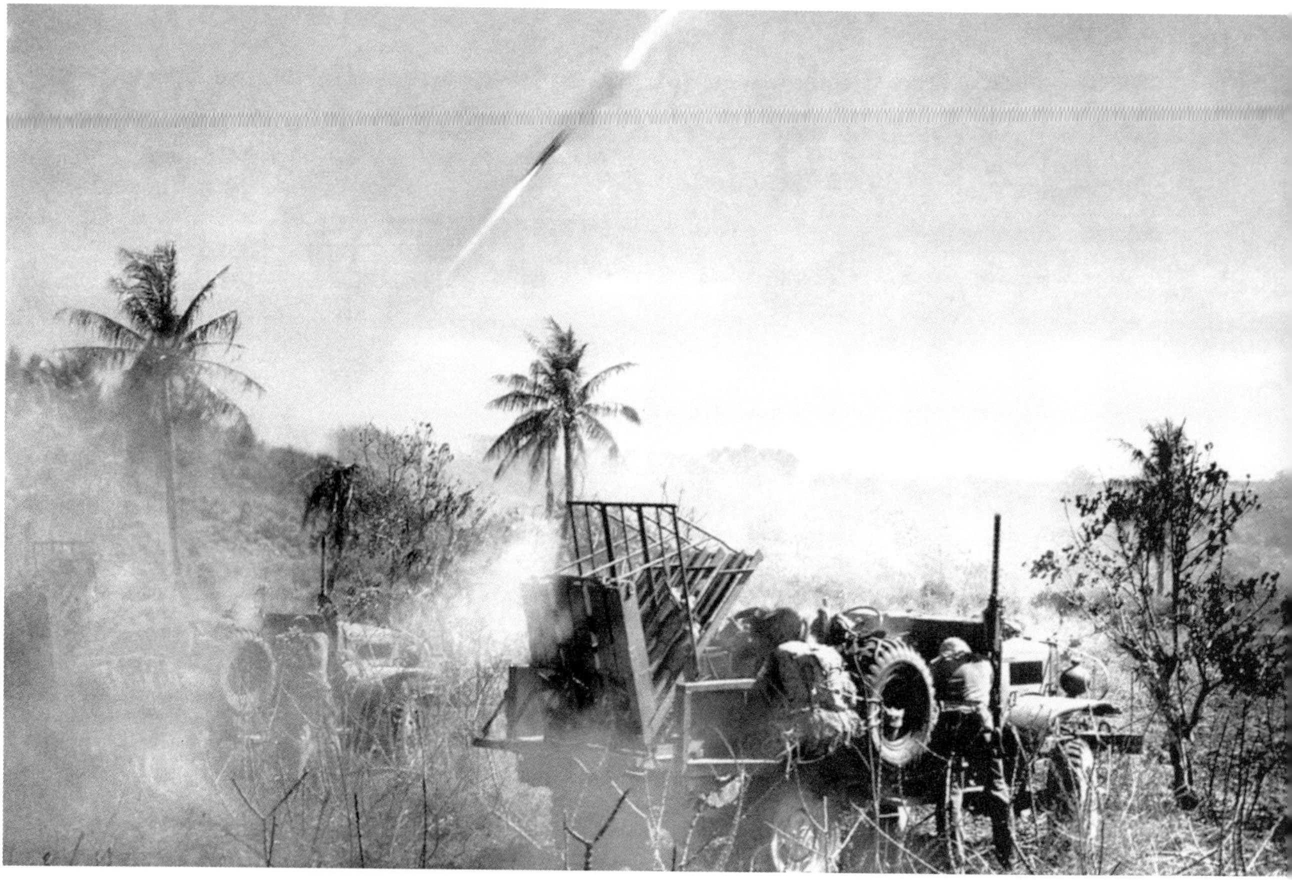

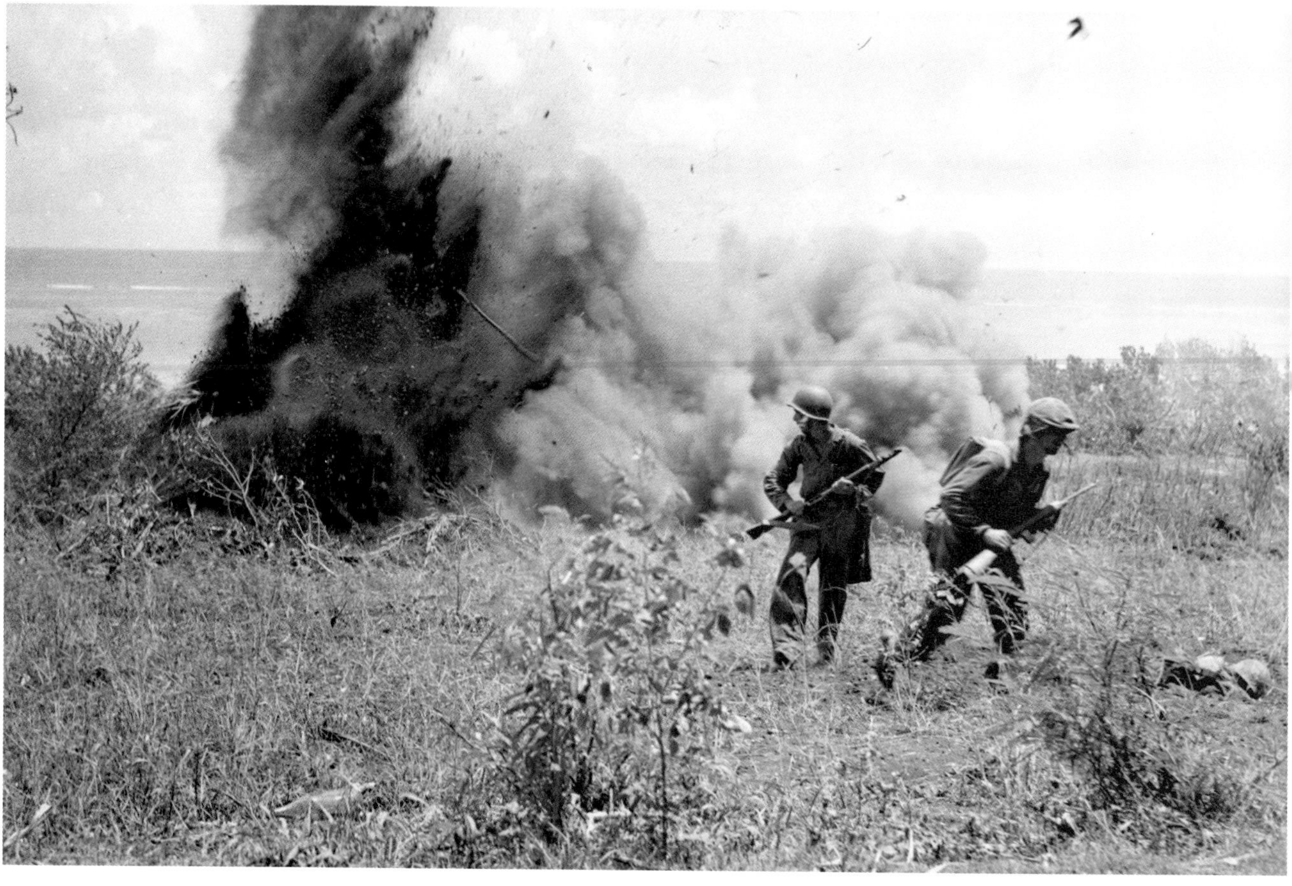

(**Opposite, above**) First fielded by the US Army in 1943 was a 4.7in rocket labelled the M8 and also listed as a barrage rocket. It could be fired from a variety of launcher systems. The version adopted by the Marines is seen here on Saipan and was designated the 4.5in Mark T45 Self-Propelled Rocket-Launcher and mounted on a 4 × 4 truck. The rocket-launcher contained twenty-eight gravity-fed M8 rockets. The individual rockets weighed 38.1lb and had a range of approximately 4,000 yards. (USMC)

(**Above**) Lieutenant General Holland M. Smith (commander of the 5th Amphibious Corps), Major General Thomas E. Watson (commanding general of the 2nd Marine Division) and Admiral Raymond A. Spruance (commander of the US Navy Fifth Fleet) – listed from left to right – discuss the Saipan tactical situation at the divisional headquarters tent on Saipan. (USMC)

(**Opposite, below**) Marine Corps engineers are caught in this photograph running from an explosive charge that has just gone off in a Japanese underground bunker on Saipan. In the Marine Division TO&E for 1944 there was an engineer battalion of 904 men. This was in turn broken down into a headquarters company of 307 men and three engineer companies of 199 men each. (USMC)

Pictured on Saipan is a knocked-out Marine Corps M4A2 medium tank with corpses of the Japanese soldiers that destroyed it. An American wartime manual described the ways in which specialized Japanese 'tank-fighters' were trained to destroy American tanks. These included climbing on the tank to damage or jam the main gun and turret, blinding the crew by covering the vision slits with mud or shelter-halves, or 'smoking it out' with flares. (USMC)

Two Marines on Saipan cautiously approach the entrance to a Japanese bunker. Prior to the Second World War and up to 1943 the Japanese Army had regarded the best defence as going on the offensive. However, by early 1944 they came to realize that this did not work well against the American firepower advantage and therefore began investing more effort in their defensive works to prolong the fighting. (USMC)

Shown is a Marine trying to comfort an obviously starving woman and her children during the later stages of the campaign for Saipan. It was estimated by the American military that there were approximately 25,000 civilians on the island prior to the invasion. Forced to take cover with Japanese soldiers in the same caves, it proved impossible to separate the civilians from their captors and thousands would perish from American firepower or by their own hands, convinced it was better than surrendering to the Americans. (USMC)

(**Above**) A Marine lies dead in a Saipan sugar-cane field. Those wounded or killed on Saipan were not lost in vain. Lieutenant General Holland Smith declared it 'the decisive battle of the Pacific offensive' for it 'opened the way to the [Japanese] home islands.' A Japanese admiral agreed, 'Our war was lost with the loss of Saipan.' It had truly been a 'strategic strike' for the United States. *(USMC)*

(**Opposite, above**) After having some time to recover and reorganize from the ordeal of securing Saipan, the 4th Marine Division was landed on the nearby island of Tinian on 24 July 1944. Pictured is a late-production model of the LVT-2 (built after March 1944) heading towards the landing beaches. It now came with an armoured cab, two shield-protected small-calibre machine guns and armoured engine air intakes. *(USMC)*

(**Opposite, below**) Prior to the initial landings on Tinian the island was subjected to a massive multi-day Marine Corps and US Army artillery barrage from the nearby island of Saipan, which had been declared secure on 9 July 1944. Pictured here is a Marine Corps 155mm M1 howitzer in action on Saipan. The artillery piece first appeared in US Army service in 1942 and in Marine Corps service in 1944. *(USMC)*

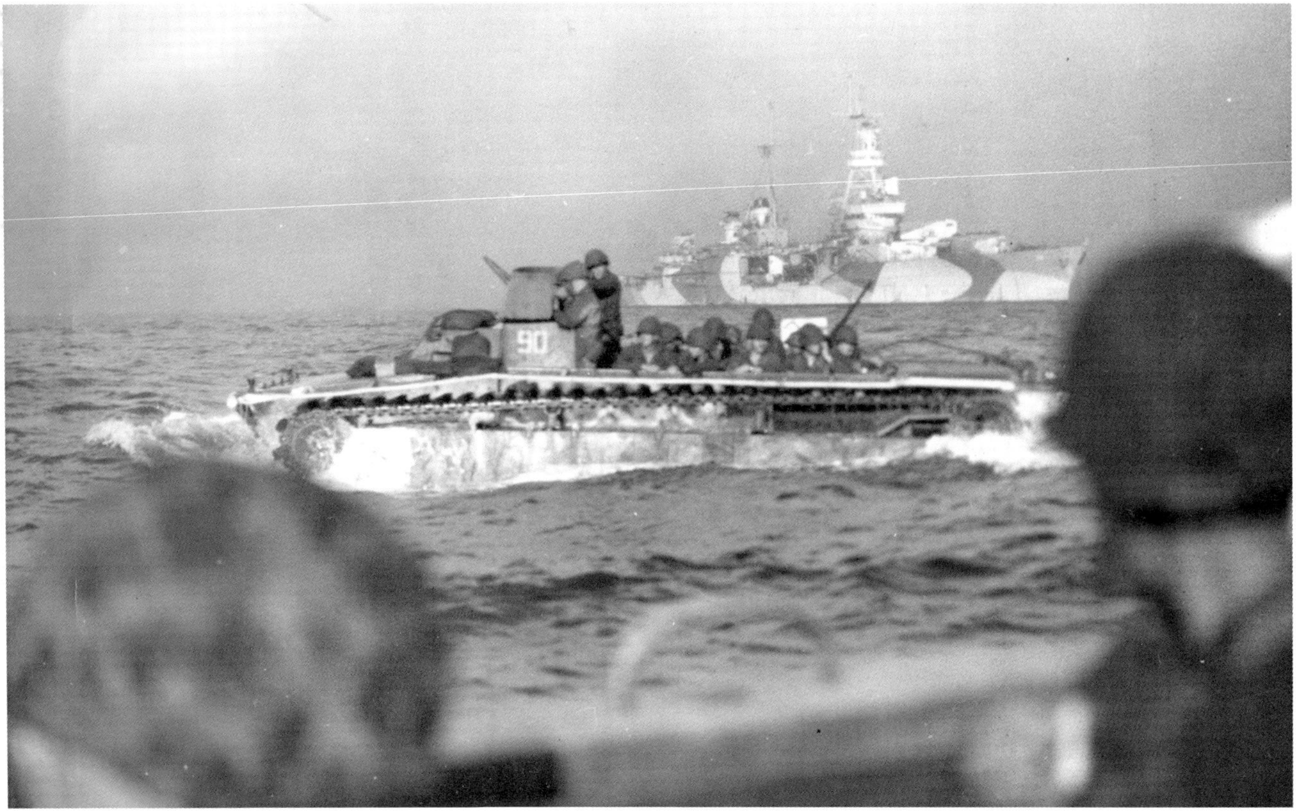
90

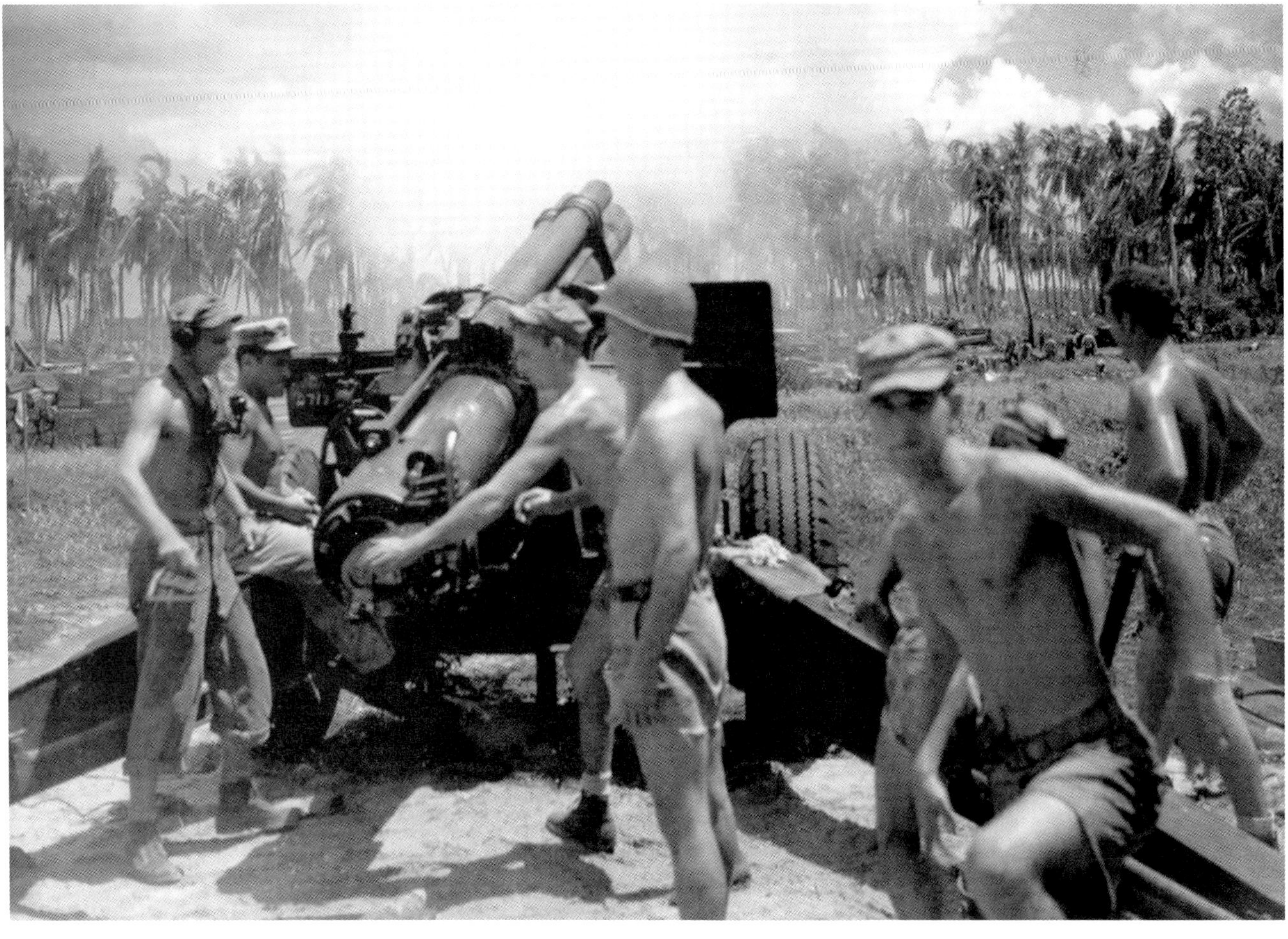

A map of Tinian marked with the location of the two landing beaches for the 4th Marine Division, which were labelled White 1 and White 2. The Japanese senior leadership on the island was convinced that an American landing would occur at Tinian Town located on the south-west portion of the island and not the two small narrow beaches on its north-west coast. This meant that the Marine landing on Tinian was met with far less Japanese resistance than in other island assaults. (*USMC*)

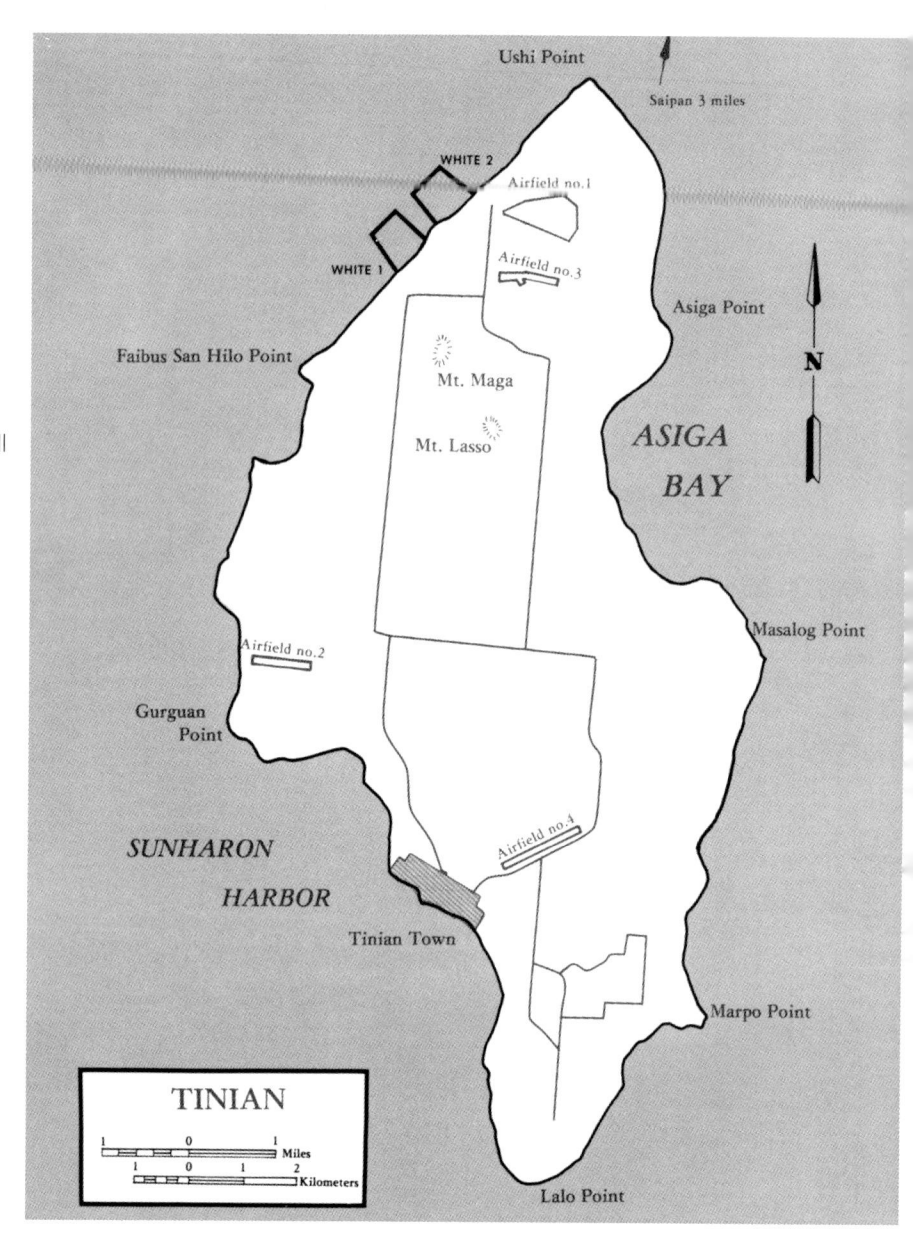

(**Opposite, above**) Marines are shown wading ashore from their landing craft at Tinian on 24 July 1944. The White 2 landing beach proved a bit more heavily defended than White 1. However, the Japanese troops encountered on White 2 were quickly dealt with and the Marines continued to pour onto the island. Enemy mines did account for three small US Navy landing craft with 100 undetonated mines disarmed by Marine Corps engineers with others assisting. (*USMC*)

(**Opposite, below**) Seen here in transit between ship and shore at Tinian are two Marine Corps 2.5-ton 6 × 6 amphibian trucks more popularly known by their nickname of the 'Duck'. They first entered US Army service in 1942 and quickly impressed all those in the Marine Corps who saw them in action. The Marine Corps took them into service in 1944. On land they had a maximum speed on level roads of 45mph and in the water 6.3mph. (*USMC*)

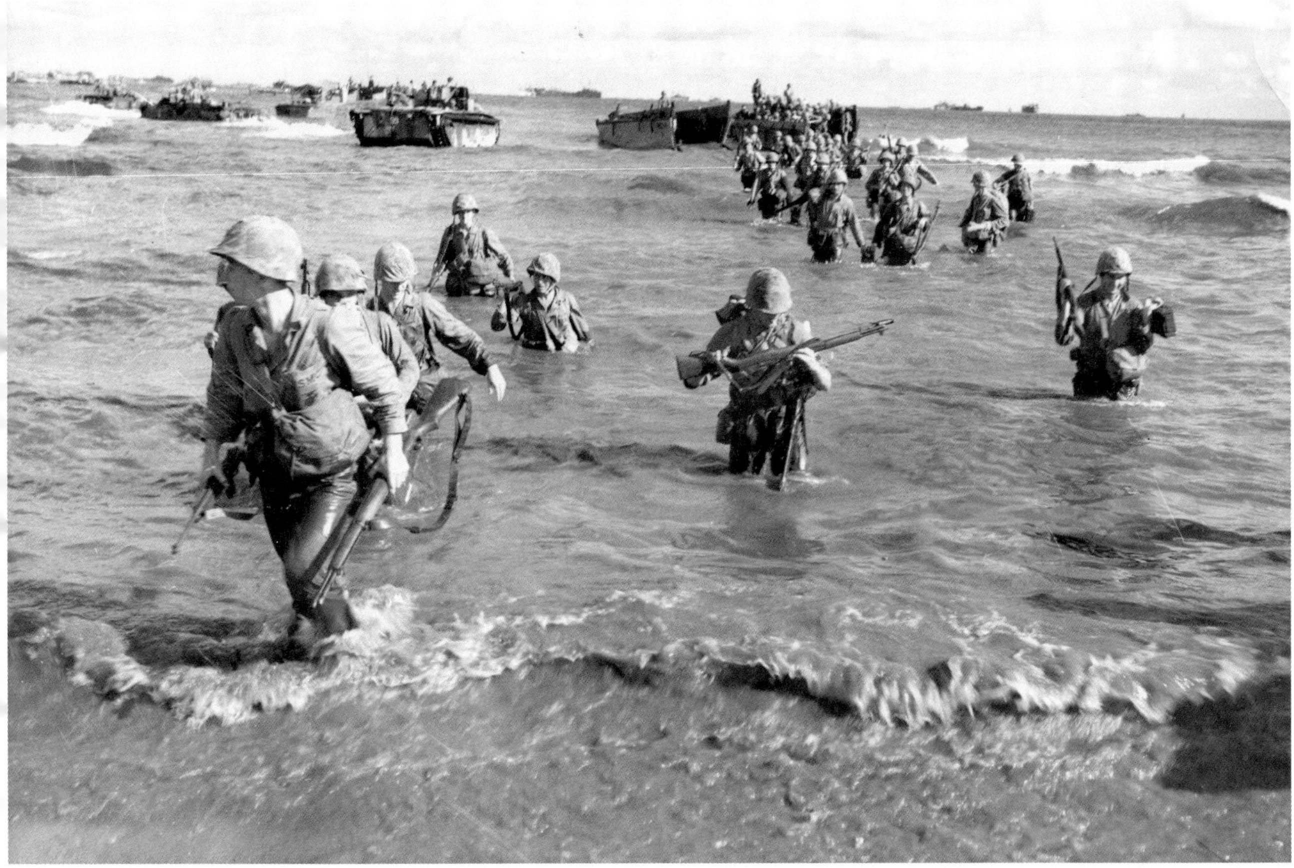

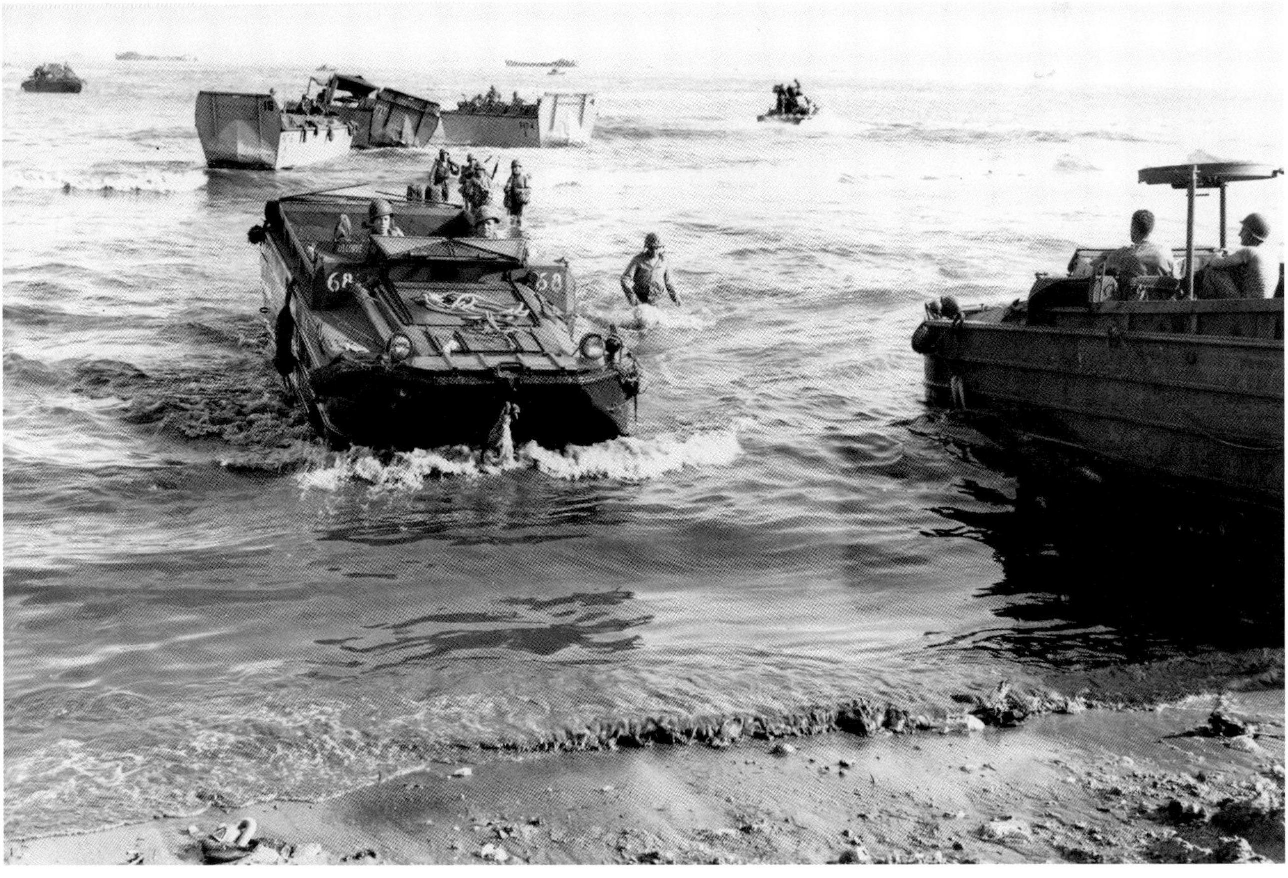

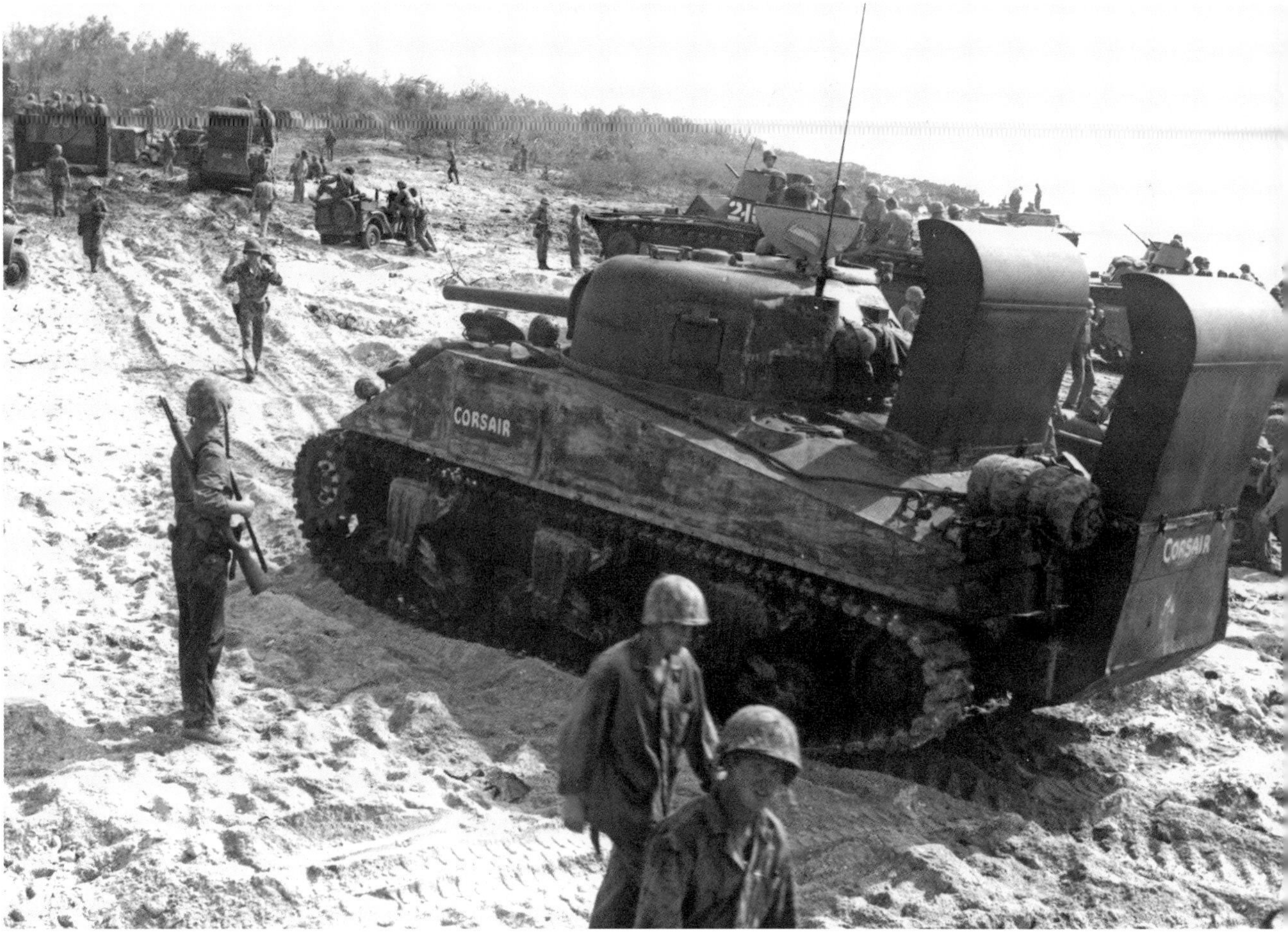
CORSAIR
CORSAIR

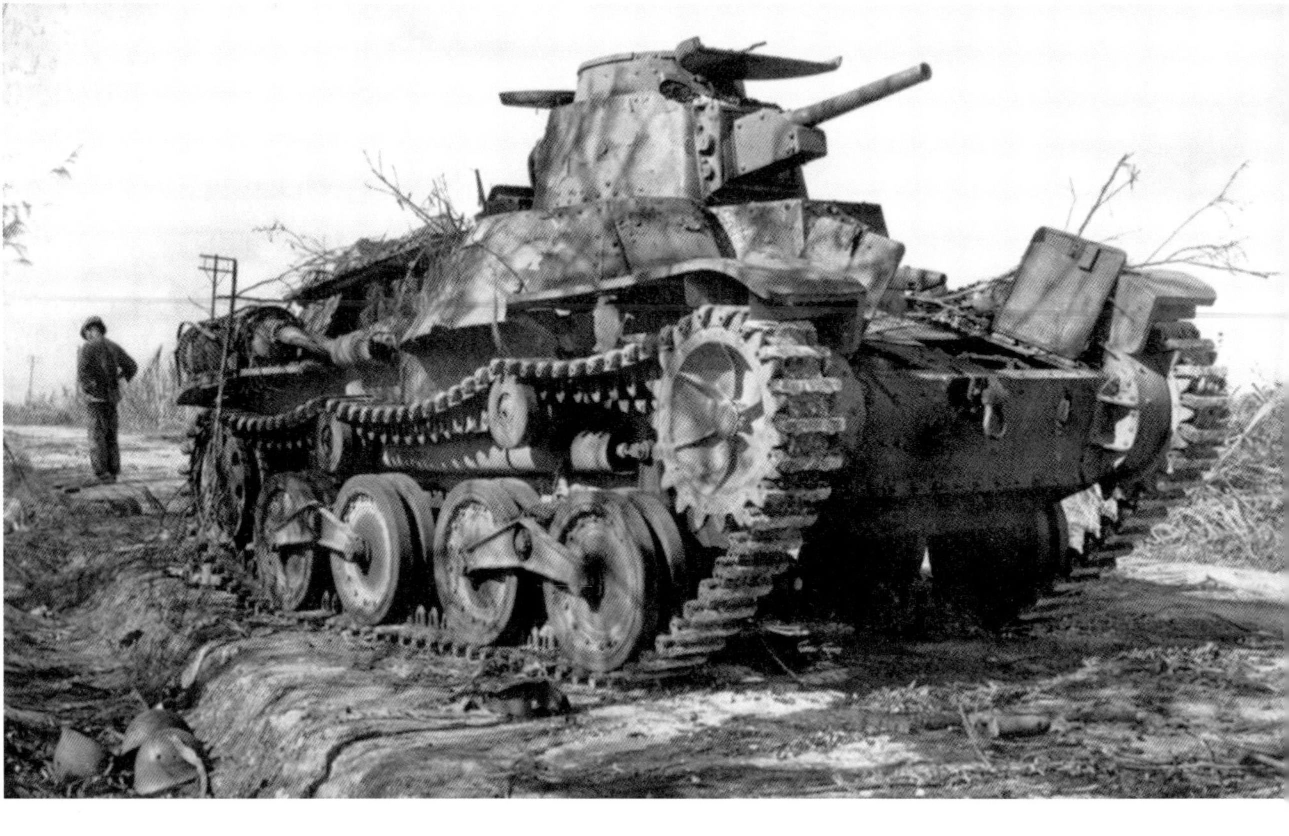

(**Opposite, above**) Having just landed on a Tinian beach is a Marine Corps M4A2 medium tank in the foreground. Its crew has not yet removed the three-part deep-water fording kit. The forward funnel positioned on the roof of the tank's engine compartment is the engine air intake. The rear funnel projecting out of the rear of the engine compartment is for engine exhaust. With waterproofing and the deep-water fording kit fitted, the M4A2 medium tank could operate in surf 6ft deep. (*USMC*)

(**Opposite, below**) Similarly to what occurred on Saipan, the Japanese launched a series of counter-attacks on the Marine landing beaches on Tinian on the first night of the invasion. One of these involved a force of approximately 600 naval infantrymen, the other three were all composed of Japanese Army troops supported by small numbers of tanks. All the counter-attacks were beaten off, leaving behind hundreds of corpses, and as shown in this picture a knocked-out Type 95 light tank. (*USMC*)

(**Above**) For the Japanese Army, the object of all manoeuvres was to close quickly with the enemy so that the supposed Japanese superiority in close combat could be realized. In this photograph, we see the results of that Japanese belief with two dead Marines in a fighting position on Saipan and two dead Japanese soldiers. The empty ammunition cans in the foreground could indicate that the two Marines were operating a machine gun. (*USMC*)

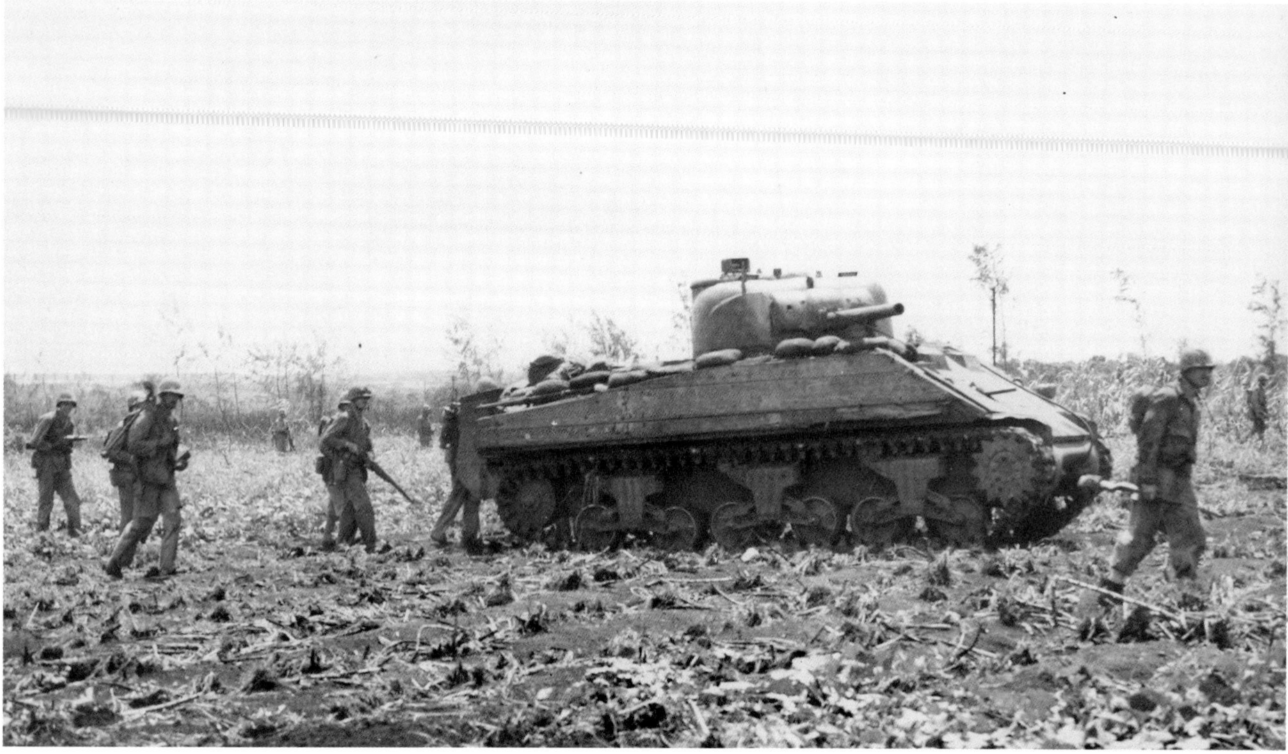

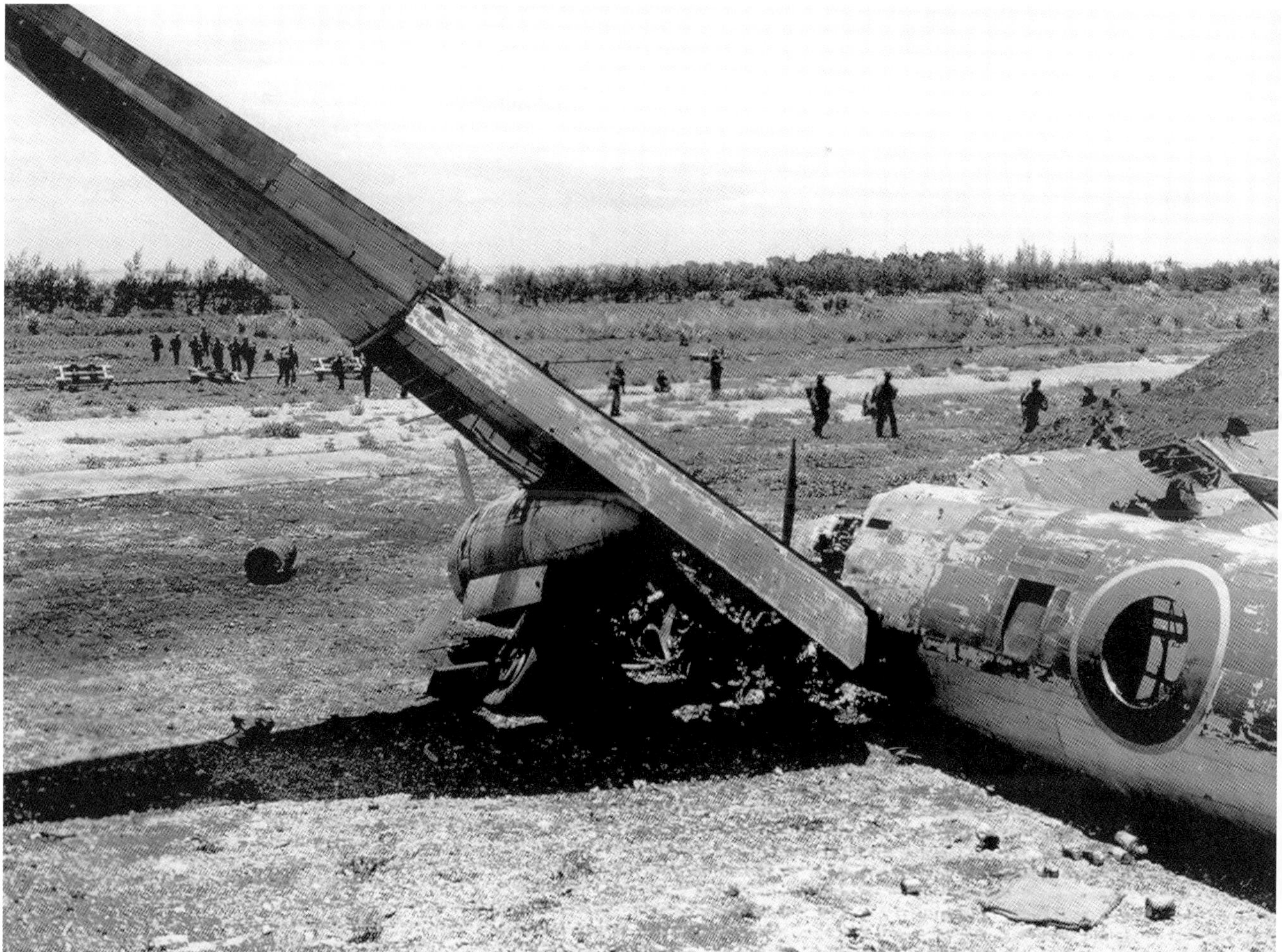

(**Opposite, above**) A Marine Corps M4A2 medium tank is shown receiving support from infantry on Tinian. A closer examination of the tank shows it to have wooden planks affixed to both its front hull and hull sides to neutralize the threat of Japanese magnetic mines. In addition, the top of the vehicle's hull, including the rear engine deck, has been covered with sandbags to offset the effect of Japanese infantry placing explosive charges on those thinly-armoured areas. (USMC)

(**Opposite, below**) A Marine patrol on Tinian comes across an abandoned Japanese-built airfield with the derelict remains of an enemy twin-engine bomber in the foreground. After the initial Japanese resistance on the landing beach labelled White 2, enemy opposition on the northern half of the island was minimal. The Marine regiments and divisions formed a skirmish line across the island and reached the centre of Tinian by 29 July 1944 with relatively light losses. (USMC)

(**Above**) Pictured in a sugar-cane field is a Marine Corps M3 series 75mm Gun Motor Carriage (GMC). Driving in a vehicle across sugar-cane fields, which covered most of Tinian, was much preferred to walking across as each stalk was stiff enough to trip a man not watching his every step. Sugar-cane fields were also rife with dangers including booby-traps and hidden Japanese soldiers. (USMC)

By 30 July 1944 the Marines had captured Tinian Town where the Japanese had originally anticipated the American landings, and had control of 80 per cent of Tinian. The remaining enemy troops had by this time withdrawn to the more defensible hills and caves of the island's southern coast. Here we see Marines trying to locate and eliminate the last hold-outs on Tinian. In the background is a US Navy destroyer that provided fire support when required. (USMC)

The crew of a Marine Corps 75mm howitzer on Tinian are shown engaging a cave containing a number of Japanese defenders. As the Marines reached the southern coast of the island their larger artillery pieces on Saipan were now out of range, resulting in their transfer to Tinian. Prior to the Marines' assault, the last Japanese defensive line was subjected to fierce bombardment from the air, land and sea. The island was declared secure on 1 August 1944. (USMC)

Marines are shown assisting some of the locals from their cave refuge on Tinian. Not wanting a repeat of mass suicides of the civilian inhabitants as had occurred on Saipan, the Marine Corps made a major effort to reduce civilian casualties. Their work paid off and upon the end of major fighting, 8,000 non-combatants surrendered to the Marines with another 3,000 dribbling in over the next three months from various hiding places on the island. (USMC)

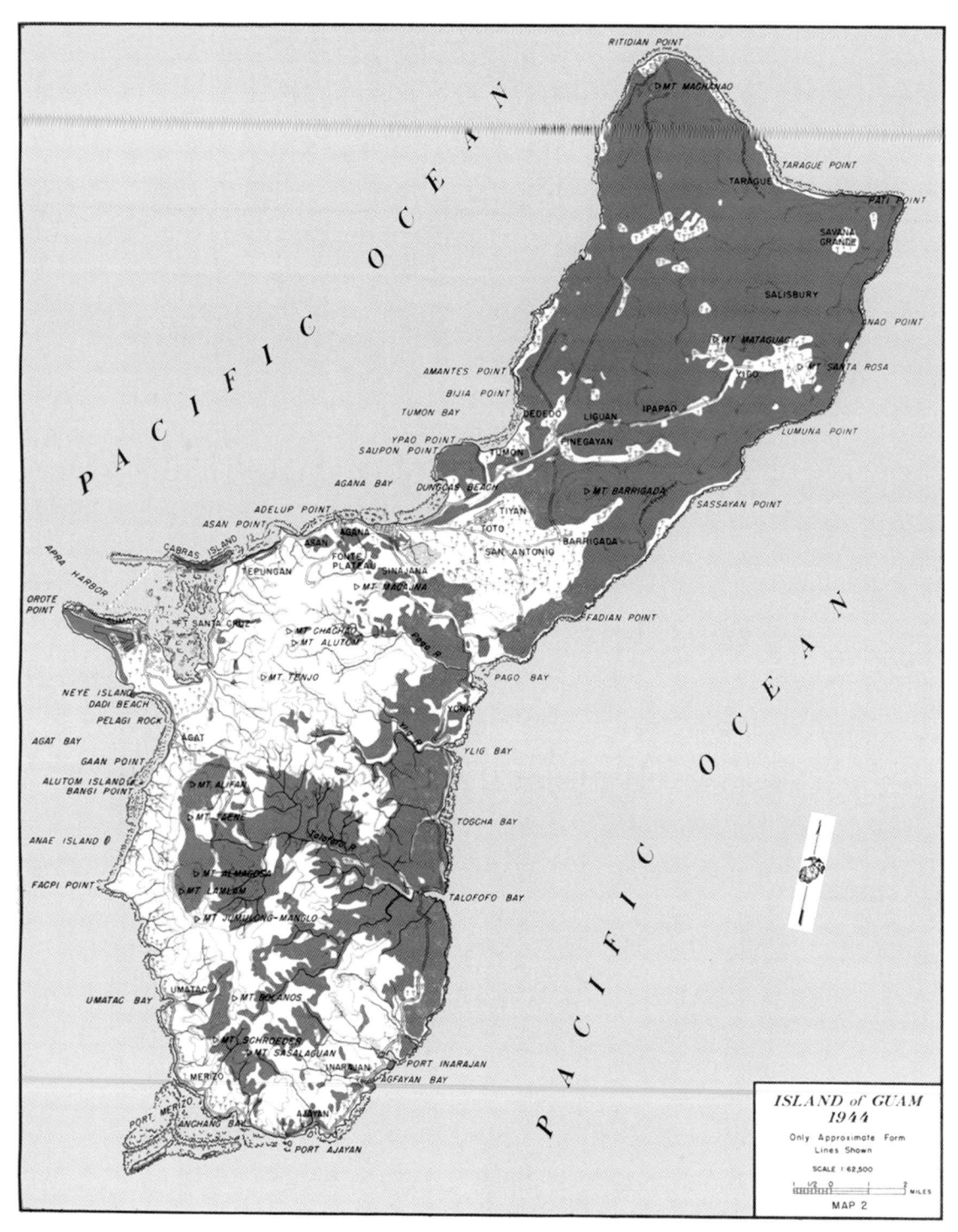

ISLAND of GUAM
1944
Only Approximate Form
Lines Shown
SCALE 1:62,500

MAP 2

The island of Guam is 212 square miles in size and was one of the three islands in the Marianas slated for seizure by American armed forces. It is located approximately 150 miles south of Saipan and Tinian. Some 32 miles long, its widest point measures 12 miles and its narrowest 4 miles. The two Marine invasion beaches were located on either side of the Orote Peninsula on the western side of the island. (*USMC*)

Pictured is a US Navy cruiser during the thirteen-day pre-invasion bombardment of Guam. A US Navy gunfire control officer claimed that they had accounted for every known Japanese gun that could pose a threat to the Marines. This did not turn out to be entirely accurate as the Japanese had built extensive fortifications on the reverse slopes of the hills that surrounded the invasion beaches and were thus untouched by naval gunfire. (USMC)

Due to Guam's geography, it was not difficult for the Japanese defenders to anticipate probable landing sites and they therefore built up their defensive positions in these locations. Pictured on a Guam invasion beach are Marines jumping over the side of an LVT-1. It was not until the introduction of the LVT-4 that the Marines had an amphibious tractor with a rear ramp. (USMC)

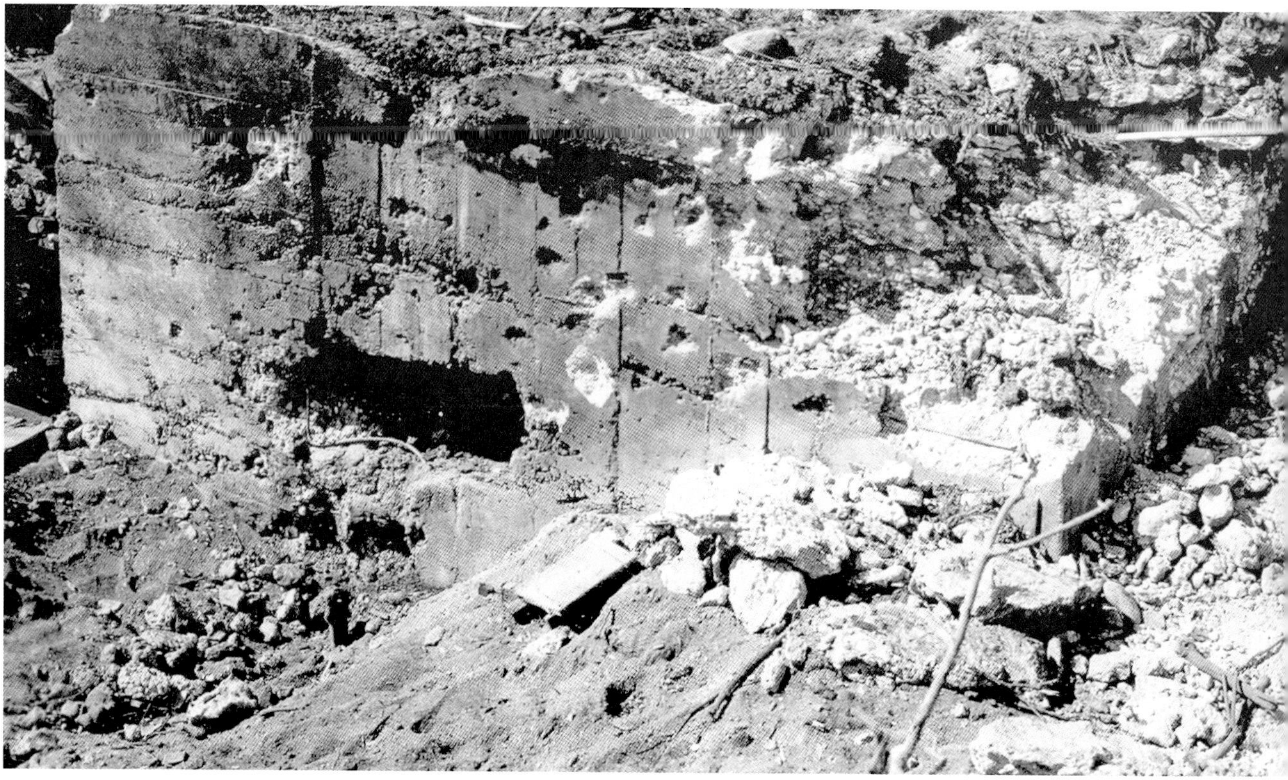

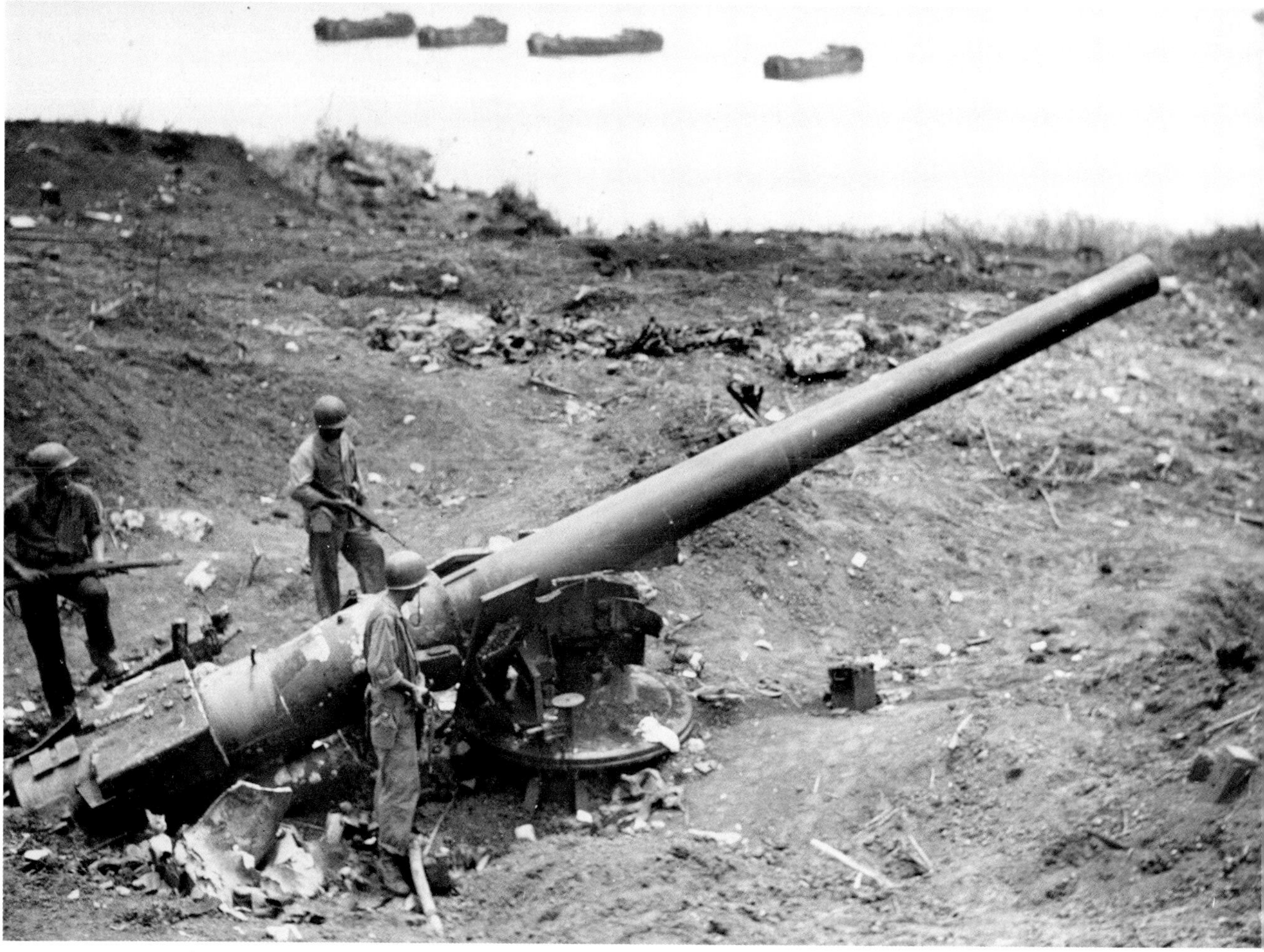

(**Opposite, above**) In this picture, we see a Japanese reinforced concrete bunker on Guam that was identified by aerial reconnaissance aircraft prior to the Marine landings and destroyed by a direct hit from a large-calibre naval gun. Such Japanese fortifications were normally tied into nearby bunkers by an extensive trench system and had interlocking fields of fire to prevent a flanking attack on any of them. (*USMC*)

(**Opposite, below**) Marines look over a knocked-out large-calibre Japanese coast artillery gun on Guam that was no doubt a redundant naval warship gun. What is not obvious is that the US Navy, pre-invasion bombardment, stripped away its camouflage netting that would have been put in place to hide it from American reconnaissance aircraft. (*USMC*)

(**Above**) Seen here on a Guam beachhead is a small portable switchboard unit. Each Marine Corps rifle regiment had a communication platoon, which formed part of each rifle battalion headquarters. It provided battalion commanders with the means to communicate to subordinate, adjacent and higher units. It consisted of a platoon headquarters, message centre and messenger section, a wire section, a radio and visual (panel) section to mark unit positions for friendly aircraft. (*USMC*)

The five-man crew of a Marine Corps M4A2 medium tank poses for the photographer during the battle for Guam. The leather helmets worn by the crew were a US Army design and included hinged ear flaps to allow for the insertion of a hard plastic earphone in each flap. To allow for the crew members to talk to each other within the tank, they were provided with either a throat microphone or a separate hand-held microphone. (USMC)

An official photograph of Marine Private Luther Skaggs Jr, who was presented with the Medal of Honor for his actions on Guam. A portion of his citation reads: 'Skaggs was critically wounded when a Japanese grenade lodged in his foxhole and exploded, shattering the lower part of one leg. Quick to act, he applied an improvised tourniquet and, while propped up in his foxhole, gallantly returned the enemy's fire with his rifle and hand grenades for a period of eight hours.' (USMC)

The Marine Corps had not really seen a big requirement for man-portable flame-throwers prior to America's entry into the Second World War. However, their employment at Guadalcanal impressed everybody with their usefulness in destroying Japanese defensive positions. By the time of the Saipan invasion the M2-2 flame-thrower with a 60-yard range was in use. An example is seen here during the fighting on Guam. (*USMC*)

(**Above**) Marines are shown on Guam running a cleaning rod through the barrel of a 155mm Gun M1. One of the Marine generals involved in the Guam campaign had this to say about the artillery support: '... artillery was the most effective weapon employed during the operation. Close support was given to the infantry in both attack and defense and harassing fires at night were particularly effective. The troops have great confidence in the power of our own artillery.' (USMC)

(**Opposite**) A very tired-looking Marine squad leader armed with an M1 carbine is seen leading a patrol on Guam. By 28 July 1944 the Marine units that had landed on either side of the Orote Peninsula had linked together and declared the entire peninsula secure the next day. The capture of the Orote Peninsula had cost the Marines 115 men killed, 721 wounded and 38 missing in action. The enemy toll was 1,633 dead. (USMC)

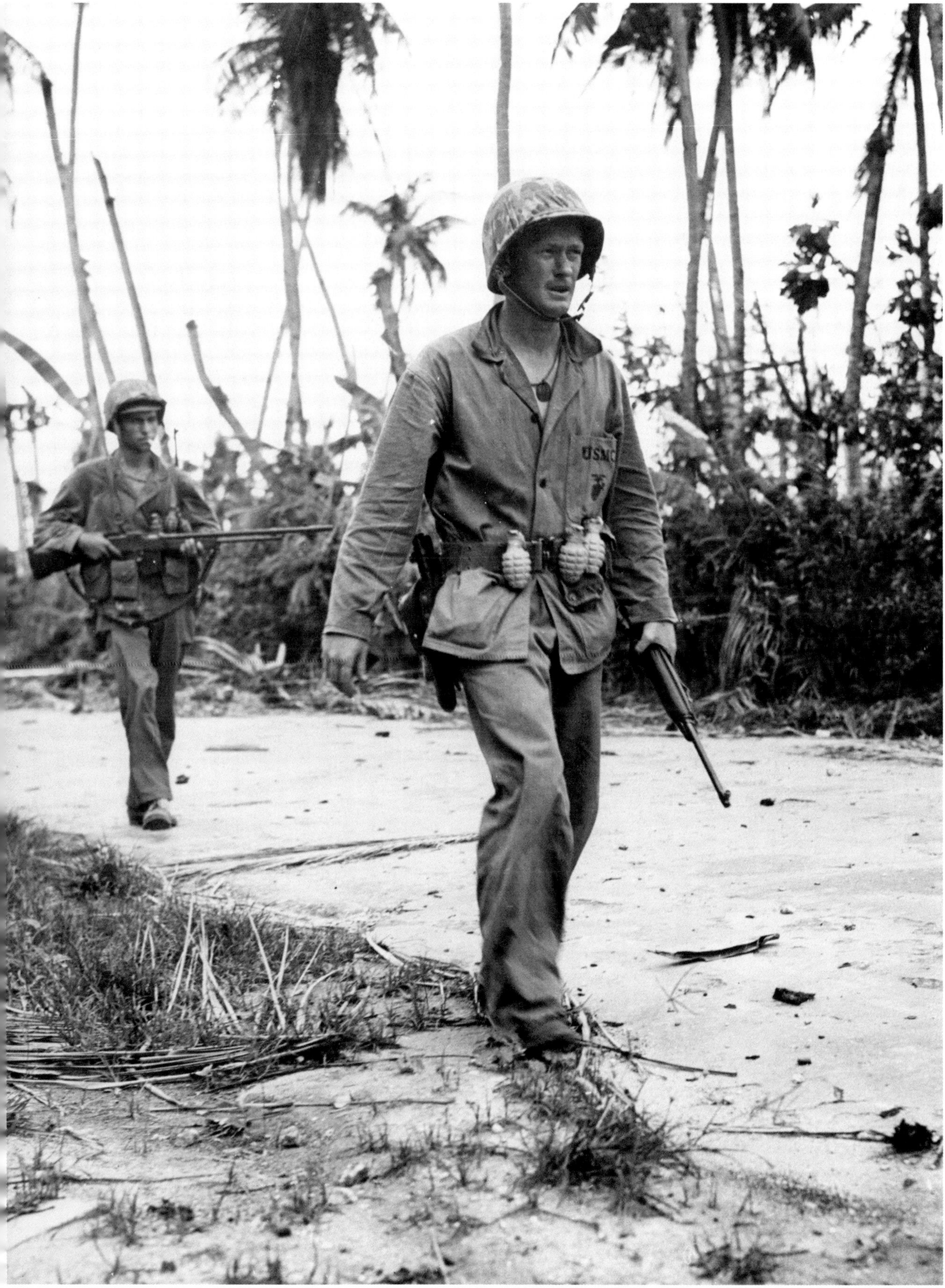
USMC

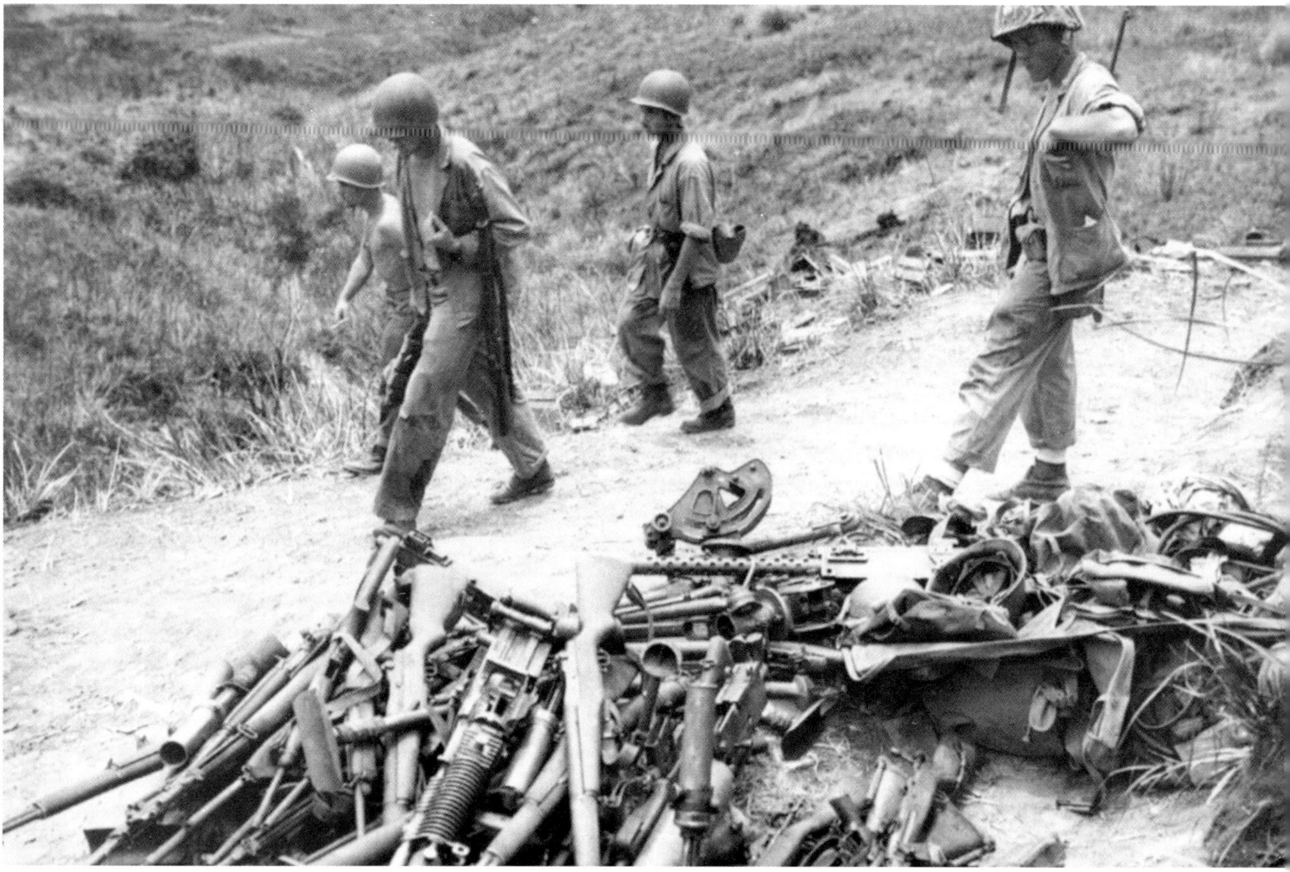

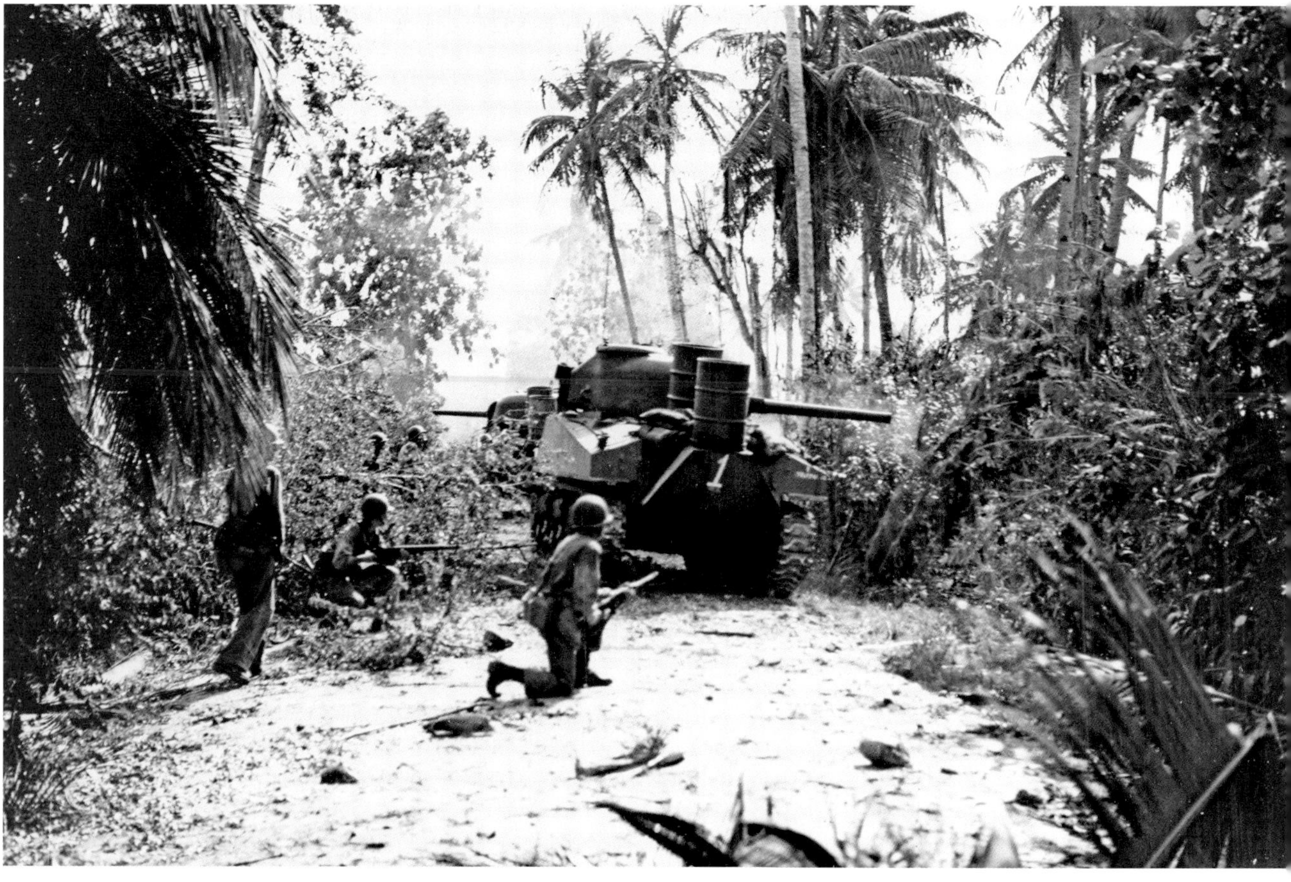

(**Opposite, above**) In this image we see a Marine Corps collection point for leftover weapons following a battle on Guam. The Japanese weapons would be destroyed and the American weapons restored to operational condition and reissued. On the top of the weapon pile in the foreground is a Japanese 7.7mm heavy machine gun Model 92 and what appears to be the barrels of the Japanese 50mm grenade-launcher Model 89. The Marines incorrectly referred to this as the 'knee mortar'. (USMC)

(**Above**) A Marine on Guam has found time in between fighting the Japanese to sack out in his foxhole. The Marines tasked with the capture of Guam belonged either to the 3rd Marine Division or the 1st Provisional Marine Brigade. The latter was formed on Guadalcanal in mid-1944 from the non-divisional 4th and 22nd Marine regiments. Upon the conclusion of the battle for Guam it returned to Guadalcanal and was the base upon which the 6th Marine Division was formed. (USMC)

(**Opposite, below**) Marine infantrymen are shown on Guam in support of a Marine M4A2 medium tank searching out Japanese positions. The large barrels visible on the rear engine decks of both tanks are for fresh water, a precious resource in battle together with food, fuel and ammunition. As the biggest threat to Marine tankers was close-in Japanese attacks, they tended to keep all the hatches closed most of the time, which meant that the heat build-up inside them was terrible. (USMC)

As the Japanese defenders of Guam retreated to the more mountainous portions of the island, the Marines had to follow. The Marine in front here is carrying the approximately 53lb tripod for the water-cooled .30 calibre M1917A1 heavy machine gun carried by the Marine behind him. The machine gun itself (with its water jacket filled) weighed 41lb. *(USMC)*

A Marine on Guam is standing watch by his .30 calibre M1917A1 heavy machine gun. The weapon's receiver was fed by a woven fabric belt seen in the picture with a capacity of 250 rounds. For every four ball or armour-piercing rounds in the ammunition belt there was a single tracer round. The machine gun had a maximum effective direct-fire range of approximately 2,000 yards. It could also be employed in the indirect fire mode. (*USMC*)

Rear Admiral Richard L. 'Close-In' Conolly, US Navy (left), with Major General Roy S. Geiger, US Marine Corps, on Guam. Geiger took charge of the III Amphibious Corps in April 1944, which oversaw all the Marine Corps units assigned to the Guam campaign. He started his career with the Marine Corps as a pilot during the First World War and thereafter rose in rank. He would be the first Marine aviator to command a major ground formation during the Second World War. (USMC)

A Marine Corps psychological warfare team is shown using a small loudspeaker to convince both the remaining Japanese troops on Guam and the local civilian inhabitants of the island in hiding to show themselves. By this time, the Japanese troops on the island were short of everything including ammunition, food and water. Some Japanese troops resorted to making spears by attaching bayonets to bamboo poles. (USMC)

In this picture we see Marines pulling a Japanese Navy man from his hiding place on Guam. Marine front-line riflemen generally preferred the M1 rifle due to its range and knock-down power. The lighter M1 carbine in the foreground was typically issued to the Marines that operated crew-served weapons such as mortars, machine guns and artillery pieces. Marine Corps infantry squad leaders sometimes armed themselves with sub-machine guns. (*USMC*)

With the end of organized large-scale Japanese resistance on Guam, the island was declared secure on 10 August 1944. This prompted many of the remaining Guamanians to leave their hiding places as seen here and seek food and medical care from the Marines and US Army troops on the island. To everybody's surprise a Japanese Army sergeant was found still hiding on Guam in 1972, a total of twenty-eight years after the island was captured by the American military. (*USMC*)

Chapter Four

The Last Few Battles

Even before the Mariana Islands were secured, in August 1944 the leadership of the US Navy's Central Pacific advance was trying to decide what its next step would be. One choice was to advance northward towards the Bonin Island chain, seizing islands with suitable airfields that would bring American military might progressively closer to the Japanese home islands.

On the other hand, the leadership of the US Army's South-West Pacific advance had plans to invade the Philippines from its bases in New Guinea. They were concerned that Japanese aircraft flying from the Palau Island chain could pose a serious danger to their invasion plans. This led to the decision at the highest level that the Palau Island chain had to be secured before moving northward towards the Japanese home islands.

Two islands in the Palau Island chain with airfields were selected for seizure by the US Navy. They were Peleliu and the nearby smaller island of Angaur. To accomplish this goal, the US Navy had available the 1st Marine Division and the US Army 81st Infantry Division. The Marine division was tasked with the capture of Peleliu and the army division the capture of Angaur. The Japanese had not taken any chances and assigned the defence of both islands to one of its best infantry divisions.

The Battle for Peleliu

The landings on Peleliu took place on 15 September 1944, in the wake of a strong three-day preparatory bombardment. In spite of all the firepower directed at the Japanese beach defensive system, it remained relatively undamaged as the Japanese had made an extra effort to harden beach defensive fortifications. As the Marines approached the landing beaches they were met with an unexpected storm of fire. It accounted for the loss of a great many of the Marines' LVTs and amphibious DUKW trucks known as 'Ducks'.

In spite of the enhanced invasion beach defensive system, the Marines still managed to push inland a short distance on the first day of the invasion. As one Marine infantry regiment neared the island's airfield that day, the Japanese force led by thirteen tanks counter-attacked in daylight. A description of that counter-attack appears in this passage from a Marine Corps Historical Branch publication titled *The Seizure of Peleliu* by Major Frank O. Hough:

> … an air observer spotted enemy tanks forming in defilade east of the ridges a short distance above the airfield…infantry clustered atop them wherever a handhold could be had. They [Japanese tanks] passed through their advancing foot soldiers about 400 yards forward of the Marine positions, and for a moment the attack assumed aspects of genuine formidability. But only for a moment. Instead of coordinating their movement to that of the infantry, the enemy tank drivers opened their throttles wide and lit out for the American lines like so many of the proverbial bats; too fast to support their assault troops or for those troops to support them …
>
> Meanwhile the men of 1/5 had opened with everything they had: 37mm guns, bazookas, AT [anti-tank] grenades; all organic infantry weapons plus the 75s of the [Sherman] tanks which Colonel Boyd had posted in support. A navy dive bomber, happening upon the scene, came in low and dropped a large bomb into what appeared to be the midst of the on-swarming enemy. In the face of all this fire, the tank-riding infantry, so many sitting ducks, simply seemed to disintegrate into thin air. Tanks began exploding and burning, but the survivors kept coming. They struck the 1st Battalion lines in the narrow sector held by the left platoon, of Company B. And overran them.
>
> The remarkable aspect here was that, while the enemy tanks overran the lines and penetrated 150 yards beyond – one of them nearly reached the beach before being liquidated – nowhere did they cause a break in the front. If any Marines felt an urge to quit their positions, they scarcely had time, so rapidly did these events take place. Two men were caught in the path of one of these onrushing machines and crushed to death. A few others were burned or wounded by flying fragments as tanks were destroyed in their midst. The rest dodged by one means or another and kept on fighting.

When the attack petered out, all but two of the tanks were utterly destroyed. The remaining two were subsequently knocked out as they counter-attacked another portion of the Marines' lines that same day. The Japanese counter-attacks would continue in ever-diminishing intensity through the first night into the next morning.

On the second day of the invasion, the Marines captured the island's airfield despite heavy Japanese artillery fire. On the third day, small Marine Corps L-2 observation planes nicknamed the 'Grasshopper' began flying out of the airfield. Their job was to spot targets for both Marine Corps artillery and naval gunfire. On 26 September, a Marine Corps fighter squadron flying F4U Corsairs arrived on the airfield and took on the role of CAS. Besides high-explosive (HE) bombs, the Marine aviators also dropped the recently-introduced jellied gasoline weapon known as napalm.

The Marines Run into Unexpected Resistance

As the days ran on, the Marines slowly increased the area under their control. However, instead of Japanese resistance becoming progressively weaker as had occurred on other islands, their resistance grew ever fiercer as the Marines approached the more rugged portion of the island known as Umurbrogol Mountain.

Pre-invasion aerial photography had not disclosed just how rough the terrain was in the Umurbrogol Mountain area. From a Marine Corps Historical Branch publication titled *The Bloody Beaches: The Marines at Peleliu* by Brigadier General Gordon D. Gayle comes this description of what the Marines had to deal with:

> … the Umurbrogol area was in fact a complex system of sharply uplifted coral ridges, knobs, valleys, and sinkholes. It rose above the level remainder of the island from 50 to 300 feet, and provided excellent emplacements for cave and tunnel defenses. The Japanese had made the most of what this terrain provided during their extensive period of occupation and defensive preparations.

Not known at the time was that the Japanese military had given up on trying to stop American assault forces on landing beaches, merely attempting to slow them down as much as possible. There would be no more suicidal banzai attacks if they could help it. Instead, the Japanese relied on defensive fortifications built inland to prolong the fighting on every island for as long as possible. By doing so they would raise the cost in American lives to hopefully unacceptable limits and deter a potential invasion of the Japanese home islands.

Having suffered 70 per cent casualties in trying to take the area around Umurbrogol Mountain, a senior Marine Corps officer sent in elements of the US Army 81st Infantry Division to relieve the hard-pressed Marine infantry regiment. With the Marine Corps' losses growing heavier by the day among the other infantry regiments on the island and no replacements possible, the seizure of the island was assigned to the US Army 81st Infantry Division on 30 October 1944. It had completed the capture of the small nearby island of Angaur between 17 September and 22 October 1944.

It would take the US Army's 81st Infantry Division until 27 November 1944 to secure Peleliu from organized Japanese resistance. Of the approximately 11,000 Japanese defenders, almost all were killed in the fighting with only 19 captured alive. Marine Corps' losses were 1,252 men killed and 6,526 wounded. US Army losses were pegged at 3,300 men.

As events transpired, it turned out that the capture of the islands of Peleliu and Angaur had been unnecessary. The US Army's South-West Pacific advance invaded

Leyte Island in the Philippines on 22 October 1944 with no enemy opposition mounted from the Palau Island chain. From a Marine Corps historical monograph comes the following comment:

> But there is an enduring question of whether the capture of Peleliu was essential, especially in view of Admiral William F. Halsey's recommendation through Admiral Nimitz to the Joint Chiefs of Staff on 13 September 1944, two days before D-Day, that the landing be cancelled. By that time, it was too late. And Peleliu was added to the long list of battles in which Marines fought and suffered, and prevailed.

Marine Aviation in the Philippines

On 11 June 1944, all the land-based Marine Corps aviation squadrons that had fought in the Solomon Islands campaign passed to the control of the US Army-led South-West Pacific advance. The major goal of that advance at the time was the re-conquest of the Philippines, which began on 20 October 1944 with the invasion of Leyte Island.

Fierce Japanese aerial resistance prompted the US Army to request the deployment of Marine night-fighter squadrons equipped with radar-equipped F6F Hellcats in November 1944. These were supplemented by Marine daylight-only units equipped with the F4U Corsair.

With the conquest of Leyte completed by the end of 26 December 1944, the South-West Pacific advance prepared for the invasion of the main island of Luzon slated for 9 January 1945. Marine pilots would provide protection for the invasion fleet taking part in that invasion by striking at Japanese airfields on Luzon and other Philippine islands.

Besides the F4U Corsair-equipped Marine aviation squadrons, a number of SBD (Scout Bomber, Douglas) Dauntless dive-bomber-equipped Marine squadrons provided close air support (CAS) to US Army divisions to great effect.

On 17 April 1945, with the battle for Luzon still raging, the South-West Pacific advance invaded the Philippine island of Mindanao. This operation was supported by Marine dive-bomber squadrons. When the island was secured on 30 June 1945, all but one of the SBD-equipped squadrons was deactivated. The remaining Marine squadron was equipped with the newer SB2C dive-bomber, officially nicknamed the 'Helldiver'. The entire Philippines island chain was declared secured on 5 July 1945.

The Battle for Iwo Jima

With the seizure of Peleliu and Angaur in the Palau island chain, the US Central Pacific campaign's leadership once again looked northward at the Bonin Island chain, located approximately 650 miles south of the Japanese home islands. Among the Bonin

Islands was a sub-group of three islands known as the Volcano Islands, the largest of which was Iwo Jima.

The 8-mile-square Iwo Jima was selected as the next Central Pacific campaign objective for several reasons, all of which reflected the importance of air power. First, capturing Iwo and its existing airfields denied the Japanese a base from which to intercept American bombing missions over Japan that were launched from the Marianas. Second, American fighters based there could escort and defend the bombers on the way into, and returning from, the Japanese home islands. Third, bombers unable to return to the Marianas due to battle damage or mechanical failures could attempt to land 590 miles sooner, saving the bomber and its crew.

The downside of trying to capture Iwo Jima was that it had been heavily fortified and defended by a garrison of approximately 20,000 men. They were armed with anti-tank guns, anti-aircraft guns and rocket-launchers. Fortunately, a US Navy blockade around Iwo Jima kept a great deal of weaponry and munitions from ever reaching the island. Among the important items that did not reach the defenders were barbed wire and the optical gunsights for some of their weapons.

From a Marine Corps Historical Branch publication titled *Western Pacific Operations* by authors Garand and Strowbridge appears this passage detailing the type of defensive system put into place by the Japanese before the Marines were sent in to capture the island:

> The Japanese were quick to discover that the black volcanic ash that existed in abundance all over the island [Iwo Jima] could be converted into concrete of superior quality when mixed with cement. Pillboxes near the beaches north of Mount Suribachi were constructed of reinforced concrete, many of them with walls four feet thick. At the same time, an elaborate system of caves, concrete blockhouses, and pillboxes was established. One of the results of American air attacks and naval bombardment in the early summer of 1944 had been to drive the Japanese so deep underground that eventually their defenses became virtually immune to air or naval bombardment.

A total of 60,000 troops from three Marine divisions – the 3rd, 4th and 5th – were allocated for the capture of Iwo Jima. They were to be landed by a supporting force of 800 US Navy ships manned by approximately 22,000 naval personnel. The island had been subjected to air attacks and surface bombardment since June 1944, which had progressively increased in frequency. On 16 February 1945, the pre-invasion bombardment of Iwo Jima began in earnest.

The Marines' Conquest Unfolds

On the morning of 19 February 1945, the 4th and 5th Marine divisions began landing on Iwo Jima. Unlike Peleliu, the Marines initially met very little resistance coming ashore other than a minimal amount of mortar and artillery fire. As the first day of the invasion progressed, however, Japanese opposition became ever tougher. Adding to the losses of the Marines on the island was a never-ending barrage of artillery fire.

By the end of the first day, despite heavy losses, the Marines had advanced across the width of the island at its narrowest point. With that accomplishment, they isolated the Japanese troops on the southern end of the island centred around Mount Suribachi from those on the northern end. It was the latter end of the island that had the three airfields, which were the main goal of the invasion.

At dawn on 20 February 1945, the Marines became involved in two distinct operations. One was the capture of Mount Suribachi and its dug-in artillery pieces at the southern end of the island. The other was an advance to the northern end of the island to seize the important airfields and eliminate all enemy resistance in its path.

By Day Two of the invasion the Marines had seized one of the island's three airfields. On the third day of the invasion the 3rd Marine Division began landing on Iwo Jima, and part of a second Japanese airfield fell that same day as a small number of Marines began to climb the steep slopes of Mount Suribachi. To their great surprise, they encountered little Japanese resistance. On their arrival at the summit they decided to raise an American flag. This resulted in the most famous and iconic photograph of the Pacific Theatre as a civilian photographer was present and shot the dramatic image of six Marines raising the flag.

As Major Robert Neiman, commanding C Company, 4th Tank Battalion, later recorded with regard to what he witnessed that day:

> When we saw the flag raised on Mt. Suribachi, it had a great positive effect on morale of all the Marines on Iwo and the nearby ships, and of course my own morale. Suribachi stood clearly visible to those of us on the ground, by far the highest point on Iwo. From its summit the Japanese had seen every move we made and gave him a magnificent observation post for directing the gunners up north as well as direct fire on us, so that we were trapped between two fires. Both the 4th and 3rd Divisions faced north with part of the 5th Division, and Suribachi was at our backs except for the troops of 5th Division charged with taking it. So when the flag went up it meant that all the marines would no longer have to worry about what was at their back, firing on them, and were no longer caught in the middle. Until that point the issue of the battle seemed in doubt. With the flag going up, we knew that we were winning and that we would eventually take the island, however many more days remained. When that flag went up, all the marines rose up and cheered, just as if their team had just scored a go-ahead touchdown at the most important football game of their lives. Even those in foxholes stopped, looked up and cheered, almost a surreal moment in midst of the battle.

The fierceness of the fighting on Iwo Jima has been dramatized in several Hollywood movies. The oldest and best-known is the 1949 film titled *Sands of Iwo Jima* starring the legendary American actor John Wayne. In more recent times another famous American action star, Clint Eastwood, directed and produced two movies about the island's fall. One titled *Flags of Our Fathers* was from the American viewpoint. The other was titled *Letters from Iwo Jima* and reflected the island battle from the Japanese perspective. Both were released in 2006.

The Fighting Goes On

By 25 February 1945 the Marines had captured about half of Iwo Jima, including the remainder of the second airfield. As they closed in on the northern end of the island the Japanese resistance never lessened in ferocity. The Marine infantry, successfully advancing, was greatly assisted by Marine tankers. This is expressed in an extract from a Marine Corps wartime report titled 'Armored Operations on Iwo Jima':

> Much of the success of tank operations on this island was due to the spirit of the individual tank commanders and their will to take more than a normal risk to aid those they were supporting. There was much discussion as to whether or not a certain area was tank terrain. The attitude of most of the tankers was that if they could get their tank in it and fire on the enemy, then it was tank terrain for them. In close country, the tanks did not rely upon the infantry to protect them but covered each other from a column formation. This action was quite successful.

As the end of February neared, Marine Corps L-5 Grasshopper observation aircraft began flying out of one of the captured airfields to direct both artillery and naval gunfire. Fierce ground fighting on the island continued into the first day of March. By nightfall of the second day of March, the Marines had captured the last of the three airfields. Those Japanese troops remaining were confined to an area fringing the north-eastern end of the island.

On 4 March the first of many USAAF four-engine bombers made an emergency landing on the first airfield captured by the Marines. Three days later, the first USAAF land-based fighter planes landed and began escorting their bomber brethren over the Japanese home islands. They also took over the air-support role from the US Navy's carrier aircraft on 8 March. The second captured airfield became operational on 16 March. Marine ground-attack missions on Iwo Jima were fairly limited, with the bulk of close-support missions flown by either US Navy fighters or USAAF fighters.

On 16 March 1944, Iwo Jima was declared secured from organized enemy resistance. Again, nobody told the Japanese defenders this important news and stiff fighting continued until 26 March 1945. On 4 April 1945, the US Army took over the garrison duties of the island with the departure of the three Marine divisions' personnel, which had begun on 17 March 1945. The US Army would continue to deal with small Japanese attacks and stragglers until May 1945.

Losses

Among the 60,000 or so Marines tasked with the capture of Iwo Jima, the casualty rate was terrible. This was the first time that Marine losses in the capture of an enemy-occupied island were higher than those of its defenders. From a Marine Corps Historical Branch publication titled *Coral and Brass* by Marine General Holland M. Smith comes this summary of the Iwo Jima operation:

> Iwo Jima was the most savage and the most costly battle in the history of the Marine Corps. Indeed, it has few parallels in military annals. In the first five days, we suffered casualties at an average of more than 1,200 a day. One out of every three Marines who set foot on the island was killed or wounded. In the first 50 hours, our casualties were more than 3,000, and in a campaign lasting 26 days, with many more days of mopping up, our total casualties were 21,558, of whom 5,521 were killed or died of wounds. Divisions ended the battle with less than 50 per cent combat efficiency.

Of the approximately 20,000 Japanese defenders on Iwo Jima, most were killed in combat, with some committing suicide. Roughly 200 impressed Korean labourers were captured with a handful of Japanese soldiers. There were no civilian losses on Iwo Jima as all civilians had been evacuated before the American invasion so there would be fewer mouths to feed.

The Battle for Okinawa

Following the seizure of Iwo Jima, the next step towards the Japanese home islands was the island of Okinawa, considered part of Japan. The large island, covering 485 square miles, formed part of the Ryuku Island chain and was located 340 miles south-west of the Japanese home islands. Its selection as an objective was based on the fact that it had suitable airfields and a number of anchorages for ships.

From Okinawa, USAAF bombers and fighters would be able to reach the home islands of Japan as well as Japanese-occupied China, Indo-China, Taiwan and Singapore. The flipside of this meant that when the island was going to be assaulted, the US Navy invasion fleet would be in range of numerous airfields located on the Japanese home islands. It would also be under threat from what was left of the Japanese Navy.

The Enemy Prepares

As with Iwo Jima, the Japanese knew by mid-1944 that sooner or later Okinawa would face an American invasion. The Japanese engineered/built an impressive array of defensive fortifications, including approximately 96 miles of underground tunnels.

There was more Japanese artillery, including rocket-launchers, on the island than any other island that had been seized by the Marine Corps.

The Japanese commander of Okinawa had at his disposal approximately 70,000 Army troops (figures vary depending on the source) and 3,500 naval ground troops in addition to 7,000 Japanese Navy civilian personnel. An additional 40,000 men raised from the local population were formed into construction and militia units. The latter included teenage boys as young as 14 organized into what were called the 'Blood and Iron for the Emperor Duty Units'.

The Forces Brought to Bear

US Navy planners appreciated that resistance on Okinawa – on Japan's doorstep – would be ferocious and/or fanatical, and that the Japanese had had many years to prepare. Furthermore, it was the largest island apart from those of the Philippines and more readily supported from Japan. The likely difficulty of its capture was not lost on the planners. For the job, they were assigned four US Army divisions and three Marine divisions: the 1st, 2nd and 6th. The 6th Marine Division was formed overseas in September 1944. Combat experience had shown that the divisions were under-strength under the third Marine division TO&E, so all three divisions were re-organized to bring each to a complement of 19,716 men; an increase of more than 2,000 Marines.

All four US Army divisions and the three Marine divisions fell under the command of what was referred to as the Tenth Army, led by a US Army general. Of the approximately 540,000 men assigned to the Tenth Army, a total of 88,000 were Marines, who in turn were backed by roughly 18,000 US Navy support troops comprising both Seabee construction units and medical personnel. The invasion of Okinawa was referred to as Operation ICEBERG.

The Fighting Begins

Following the fairly standard aerial and naval bombardment that had begun months earlier, the American Tenth Army landings began on the morning of 1 April 1945 with four divisions: two army and two Marine, the 1st and 6th. To confuse the enemy as to American intentions and raise concerns about the threat of flanking attacks, troopships carrying the 2nd Marine Division feinted landings around southern Okinawa to tie down Japanese infantry reserves.

As with Iwo Jima, the landings were met by light enemy resistance. With 50,000 troops ashore on the first day, the Tenth Army managed to cross from one side of the island to the other with minimal losses. In the process, they captured two Japanese airfields. By the second day, enemy resistance stiffened, as the Tenth Army began encountering occasional Japanese strongpoints.

The Japanese believed the southern half of Okinawa to be much more defensible than the northern half and that is where they concentrated the bulk of their forces.

> **Flame-thrower Tanks**
> During the battle of Okinawa, one of the most useful vehicles in the corps' inventory was the flame-thrower tank. These were M4 series medium tanks on which the turret-mounted 75mm main guns were removed and replaced with flame-thrower guns.
>
> Using napalm-thickened fuel stored in four tanks in the hull, the flame-thrower tank had a maximum effective range of approximately 150 yards with favourable wind conditions. The Japanese soldiers so feared these tanks that they formed special suicide squads to destroy them. To protect their valuable flame-thrower tanks, Marine infantrymen always escorted them into battle. As many who served on the flame-thrower tanks wanted to retain the 75mm main gun for self-protection, a follow-on model had both the 75mm main gun and the flame gun turret-mounted. However, it arrived too late to see combat.

The Japanese attitude was underscored by their decision to evacuate all non-able-bodied civilians, out of a population of approximately 500,000, to the northern half of the island prior to the American landings. Once ashore, the senior leadership of the Tenth Army quickly grasped this fact and sent in the 6th Marine Division to secure the northern half of Okinawa. That task was completed by 22 April 1945.

Taking on the Southern Half of Okinawa

The capture of the southern half of Okinawa was initially assigned to two US Army divisions, with a third put into the line on 9 April 1945. The main goal was the capture of key enemy defensive positions located around the ancient Shuri Castle. This task proved much more difficult than anticipated.

By the end of April, the 1st Marine Division replaced one of the three US Army divisions involved in the advance on the southern half of Okinawa. On 8 May 1945, the 6th Marine Division joined the 1st Marine Division, forming the III Amphibious Corps now reinforcing the Tenth Army's attempt to secure the southern half of the island.

On 29 May 1945, the commander of the 1st Marine Division ordered the seizure of Shuri Castle, which had been bombarded by a US Navy battleship for the previous three days. It had been the headquarters for the Japanese commanding officer on Okinawa but, unknown to the Marines, had been abandoned at the beginning of the battleship bombardment. On reaching the castle, the Marines brushed aside the remaining defenders and took control.

Marine Aviation on Okinawa

Approximately 700 Marine Corps aircraft took part in the battle for Okinawa. Their primary job was to maintain air superiority over the island and the supporting US Navy fleet. This they did with a vengeance, as they claimed 625 Japanese planes during the campaign. Besides the daylight-only F4U Corsairs, there was a Marine Corps squadron equipped with radar-equipped F6F Hellcat fighters for night-time use.

Besides the air-superiority missions, both Marine and US Navy pilots also flew countless ground-attack missions, in the process dropping more than 152,000 gallons of napalm on enemy positions. The L-5 Grasshopper observation planes, as in past campaigns, provided the eyes for the Marine artillery and naval gunfire support. Something new was the use of Marine Corps Avenger torpedo-bombers in the aerial logistical role. In total, they would deliver to the Marines on the ground more than 400,000lb of rations, medical supplies and ammunition by parachute in all types of weather.

The End is Near

By the end of May 1945, after hard fighting, the Tenth Army had confined the Japanese defenders to an 8-mile-square parcel on the southern end of the island. The last of the organized Japanese defence positions on Okinawa was secured on 21 June 1945. As always, the problem of enemy hold-outs and stragglers remained. To eliminate this problem all six divisions – two Marine and four US Army – were ordered to begin an in-depth sweep of the entire island, which took place between 23 and 30 June 1945. More than 8,000 Japanese troops were killed in the sweep, with another 3,000 captured. Almost 1,000 impressed Korean labourers also fell into American hands.

A total of 107,539 non-American bodies were counted on the battlefield at the conclusion of the campaign. It was estimated that another 23,746 had been sealed up in caves by the Tenth Army forces. Another 10,775 were captured. This meant that total enemy causalities were 142,060. This was far above the original estimate of Japanese military personnel on the island, so the Tenth Army came to the conclusion that at least 42,000 of the dead were civilians killed during the fighting. Marine losses on Okinawa were 3,376 killed and 15,723 wounded.

The Closing Act

With the dropping of atomic bombs on two of Japan's major cities – the first (Hiroshima) on 6 August and the second (Nagasaki) on 9 August 1945 – the senior leadership of the Japanese government finally realized, with some in their military highly disagreeing, that the war was over and on 10 August 1945 offered to surrender. The formal surrender took place on the US Navy battleship USS *Missouri* in Tokyo Bay on 2 September 1945.

With the conclusion of the worldwide conflict, the Marine Corps took stock of its losses. These amounted to 25,207 dead from all causes and 67,207 wounded. Eighty-four Medals of Honor were awarded to Marines during their time fighting in the Pacific. Of that number, eleven were awarded to Marine Corps pilots.

Belief and Belonging
By Kenneth W. Estes, Lieutenant Colonel, US Marines

When the Second World War Marines left the United States and entered combat, the *esprit de corps* of the corps had been refined and decided for all time. The Marine Corps instilled discipline and cohesion in basic training and the unique Marine Corps culture provided a continuing bond, even with the transfers made necessary by wartime expansion, detachment and attachment to other units. Unit commanders and non-commissioned officers came and went, but the loyalty to one's buddies and platoons common to all fighting men became inflated in a Marine Corps setting that made one willing to fight in any circumstance to defend the honour of the corps at large.

In particular, the Marines sought to avenge not only Pearl Harbor, but the capture of the Wake Island garrison. The epic defence of Wake, pitting a few hundred Marines against Japanese ships, planes and hundreds of troops in a last stand inspired Marines throughout the war.

As the Pacific War continued, the first year of experiences at Guadalcanal, the other Solomon Islands and Tarawa confirmed in the mind and soul of these soldiers of the sea that the Japanese were not supermen but would fight to the last man. Moreover, the Japanese offered and received no quarter in their fight as they killed Americans who tried to surrender.

Basic training, or boot camp, presented recruits with a gruelling, unrelenting series of training days, lasting from 0400 to 2200 each day, filled with physical exercise, the pressure of task after task, close supervision by drill sergeants and myriad combat drills and general military training. At the end of it, usually eight seemingly endless weeks, the 'boots' paraded and received the compliments of their leaders, who called them 'men' and 'Marines' for the first time since they had entered the recruit training depot. From then on, the new Marines walked as equals with the legendary non-commissioned officers and officers who had fought from the Boxer Rebellion to the Banana Wars in the first third of a century filled with war and expeditions for the corps.

The veterans of the old corps still had a mighty role to play in the expanded Marine Corps of the Second World War. Although no veterans of tank actions existed in the pre-war corps, the steady hand of division commanders who had been sergeants at Belleau Wood in 1918, or gunnery sergeants and sergeants major who had fought there and in the jungle patrolling of Nicaragua and Haiti left an indelible impression on all the new enlisted men and junior officers that joined after 1940.

Like the legions of ancient Rome, the Marine Corps functioned as an elite military organization. Even after the December 1942 presidential decision ended all volunteering and converted American manpower to the Selective Service system, thereby forcing the corps to accept draftees for the first time in its history, a system of persuasion and volunteering operated within Selective Service. Slightly more than 10 per cent of Marines serving in the course of the war were the only true inductees of the draft.

The creed of the US Marine spread easily over the 669,000 men and women who would serve before the Japanese surrender. 'Once a Marine, always a Marine,' has for generations sufficed to describe the sense of patriotism, pride, discipline, loyalty and brotherhood that has carried the corps through perils and triumphs.

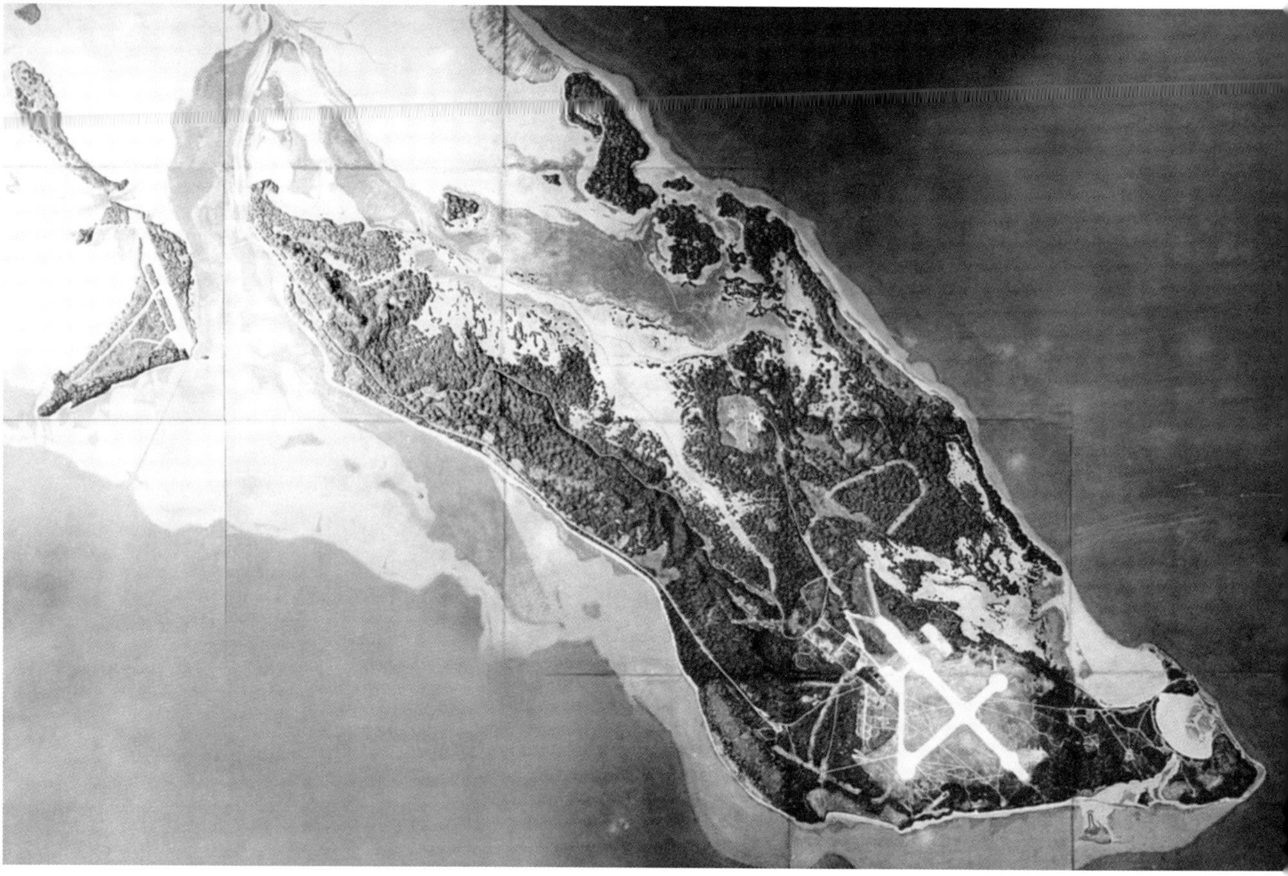

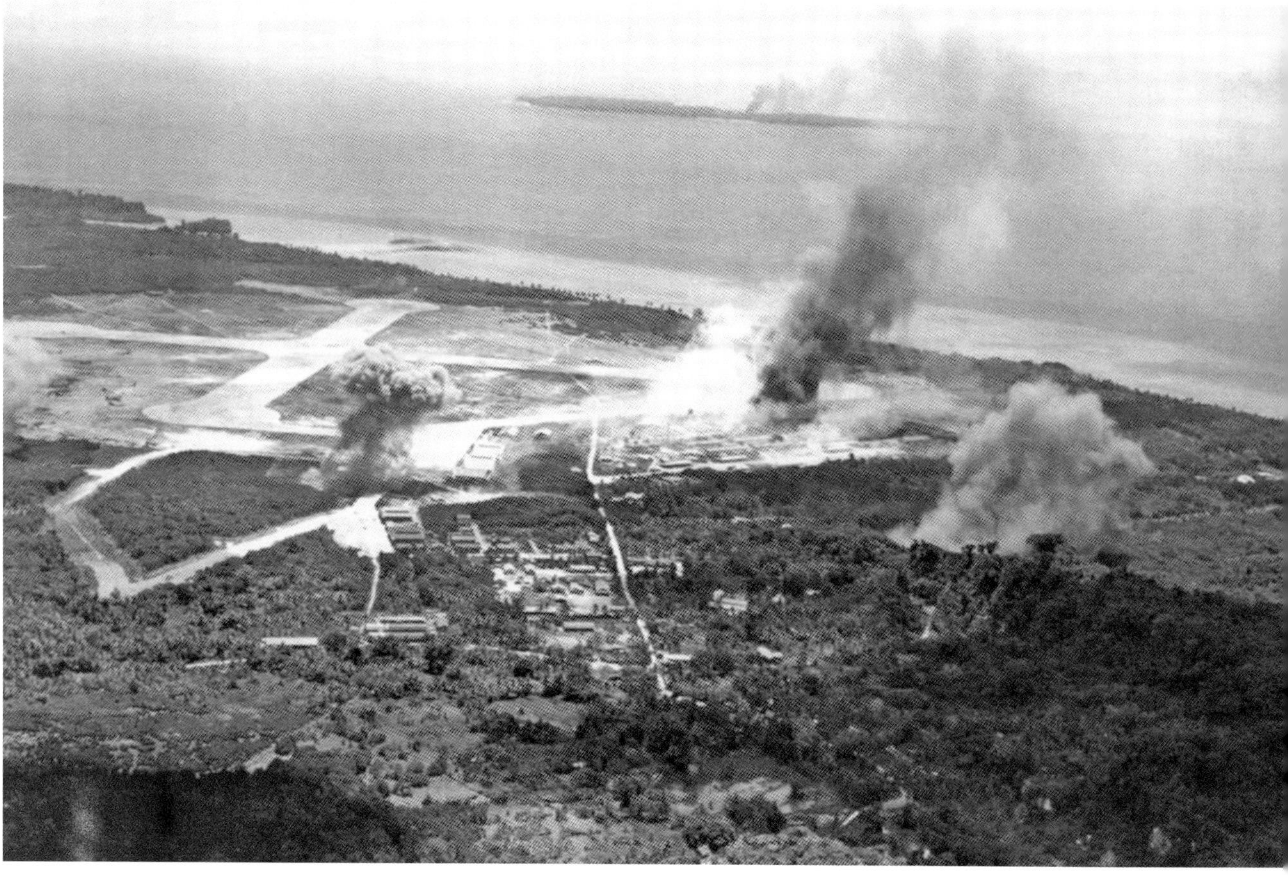

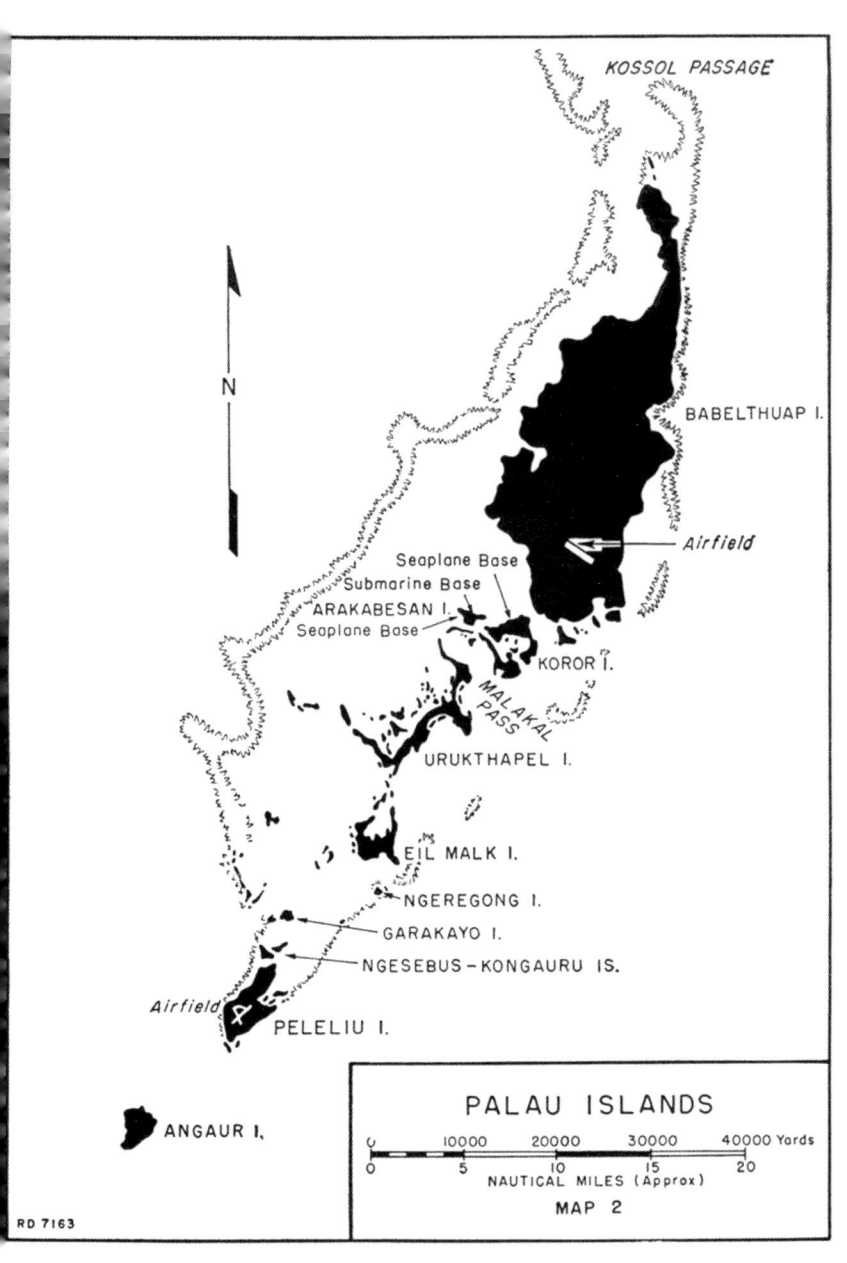

In this map, we see the relationship of Peleliu to the other islands in the Palau Island chain. Earlier in the war this series of islands was employed as a staging area and replacement centre for Japanese military forces destined to serve in the Dutch East Indies (now known as Indonesia) and New Guinea. Prior to the fall of the Marshall Islands in March 1944 and the resulting frantic Japanese build-up on Peleliu, the island was staffed only by non-combat service personnel. (*USMC*)

(**Opposite, above**) Peleliu, seen here in this wartime aerial montage, is the southernmost island in the Palau Island chain and is approximately 5 square miles in size. Visible is the large Japanese-built two-strip, hard-surfaced airfield, which was suitable for both fighters and larger multi-engine bombers. It had complete aircraft servicing facilities. In the upper left-hand portion of the picture is a Japanese auxiliary fighter-only strip on the smaller island of Ngesebus. (*USMC*)

(**Opposite, below**) In this photograph we see the large Japanese-built airfield on Peleliu being subjected to attack by US Navy aircraft prior to the initial Marine landings of 15 September 1944. Aerial attacks on the island commenced four days before the invasion and the naval bombardment two days before the landings took place. The landing beaches were located on the far side of the airfield shown in this image. (*US Navy*)

(**Above**) In the foreground here is a Marine Corps LVT-2 heading towards the invasion beaches of Peleliu. It is a late-production example with an armoured cab and rear-engine armoured air-intake covers. The engine in the rear made it necessary for the passengers to disembark in the face of enemy fire over the sides of the vehicle as it had no rear ramp. This design layout was not rectified until the introduction of the LVT-4 into Marine Corps service in June 1944. (*USMC*)

(**Opposite, above**) On a Peleliu beach, Marines are shown here bringing the wounded down for evacuation. In the background is a late-model LVT(A)-1, which can be identified by the armoured-shield-protected .30 calibre Browning machine guns just visible on the rear roof of the vehicle. The armoured amphibians such as the LVT(A)-1 and its replacement the LVT(A)-4 were organized into what were referred to as Armoured Amphibian Battalions. (*USMC*)

(**Opposite, below**) As on so many islands in the Central and Western Pacific, the Marines were met on Day 1 by a Japanese tank and infantry counter-attack. The Japanese Type 95 light tank pictured in front of a derelict LVT(A)-1 made it to one of the landing beaches before being struck by a high-explosive (HE) round from a towed M1A1 75mm howitzer and a 2.36in shaped charge rocket fired by an M1 or M1A1 Rocket Launcher Anti-tank. (*USMC*)

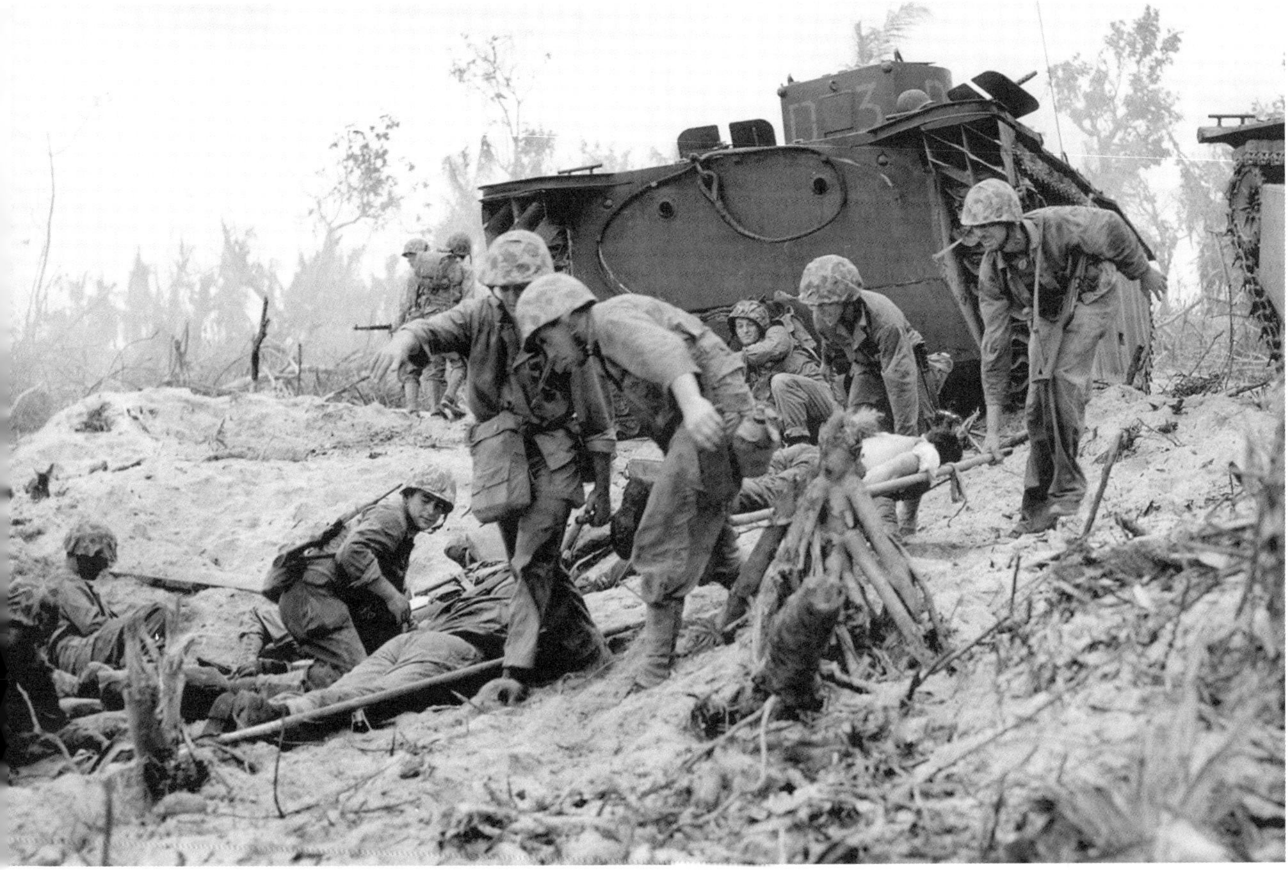

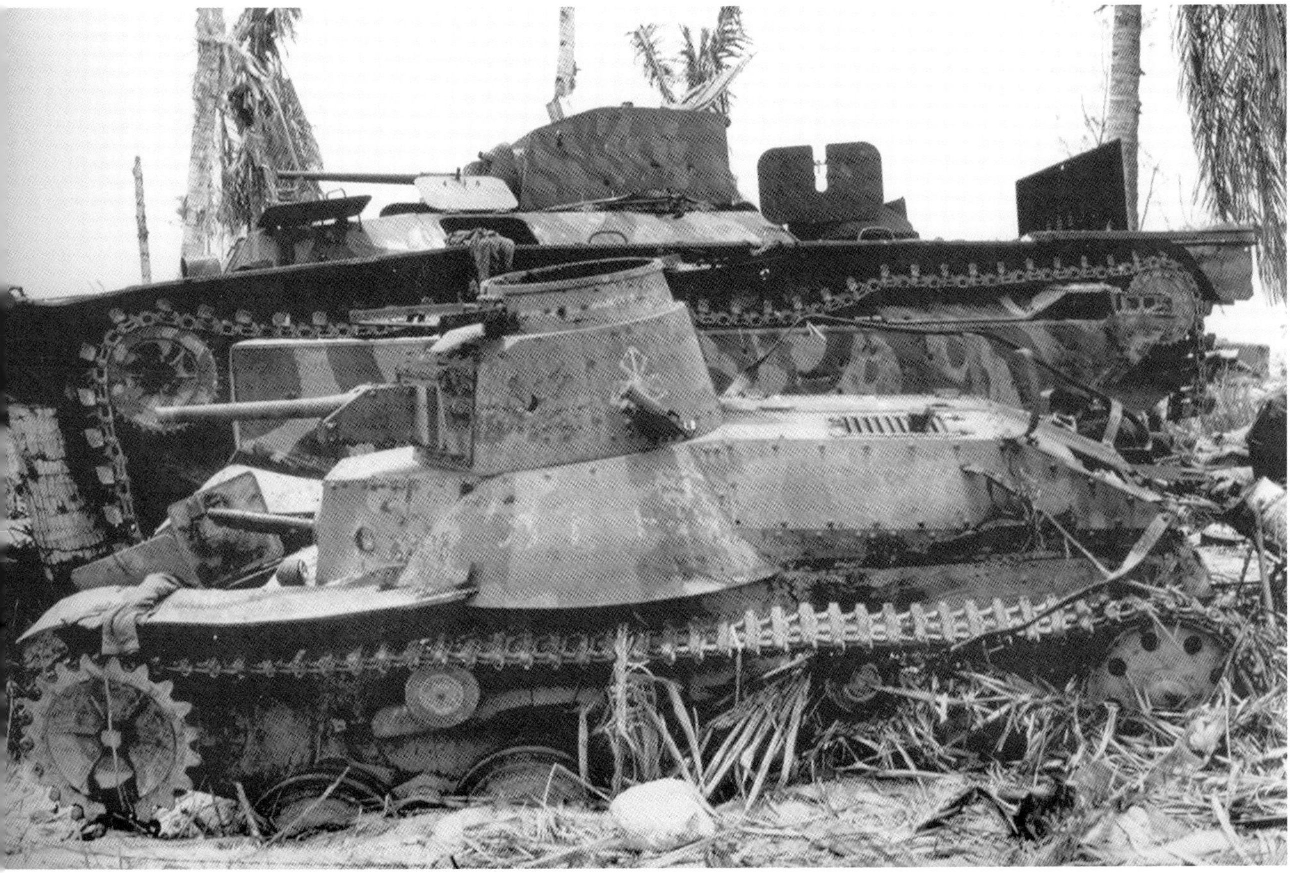

(**Above**) As the Japanese military lacked sufficient time to prepare for the impending assault on Peleliu and few of their supply ships were making it past the US Navy blockade of the island, once ashore the Marines came across a number of uncompleted Japanese fortifications such as this weaponless coast artillery position. The concrete cut-outs around the perimeter floor of the position were for ammunition storage. (*USMC*)

(**Opposite, above**) It was fairly common for Japanese troops to take advantage of terrain features or man-made objects, such as the destroyed Japanese motorized landing barge, to harass American military positions with small-arms fire whenever possible. In this case, the Marines dealt with the problem at Peleliu by dispatching two armoured amphibians, an LVT-A1 on the left and an LVTA-4 in the centre of the picture, to eliminate the threat. Seven enemy soldiers were killed and one captured. (*USMC*)

(**Opposite, below**) In spite of some Japanese defensive fortifications being incomplete due to material shortages when Peleliu was assaulted by the Marine Corps, the island defenders still managed to construct a large number of them. The Japanese pillbox pictured here, with two firing embrasures visible, was built of coral blocks held together by cement and covered with wooden logs surmounted by loose coral debris. (*USMC*)

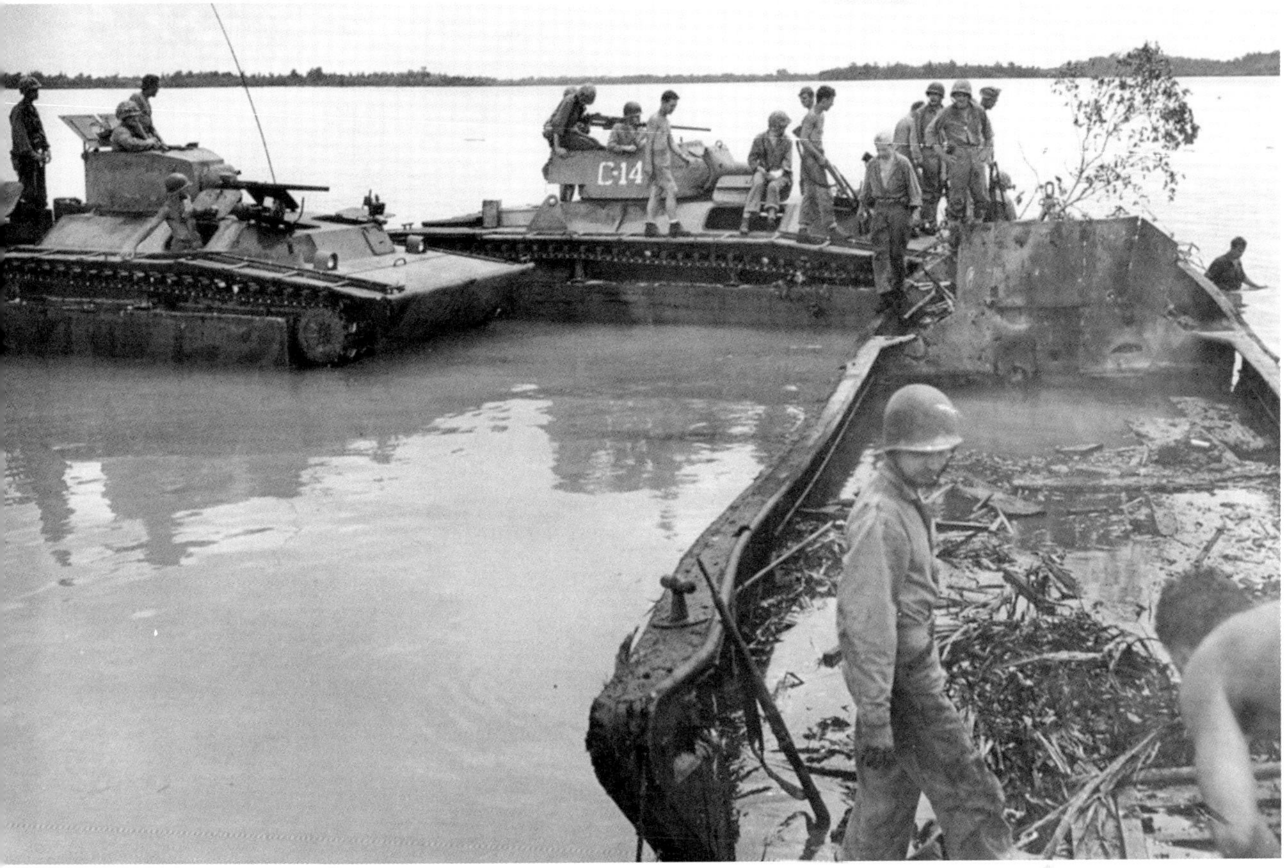
C-14

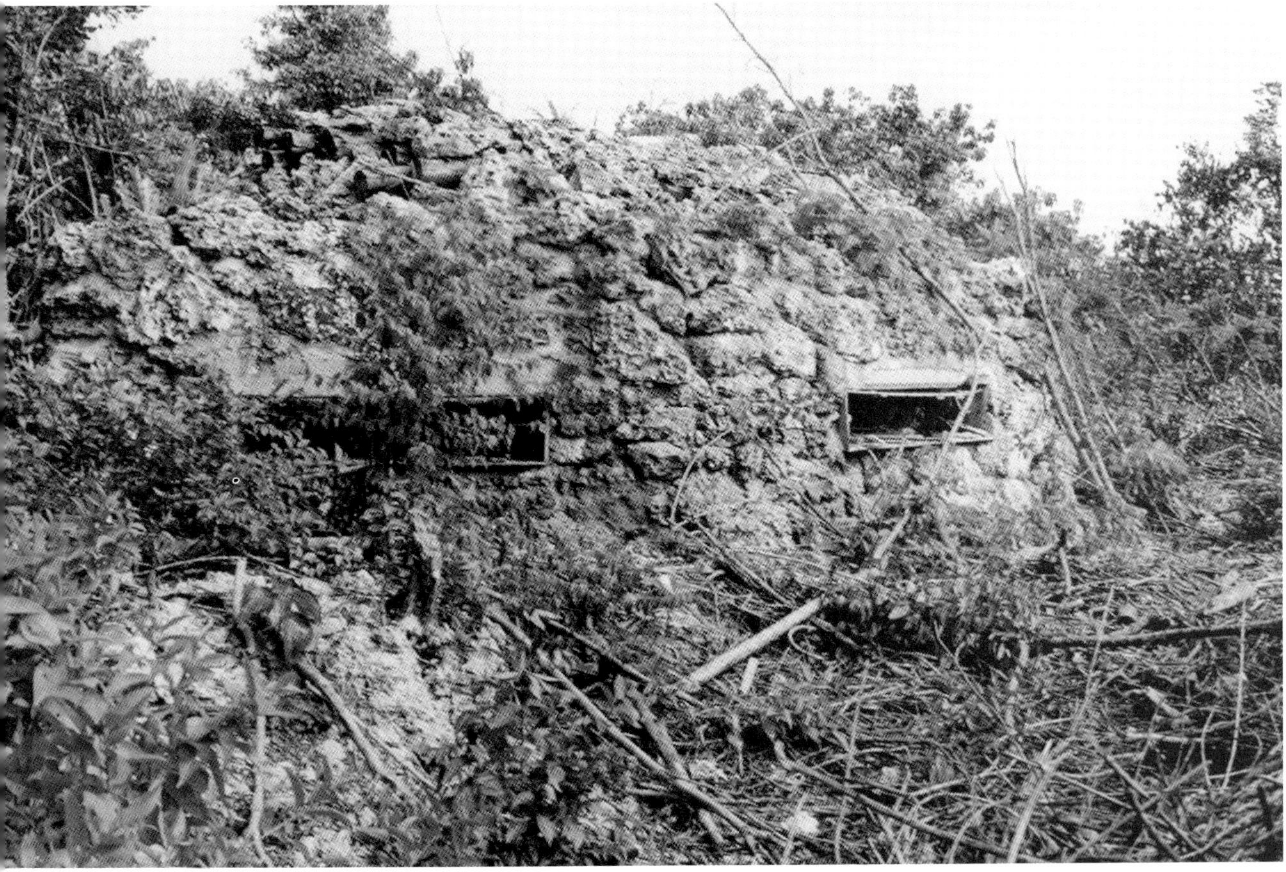

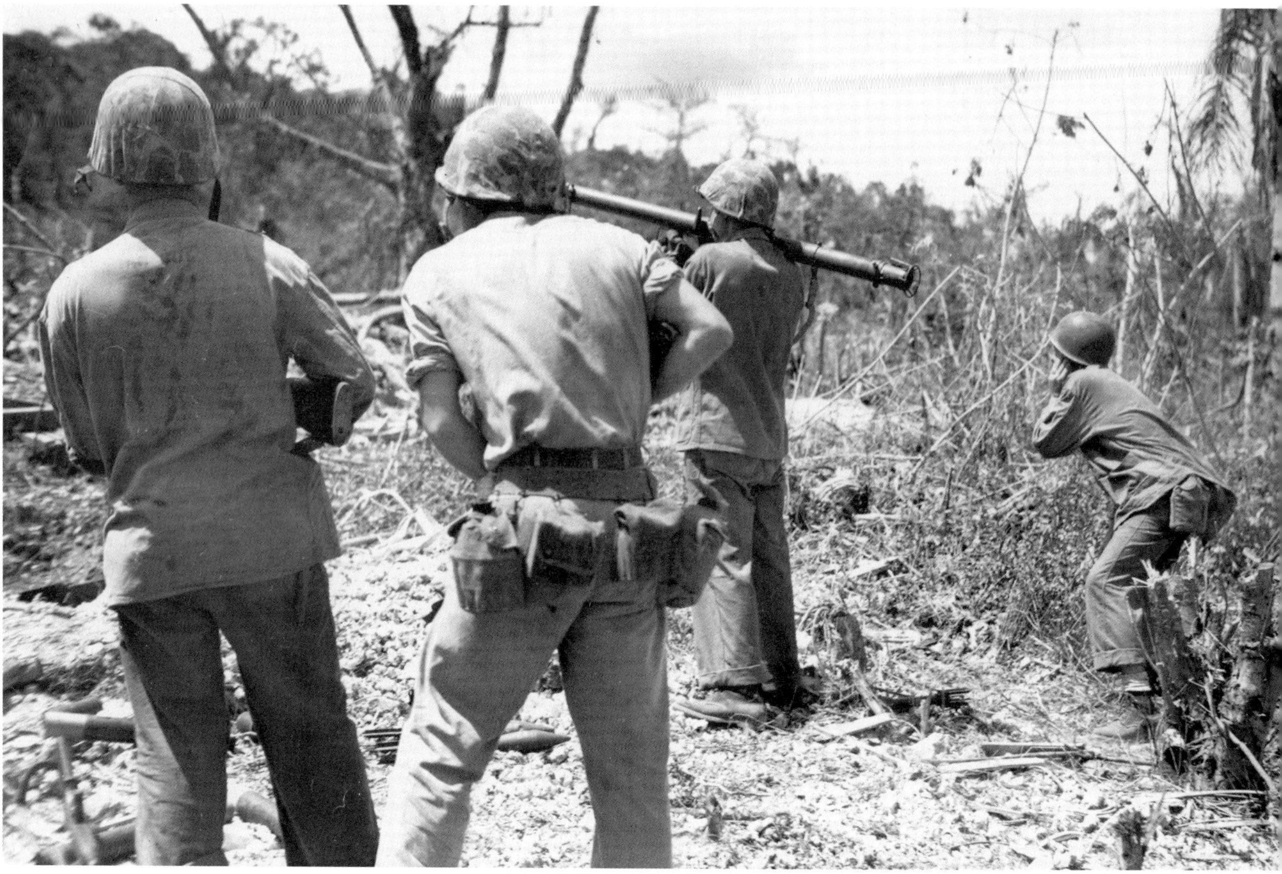

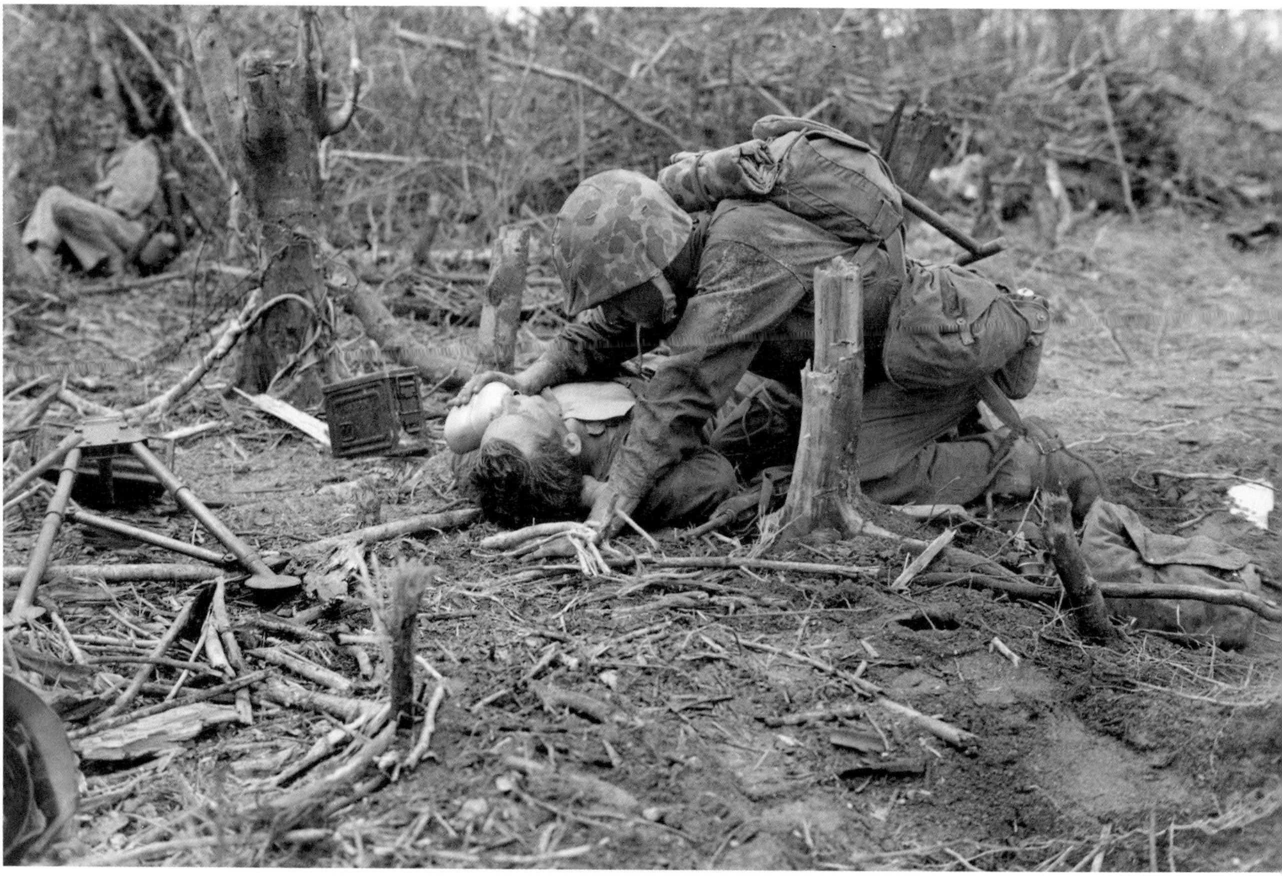

(**Opposite, above**) A Marine on Peleliu takes aim with his 2.36in M1 or M1A1 Rocket Launcher Anti-tank, nicknamed the 'bazooka' or the 'stovepipe'. Originally intended strictly as a close-range anti-tank weapon by the US Army, the small number of Japanese tanks encountered in the Central Pacific saw its primary role switched to a bunker-buster. The weapon itself was kept at the rifle battalion level and was issued to infantry squads when requested and then operated by specially-trained riflemen. (USMC)

(**Opposite, below**) The high temperatures on Peleliu added an extra degree of misery for every Marine on the island but none more so than the front-line infantrymen. In the shade, the temperature was recorded at 105 degrees and in the open up to 115 degrees. In this picture one Marine is helping another waylaid by heat exhaustion. Most of those evacuated due to heat exhaustion were returned to duty after a day or two of rest and rehabilitation. (USMC)

(**Above**) A Marine shown here is about to hurl a Molotov cocktail over a Peleliu ridgeline. Unlike a hand grenade that spews out metal fragments with a small explosive charge, the gasoline inside a Molotov cocktail can flow into an enemy foxhole or burn off the vegetation hiding an enemy position. One might assume that the Molotov cocktail is made from an empty Japanese sake bottle and is being employed in lieu of a man-portable flame-thrower. (USMC)

For the Peleliu operation the Marines modified three brand-new LVT-4s into flame-thrower units, one of which is seen here in use. The generated flame jet not only kills by incinerating those unfortunate enough to be caught in its horrible embrace but in the case of an enclosed enemy bunker or cave can asphyxiate all personnel by consuming the oxygen within. The flame jet also kills by generating high levels of carbon monoxide in enclosed spaces. (USMC)

A Marine has just fired his M7 grenade-launcher from his M1 rifle on Peleliu. There was a range of grenades available for the launcher including anti-tank, fragmentation, white phosphorus (WP) and coloured smoke. The anti-tank grenade weighed 1.23lb and had sheet steel body and tail assembly. It was filled with 4oz of an explosive material named 'Pentolite'. (USMC)

On Peleliu a Marine stands ready with his M1919A4 .30 calibre light machine gun for a Japanese counter-attack. As the Marines attempted to secure Amiangal Ridge, the heart of Japanese resistance on part of the island, they discovered that it was honeycombed with a maze of interconnected tunnels. On occasions the Japanese occupants would blast open a cave or tunnel mouth closed by the Marines to sally forth and raise havoc in areas considered secure. (USMC)

To get a towed M1A1 75mm howitzer where it was needed on Peleliu the Marines in this case resorted to good old-fashioned muscle power and what appears to be a rope-and-pulley system. As difficult and costly as the Marine efforts to secure the island were, it was equally miserable for the Japanese defenders. There was little food or water, sanitation was almost non-existent and ammunition was scarce. These conditions often pushed them to undertake suicidal night attacks that always ended in their death. (USMC)

(**Opposite, above**) A Marine Corps Piper L-4 observation plane prepares to take off from a US Navy escort carrier to fly over Peleliu. By Day 5 of the invasion they were flying from the island's captured Japanese airfield. Once in the air over Peleliu during daylight hours they made it impossible for the Japanese defenders to show themselves without bringing down either aerial attack or artillery. (USMC)

(**Opposite, below**) In this picture, we see Marines attaching a large napalm canister to the fuselage of a Marine F4U Corsair on Peleliu. The first Marine F4U Corsair squadron began operating off the island's captured Japanese airfield on 26 September 1944. Despite the weaponry employed by the Marine aviators on Peleliu in the close air support (CAS) role, they had little tactical effect on the Japanese defenders who were fighting from well-prepared underground positions. (USMC)

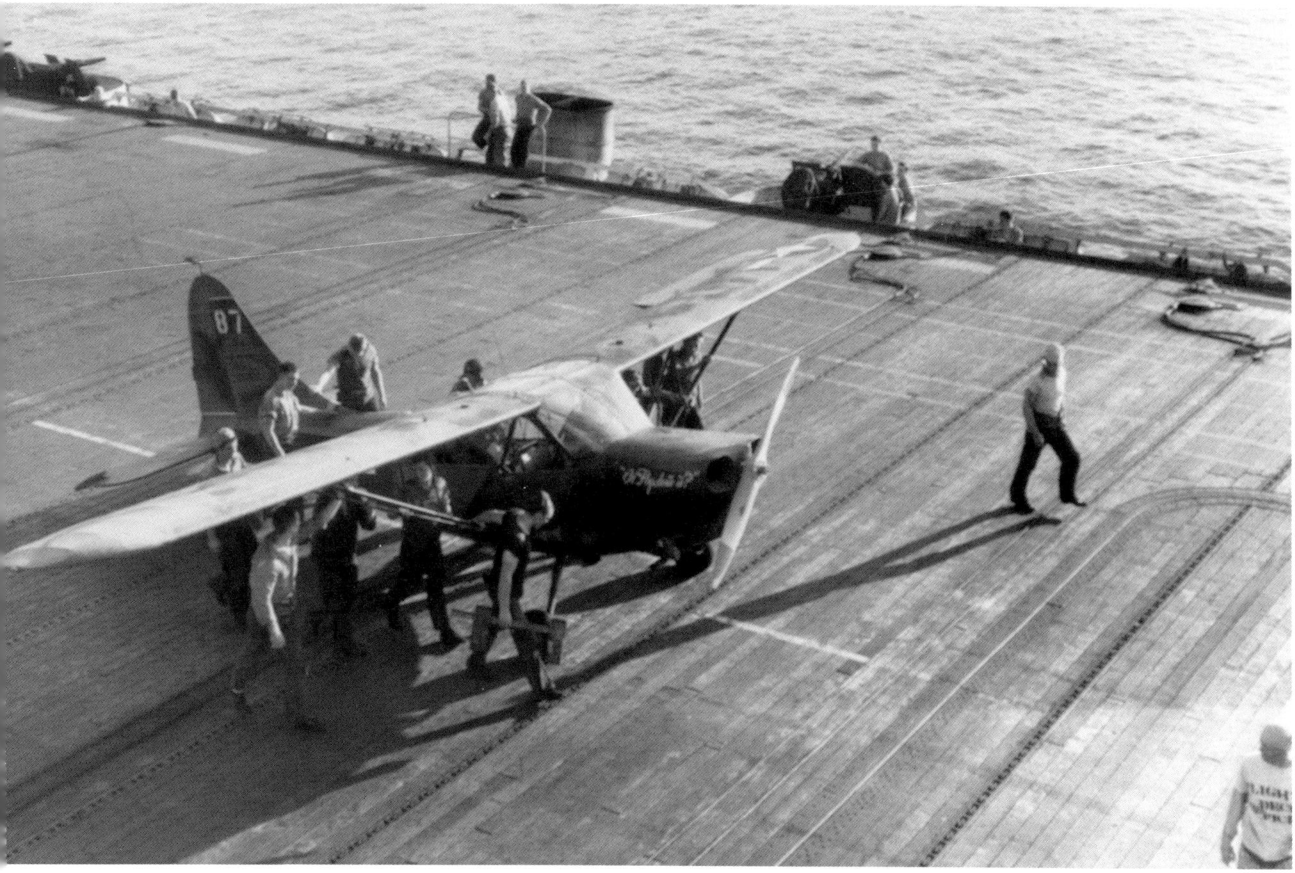
87

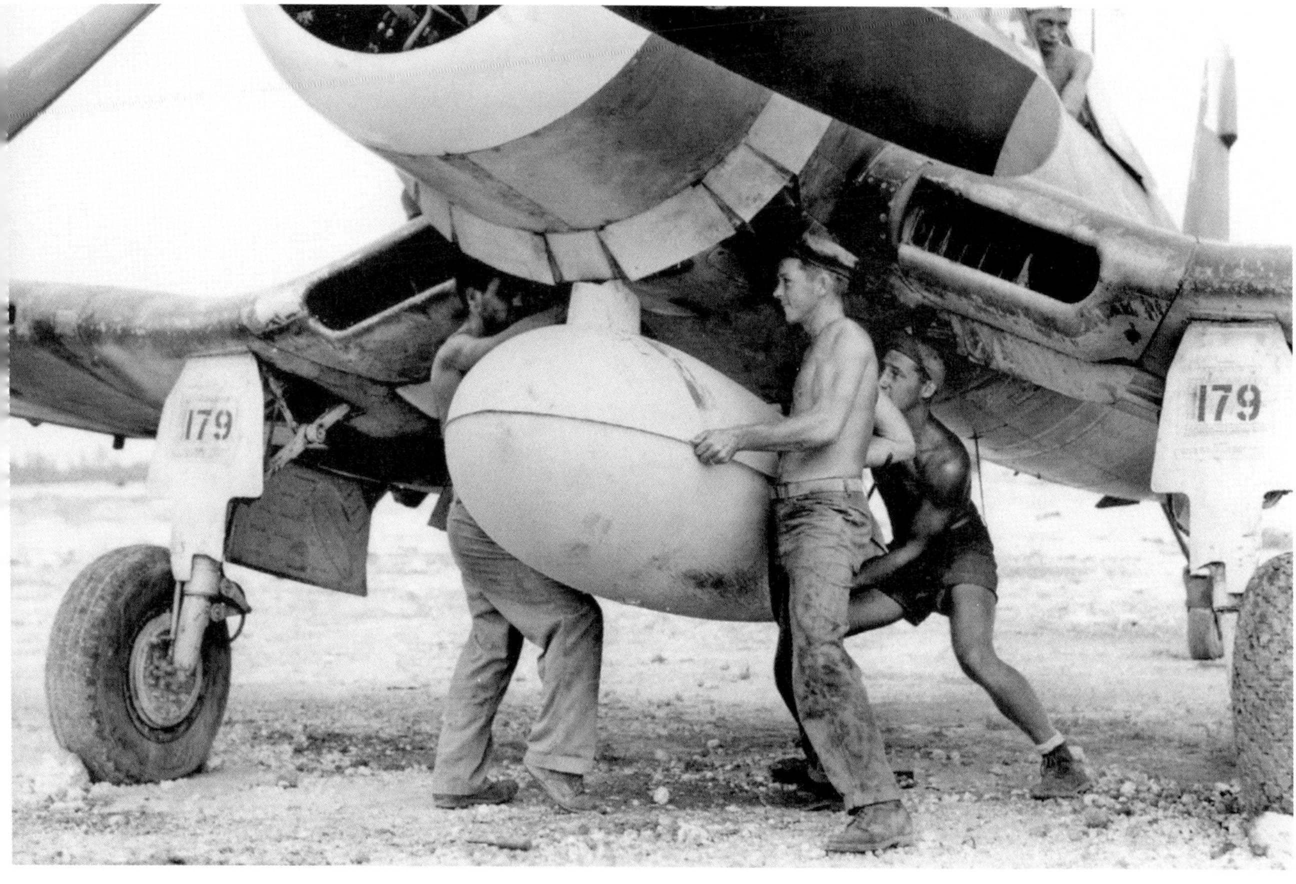
179
179

In this photograph we see twelve dead Japanese soldiers who were killed when an M4 medium tank fired a high-explosive (HE) round into a Japanese bunker on Peleliu. Marine casualties on the island totalled more than 9,000 dead and wounded. The high cost of taking the island was a sobering reminder to the American military senior leadership of what they could expect in the taking of other islands closer to the Japanese home islands. (USMC)

President Harry S. Truman is shown here shaking hands with Second Lieutenant Arthur J. Jackson after presenting him with the Medal of Honor on 5 October 1945. During the fighting on Peleliu, the then Private First Class Jackson almost single-handedly destroyed twelve Japanese pillboxes and killed approximately fifty enemy soldiers in the process. In this incredible feat of arms, he employed a Browning Automatic Rifle (BAR), phosphorus grenades and explosive charges brought to him by fellow Marines. (USMC)

US Navy and Marine Corps operation leaders for the planned invasion of Iwo Jima examine a relief model of the island. Lieutenant General Holland M. Smith, third from the left, was Commanding General Expeditionary Troops, a somewhat ceremonial title as he was in official disfavour due to having relieved a US Army general during the Saipan campaign. The real boss of the Iwo Jima invasion was Major General Harry Schmidt who was in charge of the Marine Corps V Amphibious Corps. (USMC)

Pictured here is Lieutenant General Tadamichi Kuribayashi, commander of Iwo Jima. He was a fifth-generation samurai, hand-picked for the job and endorsed by the Japanese Emperor. Under his command was a large mixed force of both army and naval troops with widely varying levels of military training and experience, ranging from veteran to recruit. He made everybody serving under him swear an oath to kill ten Americans before being killed themselves. (USMC)

An example of the type of underground passageways built on Iwo Jima prior to the Marine landings of 19 February 1945 is seen in this post-invasion photograph. The Japanese commander of Iwo Jima had wanted to have built hundreds of miles of underground passageways constructed before the American invasion. However, the Japanese defenders ran out of time and only about 3 miles of tunnels were in place when the invasion began. (USMC)

In this post-invasion image taken on Iwo Jima we see an armoured turret fitted with two 120mm dual-purpose guns, which were repurposed naval weapons. The Japanese defenders of the island had a wide variety of firepower available including artillery pieces, medium and light mortars, anti-aircraft guns, anti-tank guns, and twenty-two light and medium tanks armed with 47mm main guns. (USMC)

One of the more unusual Japanese weapons encountered by the Marines on Iwo Jima was the 320mm spigot mortar seen here post-invasion. It could hurl a 675lb high-explosive (HE) round to a maximum range of 1,440 yards. One Marine who saw combat on Iwo Jima stated that these mortar rounds in flight were referred to in his units as 'the screaming Jesus'. Other Marines on the island nicknamed the massive mortar rounds the 'flying ashcans'. (USMC)

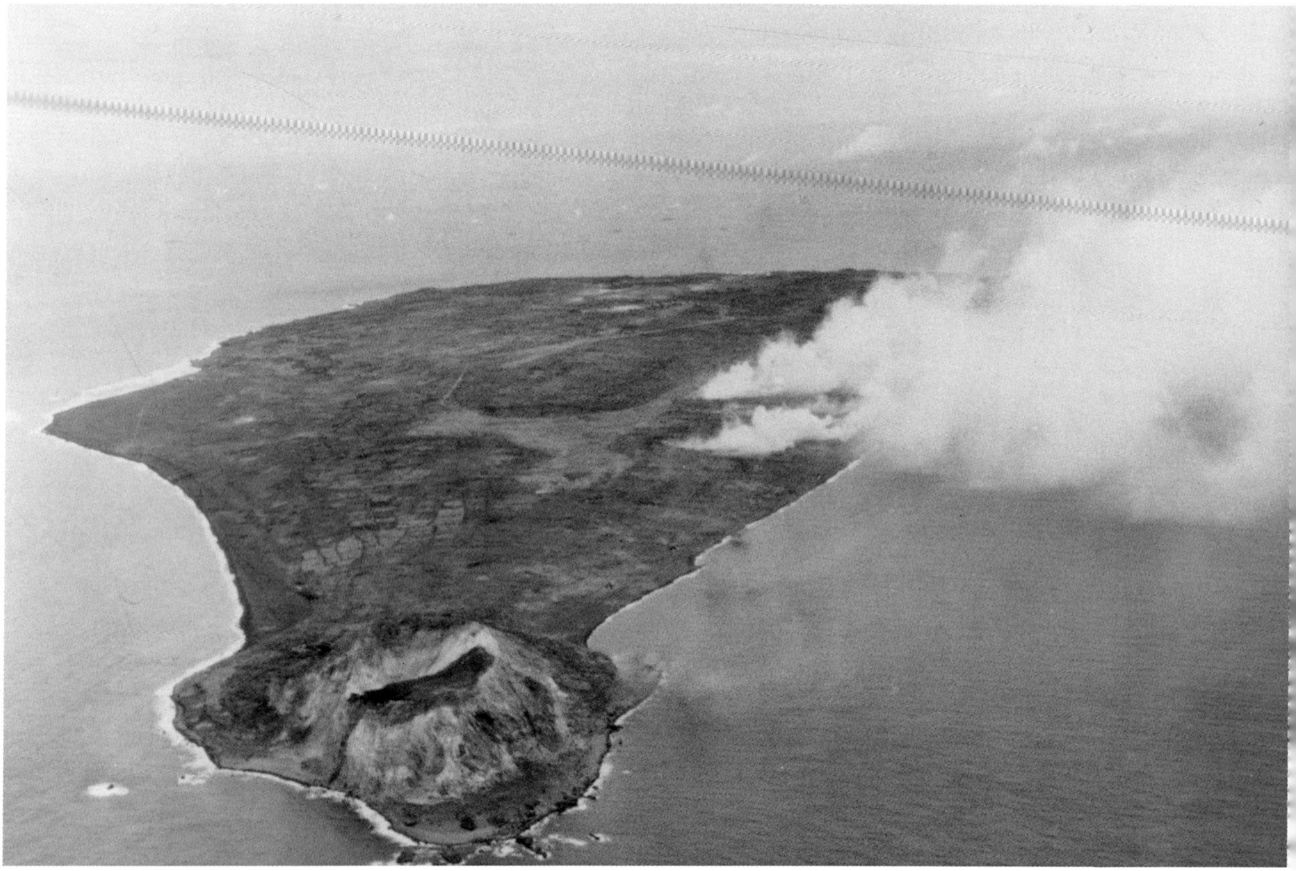

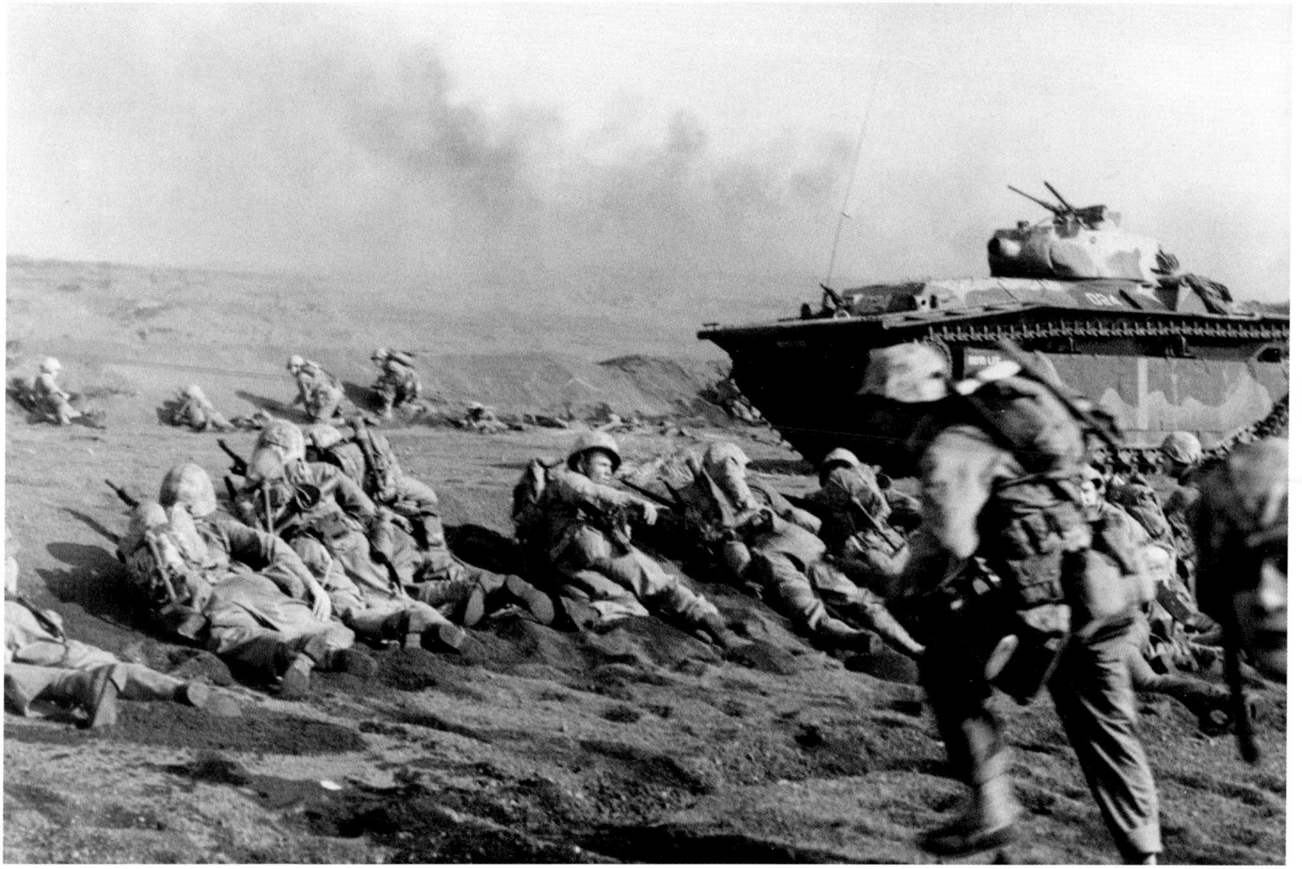

(**Opposite, above**) A picture of Iwo Jima during the pre-invasion bombardment. Visible at the southernmost tip of the island is Mount Suribachi, which has a height of 550ft and as is obvious from the photograph dominates the remainder of the island. The entire island measures approximately 4 miles along its north-east/south-west axis, while the width varies from about 2.5 miles to slightly less than half a mile at the narrow base of Mount Suribachi. Iwo Jima covers 7.5 square miles. (USMC)

(**Above**) The initial assault waves of Marines are visible heading towards Iwo Jima as the three-day pre-invasion naval bombardment of the island continues to the very last moment. The duration of the naval bombardment of Iwo Jima was a point of contention between the Marine Corps senior leadership and that of the US Navy. The Marines wanted the pre-invasion naval bombardment to last ten days. The navy responded by stating that it had neither the time nor sufficient ammunition. (USMC)

(**Opposite, below**) The Marines in this picture are attempting to form up to move inland on Iwo Jima on Day 1 of the invasion. In the background is an LVT(A)-4 armed with a short-barrelled 75mm howitzer. Sixty-eight of them were in the first wave of the Marine assault. Behind them was a combination of 380 more amphibious tractors divided between LVT-2s and LVT-4s. Despite being tracked, many of the LVTs became stuck in the soft volcanic sand of Iwo Jima. (USMC)

(**Above**) As the Marine leadership had feared, the three-day naval bombardment of Iwo Jima did not effectively destroy the bulk of the Japanese fortifications on the island. From their observation posts on Mount Suribachi the Japanese artillery, which had pre-registered every inch of the island, unleashed a hurricane of fire that covered every Marine landing beach. Two Marine machine-gunners are shown hugging the ground for protection. (*USMC*)

(**Opposite, above**) From a Marine Corps historical monograph on Iwo Jima comes this quote by Major Karch of the 14th Marines: 'It was one of the worst blood-lettings of the war … They rolled those artillery barrages up and down the beach – I just didn't see how anybody could live through such heavy fire barrages.' Pictured here are several Marines who perished on that first day of the assault. (*USMC*)

(**Opposite, below**) In the wake of the LVTs landing on Iwo Jima came the small US Navy landing craft bringing in additional personnel and equipment. In this case Marines are shown dragging ashore a small two-wheeled trailer for either a machine gun and ammunition or a mortar and ammunition. As Iwo Jima had a very narrow violent surf zone, many of the smaller landing craft were quickly swamped and then broached sideways on the landing beaches as seen here. (*USMC*)

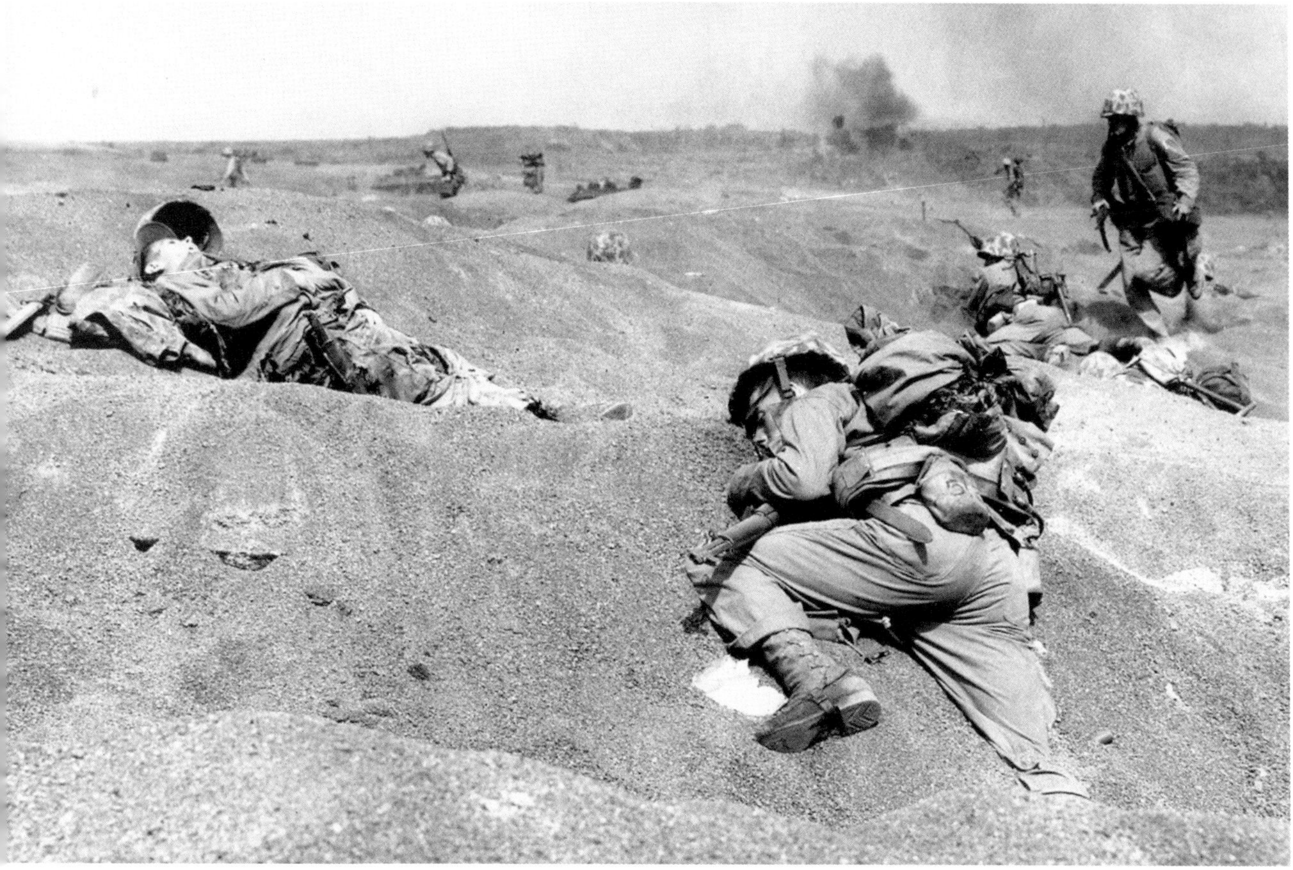

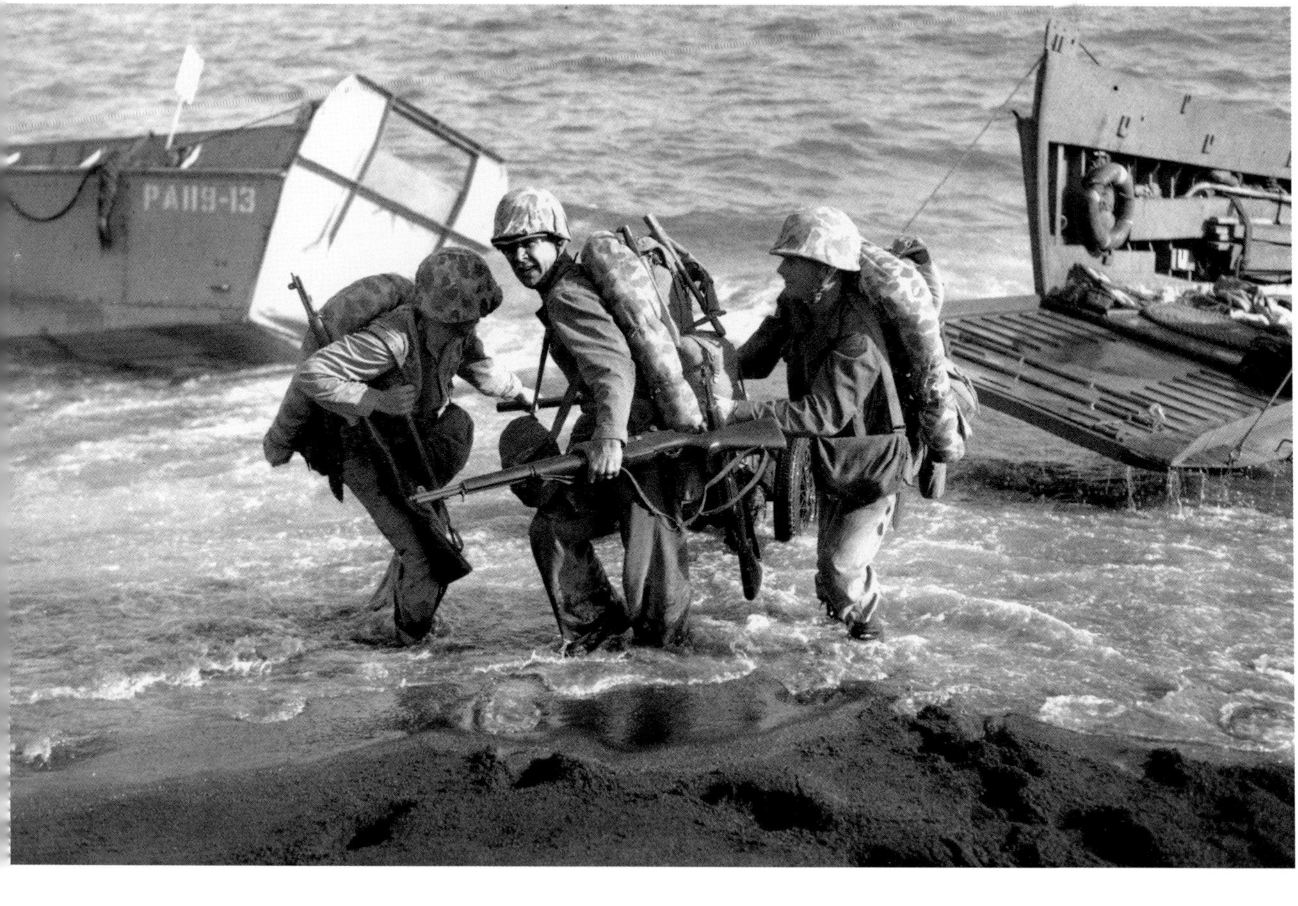
PA119-13

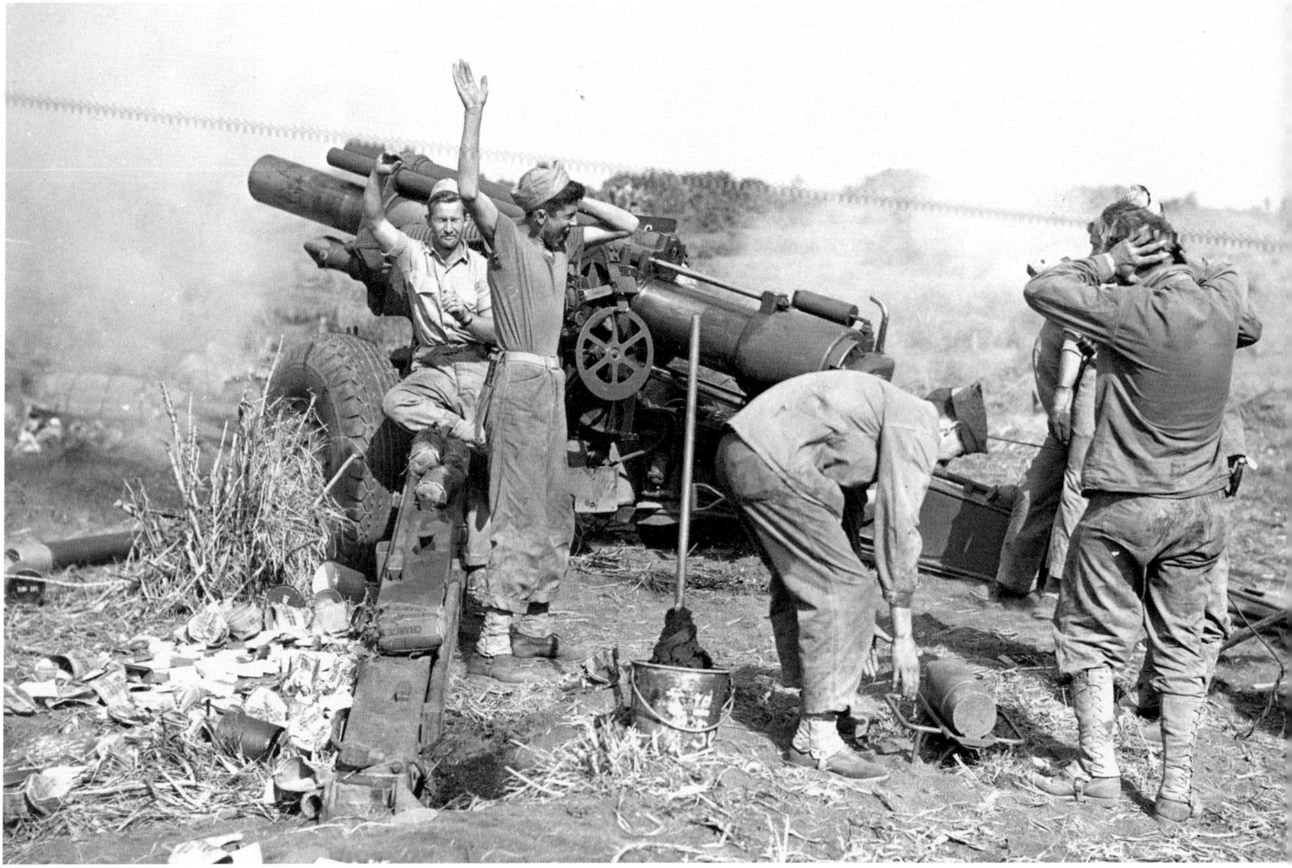

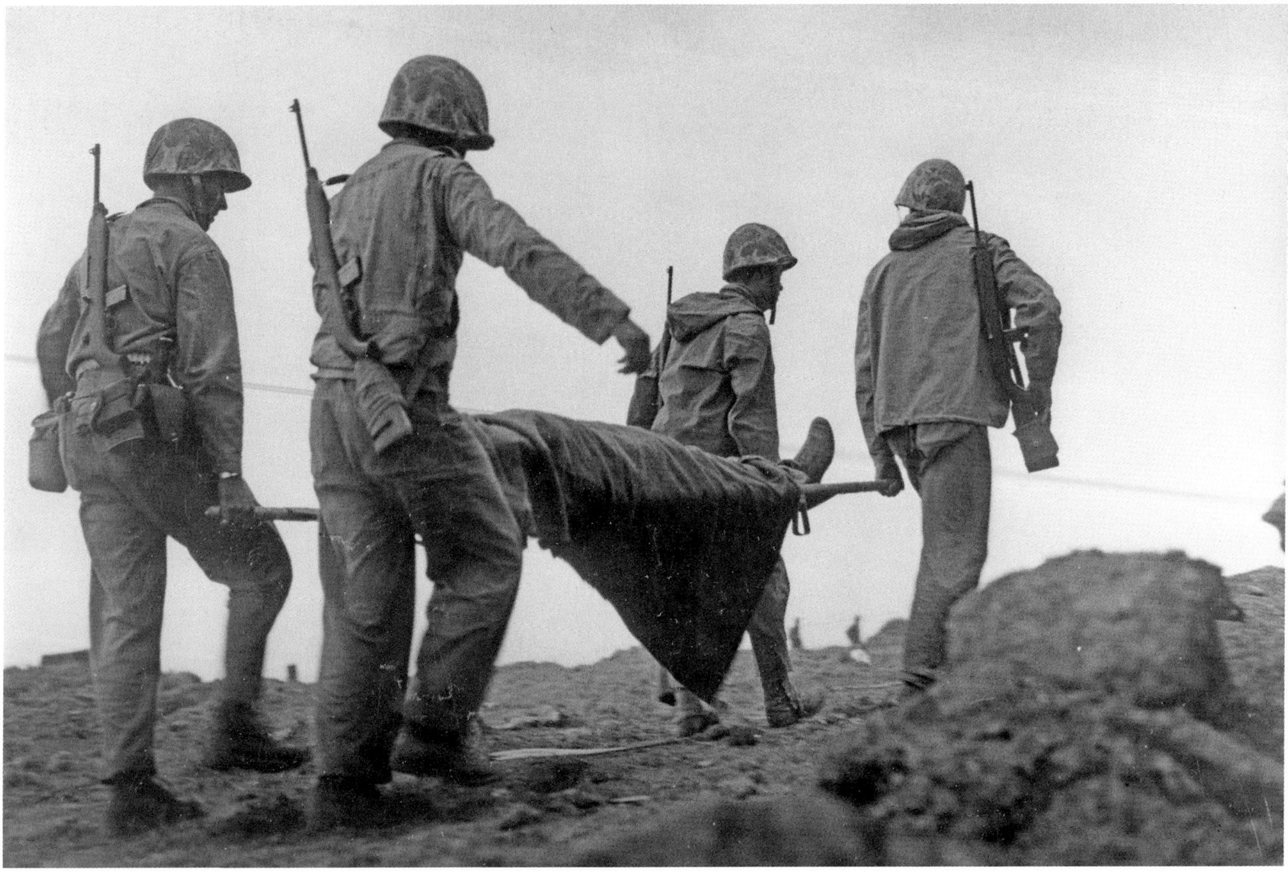

(**Opposite, above**) As always, the Marines tried to bring their own artillery onto the islands that they were tasked with securing. In this case, a 155mm howitzer M1 on Iwo Jima is shown at the moment of firing with the barrel in full recoil. It fired a 95lb high-explosive (HE) round to a maximum range of 20,100 yards. The shell was made of common forged steel and had comparatively thin walls and a large bursting charge. It was intended to be employed against personnel and material targets. (*USMC*)

(**Opposite, below**) A Marine litter party on Iwo Jima is shown here moving a casualty to a battalion aid station. The faster this was accomplished, the greater the patient's odds of surviving his wound. Litter parties often had to be escorted by riflemen to protect them from enemy stragglers. Casualties among the navy doctors and corpsmen on Iwo Jima totalled 738, of which 197 were killed. (*USMC*)

(**Above**) Shown here is a battalion aid station on an Iwo Jima beach. The distances from the front lines to the rear area aid stations were short, but the harsh terrain and heavy enemy fire made evacuation of the wounded extremely hazardous. Until bulldozers could scrape out roads for jeep ambulances, LVTs or M28 Cargo Carriers were sometimes employed to move the wounded to the rear area aid stations. (*USMC*)

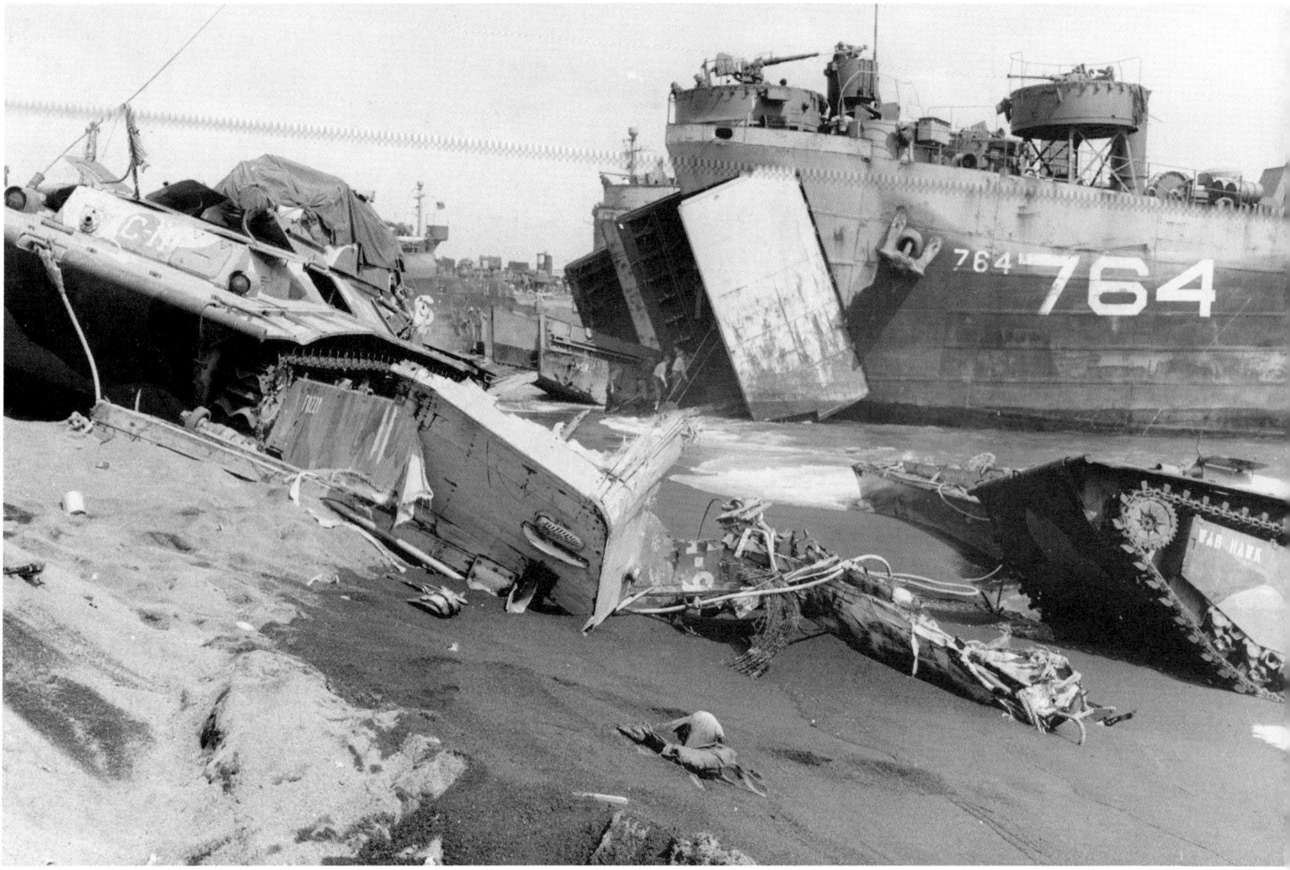
764
764

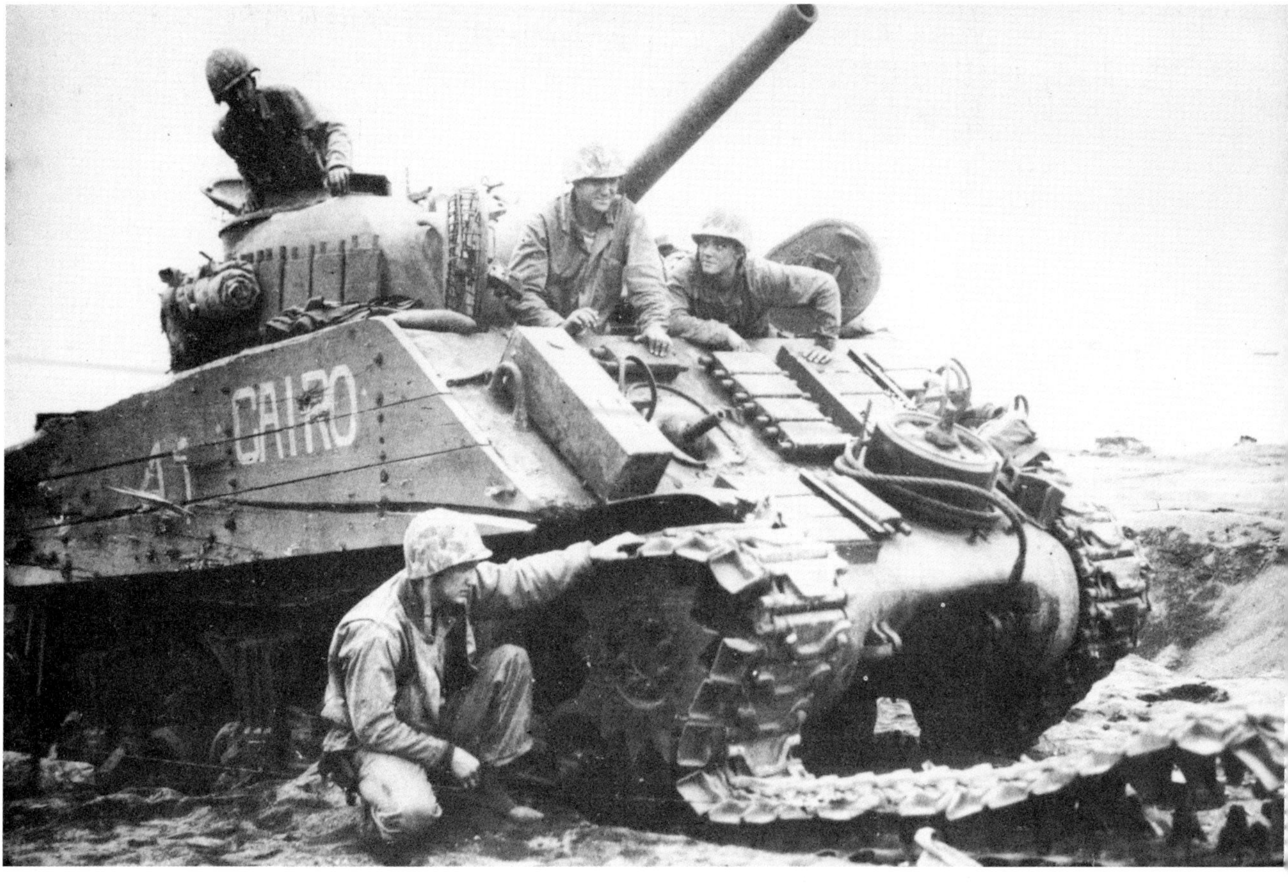
CAIRO

(**Opposite, above**) Despite the many problems in moving supplies onshore to Iwo Jima, the only serious shortage encountered during the campaign for the island was ammunition. This was due to the large number of rounds fired by Marine Corps artillery and mortar units. In the background of this Iwo Jima picture is a US Navy Landing Ship Tank (LST) and in the foreground two derelict LVTs, the one on the left being an LVT(A)-4. (*USMC*)

(**Opposite, below**) By the time the Iwo Jima invasion took place the Marine Corps had largely switched to the M4A3 medium tank. A disabled example is seen here on Iwo Jima having succumbed to both an anti-tank mine and five artillery strikes. The switch to the M4A3 medium tank was forced upon the Marine Corps because the US Army had halted production of the M4A2 medium tank with the 75mm main gun in mid-1944. (*USMC*)

(**Above**) Having dealt with suicidal attacks by Japanese infantry tank-hunting teams during previous island campaigns, the Marine 5th Tank Battalion took extra precautions before Iwo Jima as seen here on this stuck M4A3 medium tank. Besides the wooden planking on the sides of the hull and suspension system, the crews welded upright penny nails to all the hatches on the tank to provide stand-off protection from Japanese satchel charges. The gap allows the explosive force to partially dissipate, reducing damage to the vehicle and injury to the crew. (*USMC*)

Shown in action on Iwo Jima is one of the four M4A3 medium tanks of the Marine 4th Tank Battalion converted to the POA-CWS-H1 flame-thrower tank by giving up the standard 75mm main gun. This was the most successful flame-thrower tank employed by the Marines during the Second World War. The biggest threat to Marine tanks on Iwo Jima turned out to be mines and not Japanese infantry tank-hunting teams due to a lack of cover for the tank-hunters to operate successfully. (*USMC*)

For his actions during the battle for Iwo Jima, Corporal Charles J. Berry pictured here was posthumously awarded the Medal of Honor. A passage from his citation reads: 'When infiltrating Japanese soldiers launched a surprise attack shortly after midnight in an attempt to overrun his position, he engaged in a pitched hand grenade duel, returning the dangerous weapons with prompt and deadly accuracy until an enemy grenade landed in the foxhole. Determined to save his comrades, he unhesitatingly chose to sacrifice himself and immediately dived on the deadly missile.' (*USMC*)

Beside the extensive employment of flame-thrower tanks on Iwo Jima, the man-portable flame-throwers continued to serve a useful role as seen in this picture of one of them in use. The flame-thrower man visible in the picture is armed with either the late-war M2 flame-thrower or an improved version designated the M2-2. *(USMC)*

The corpse of a Japanese soldier lies outside the rear entry to his bunker on Iwo Jima. A Marine who fought on the island describes in an historical monograph what he and his buddies had to confront: 'There was no cover from enemy fire. Japs dug in reinforced concrete pillboxes laid down interlocking bands of fire that cut whole companies to ribbons.' *(USMC)*

(**Above**) Emerging from a badly-battered Japanese bunker on Iwo Jima are three of its defenders who decided that surrendering to the Marines might not be that bad a choice. They were maybe Japanese naval personnel who were pressed into serving as infantrymen by the island's commander and lacked the usual fervour that marked the Japanese Army troops. (*USMC*)

(**Opposite**) In this photograph we see the first American flag raised on Mount Suribachi on 23 February 1945 by a patrol of forty-five Marines. The small flag is attached to an iron pipe found at the location. Its appearance on the top of Mount Suribachi, nicknamed 'Hot Rocks' by the Marines who fought so hard for the island, is reputed to have raised a cheer from all the Marines who witnessed it. (*USMC*)

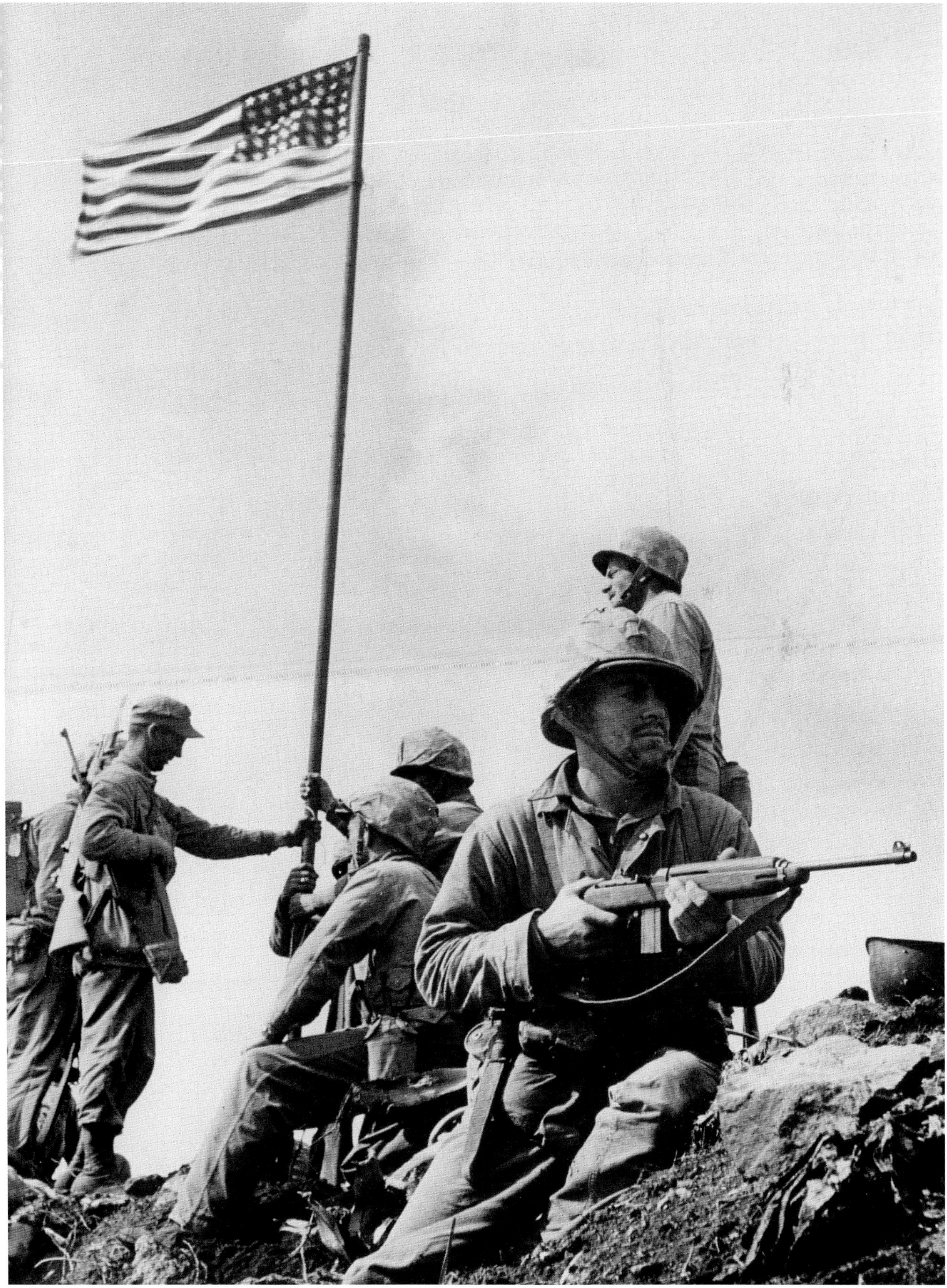

To make the point that Mount Suribachi was now in American hands, the same day another larger group of Marines was tasked with reaching its peak and raising a much larger American flag, which would be more visible to those on Iwo Jima. This group included a new civilian photographer named Joe Rosenthal. As the second flag was raised, Rosenthal snapped three pictures of the event with the image shown here becoming the best-known. (USMC)

Corporal Douglas T. Jacobson being congratulated by President Harry S. Truman just after being presented with the Medal of Honor for his actions on Iwo Jima. From his citation comes this passage: 'By his dauntless skill and valor, Private First Class Jacobson destroyed a total of sixteen enemy positions and annihilated approximately seventy-five Japanese, thereby contributing essentially to the success of his division's operations against the fanatically defended outpost of the Japanese Empire.' (USMC)

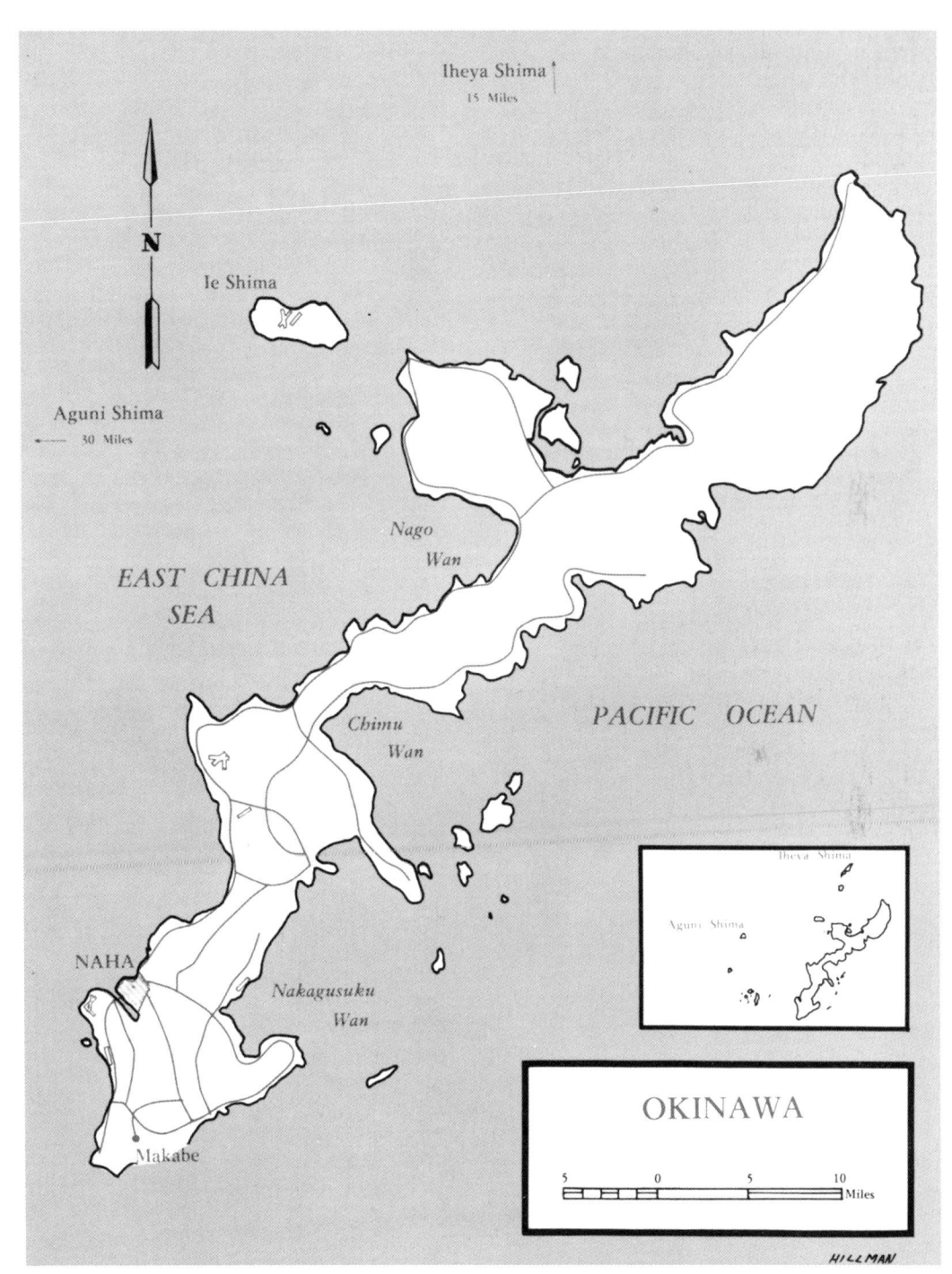

Okinawa was the last stepping-stone for the American military before the planned invasion of the Japanese home islands. It is 60 miles in length with a maximum width of 18 miles and its narrowest point just 2 miles wide. It is divided into two very different peninsulas joined by an isthmus as seen in this map. The northern peninsula is mountainous and wooded; the southern peninsula was the island's urban centre and contained all the significant military objectives such as airfields, ports and anchorages. (USMC)

With a great deal of relief and surprise, Japanese resistance to the initial Marine and US Army landings on the southern peninsula of Okinawa consisted of only sporadic mortar and small-arms fire, which inflicted very few casualties and caused no damage to the hundreds of LVTs being employed. Nor had the Japanese mined the landing beaches as they had in the past. In this picture, we see two Marines disembarking from an LVT-3 on Okinawa. (USMC)

The command of the Tenth Army, which included four US Army divisions and three US Marine Corps divisions, was assigned to Lieutenant General Simon Bolivar Buckner of the US Army who is seen on the left-hand side of the picture. Subordinate to Bolivar was Major General Roy Geiger (on the right) who was in command of the three Marine divisions of the Tenth Army. When General Bolivar was killed by Japanese fire on Okinawa on 18 June 1945, command of the Tenth Army passed to Geiger. (USMC)

In this picture taken from an aircraft can be seen one of the landing beaches on Okinawa for the two Marine Divisions, the 1st and the 6th, that assaulted the island on 1 April 1945. The Marine 2nd Division was kept on board its transport ships and later used to feint a landing to confuse the Japanese. In the foreground are Marine LVTs moving inland. By the end of Day 1 of the invasion of Okinawa the Tenth Army, which oversaw both the Marine and army divisions assigned, had 50,000 men ashore. (USMC)

(**Above**) For the Okinawa campaign the Marines committed two tank battalions: the 1st and the 6th. The 1st was still equipped with M4A2 medium tanks and the 6th with M4A3 medium tanks as seen here. Heavy losses eventually forced the 1st to take in some M4A3 tanks as replacements as there were fewer M4A2 tanks available. (*USMC*)

(**Opposite, above**) In this picture we see two Marine Corps M4A3 medium tanks working together with infantry to clear the city of Naha on Okinawa. A wartime American manual describes two reasons why the Japanese so often chose to attack American tanks with infantrymen. They lacked a sufficient number of modern anti-tank weapons and the ground over which they typically fought lent itself to the close assault of enemy tanks. (*USMC*)

(**Opposite, below**) A Marine M4A3 medium tank on Okinawa is fitted with an M1 bulldozer kit. The Japanese Army commander of Okinawa paid tribute to the effectiveness of the Marine Corps and US Army M4 series medium tanks that fought on the island in a lesson-learned report to his superiors: '… the enemy's power lies in his tanks. It has become obvious that our general battle against the American forces is a battle against their … tanks.' (*USMC*)

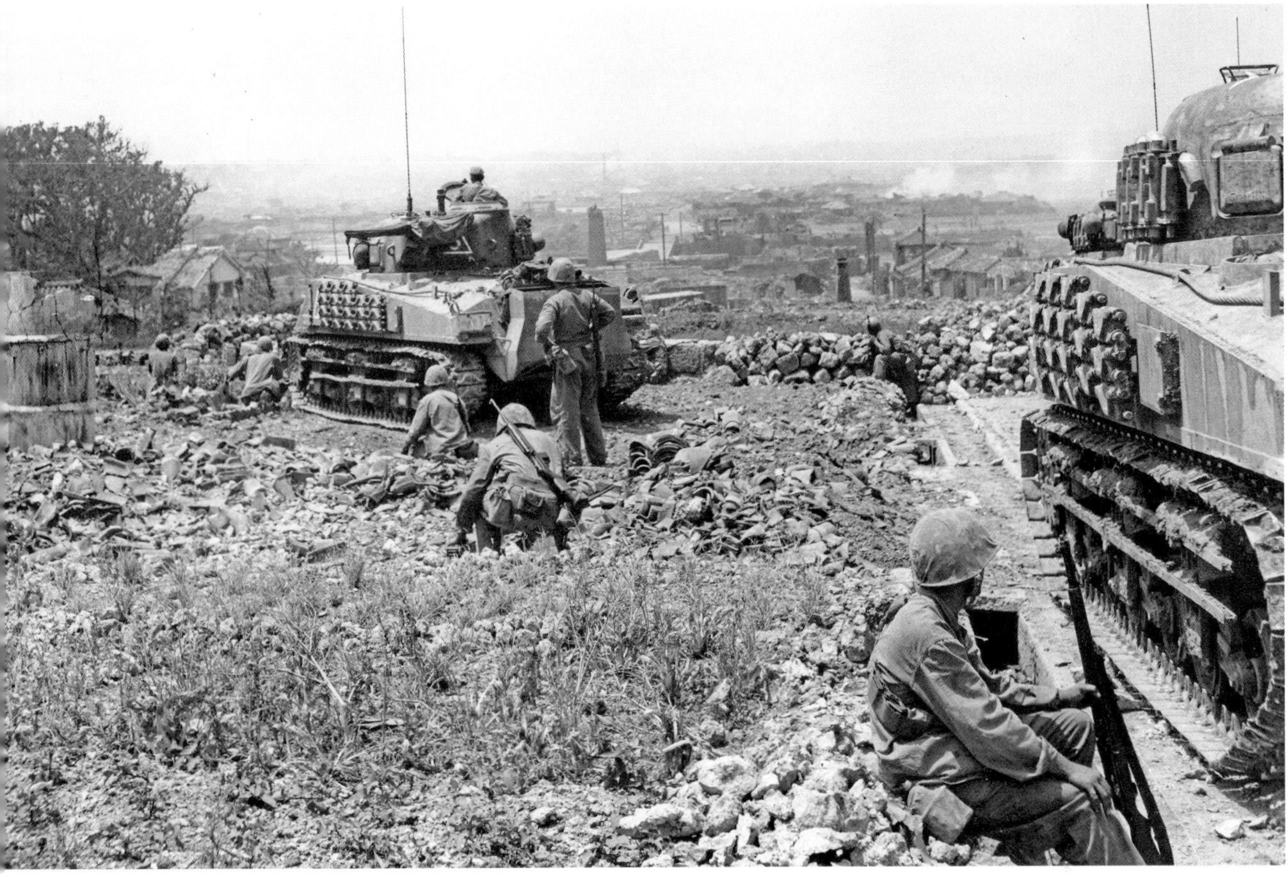

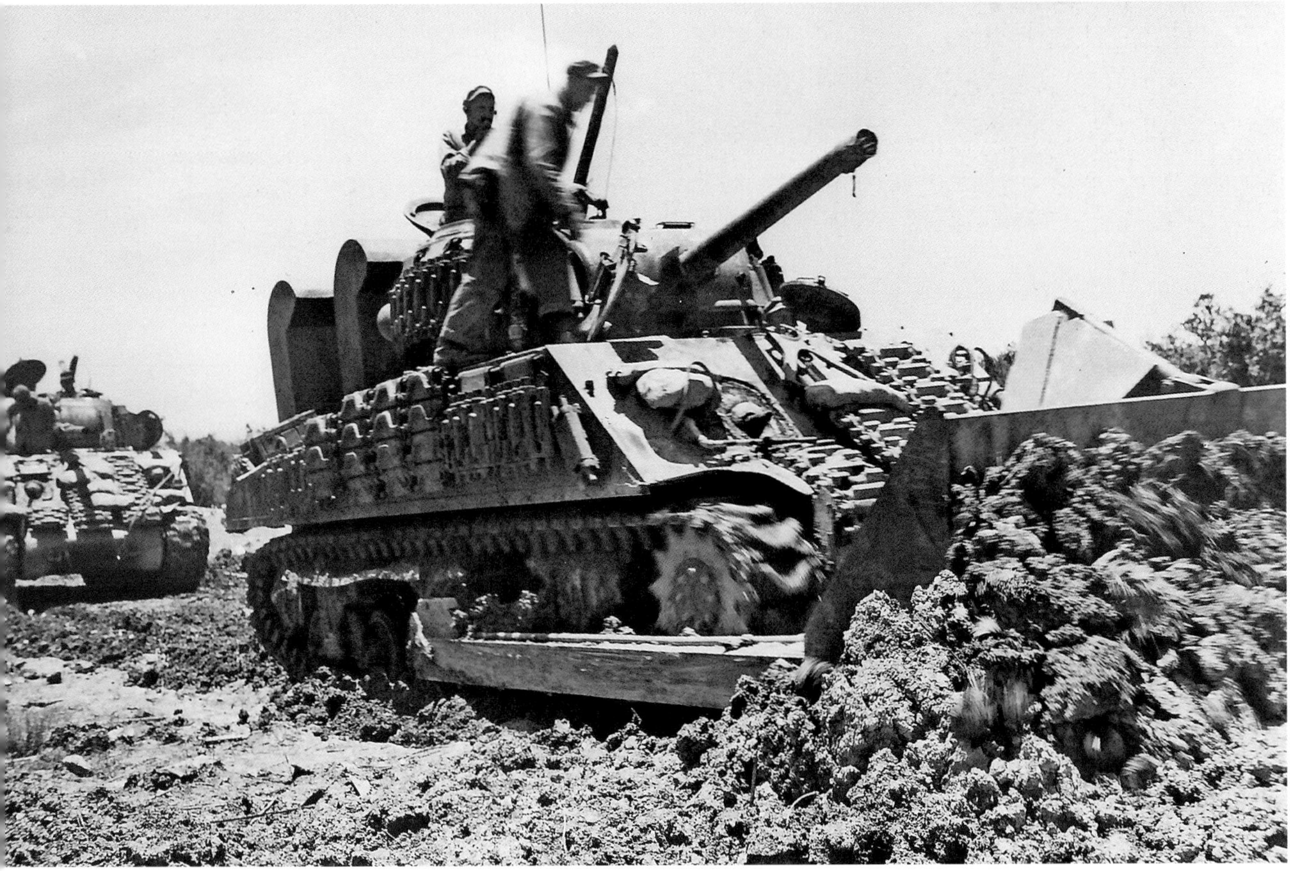

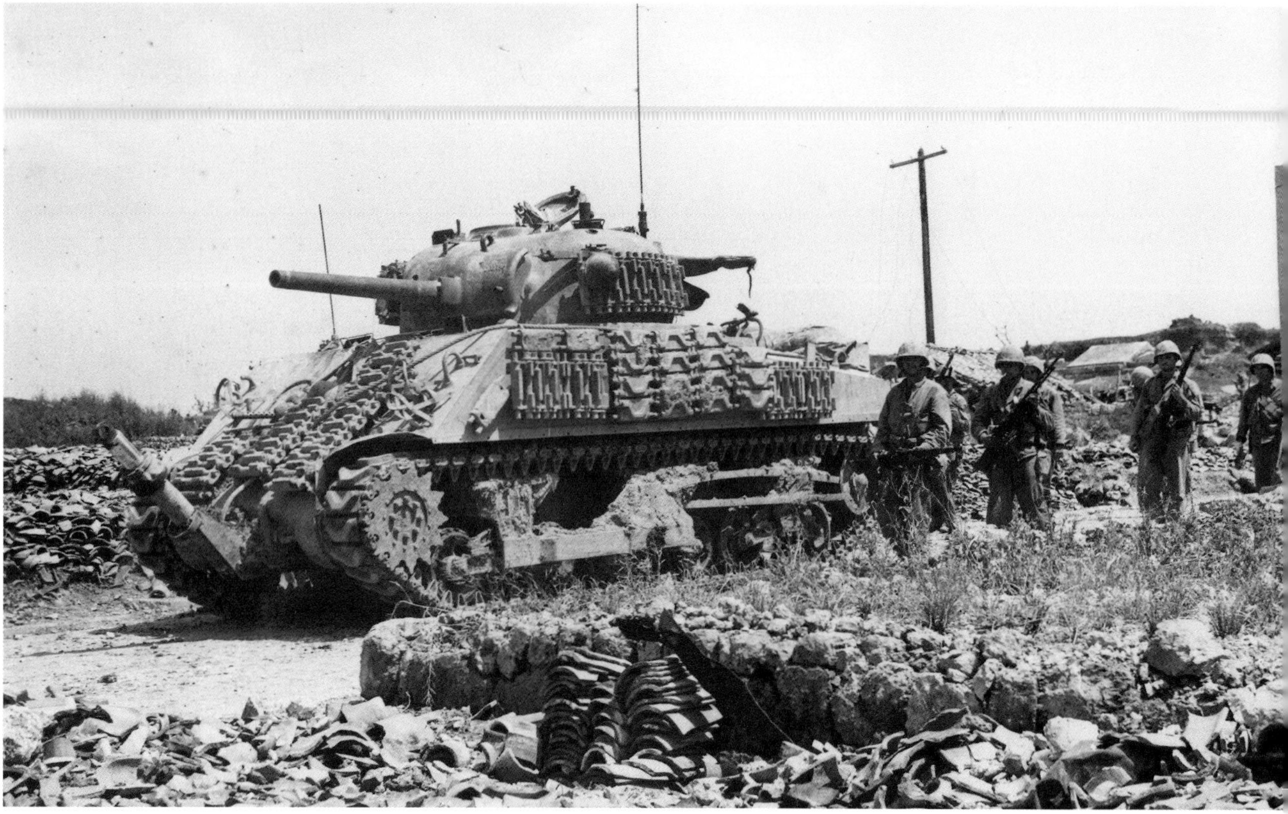

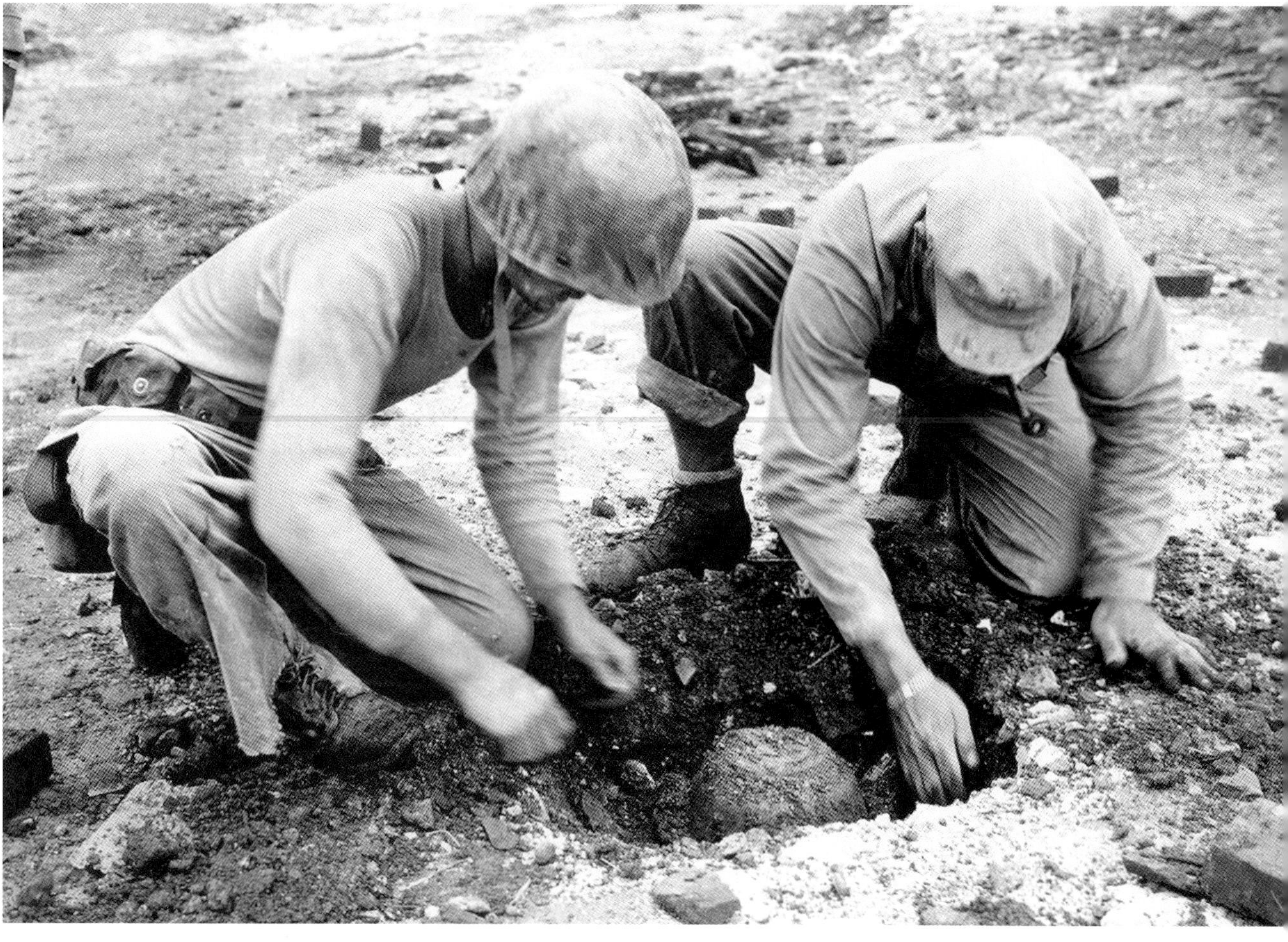

(**Opposite, above**) Here, missing its dozer blade but retaining the hydraulic piston and mounted attachment frame, is a Marine Corps M4A3 medium tank on Okinawa. By this point in the war the Marine Corps had worked out many of the kinks with tanks and infantry working together. From a Marine Corps after-action report on Okinawa: 'Tanks fought at all times as infantry tanks and functioned as a major direct fire close-support weapon.' (*USMC*)

(**Opposite, below**) In this picture two Marine Corps engineers are attempting to disable a Japanese mine. From an after-the-battle report written by a Marine tank unit on Okinawa come these comments: 'Japanese mining was erratic. In one case the mines were marked with stakes. In another case a complete field beside a road was mined while the road was left untouched. Tanks on the beach were able to pick their way through [mine] fields because the mines were spaced too far apart.' (*USMC*)

(**Above**) Besides the employment of their standard inventory of anti-tank mines on Okinawa, the Japanese also created a number of improvised anti-tank mines using large redundant aerial bombs containing hundreds of pounds of explosive. The consequences of detonating one of these improvised anti-tank mines can be seen here with this destroyed Marine Corps M4A3 medium tank. It is doubtful that the vehicle crews survived such encounters. (*USMC*)

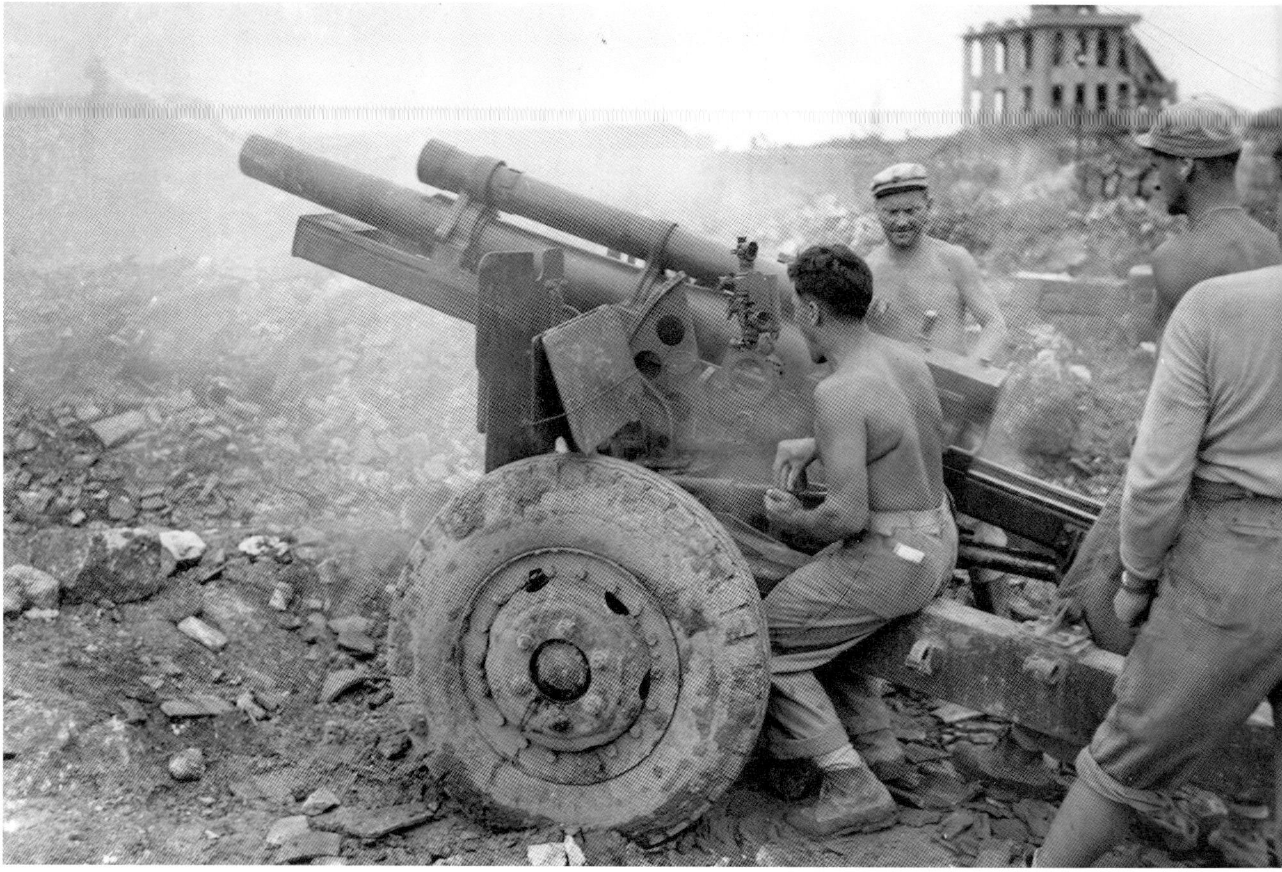

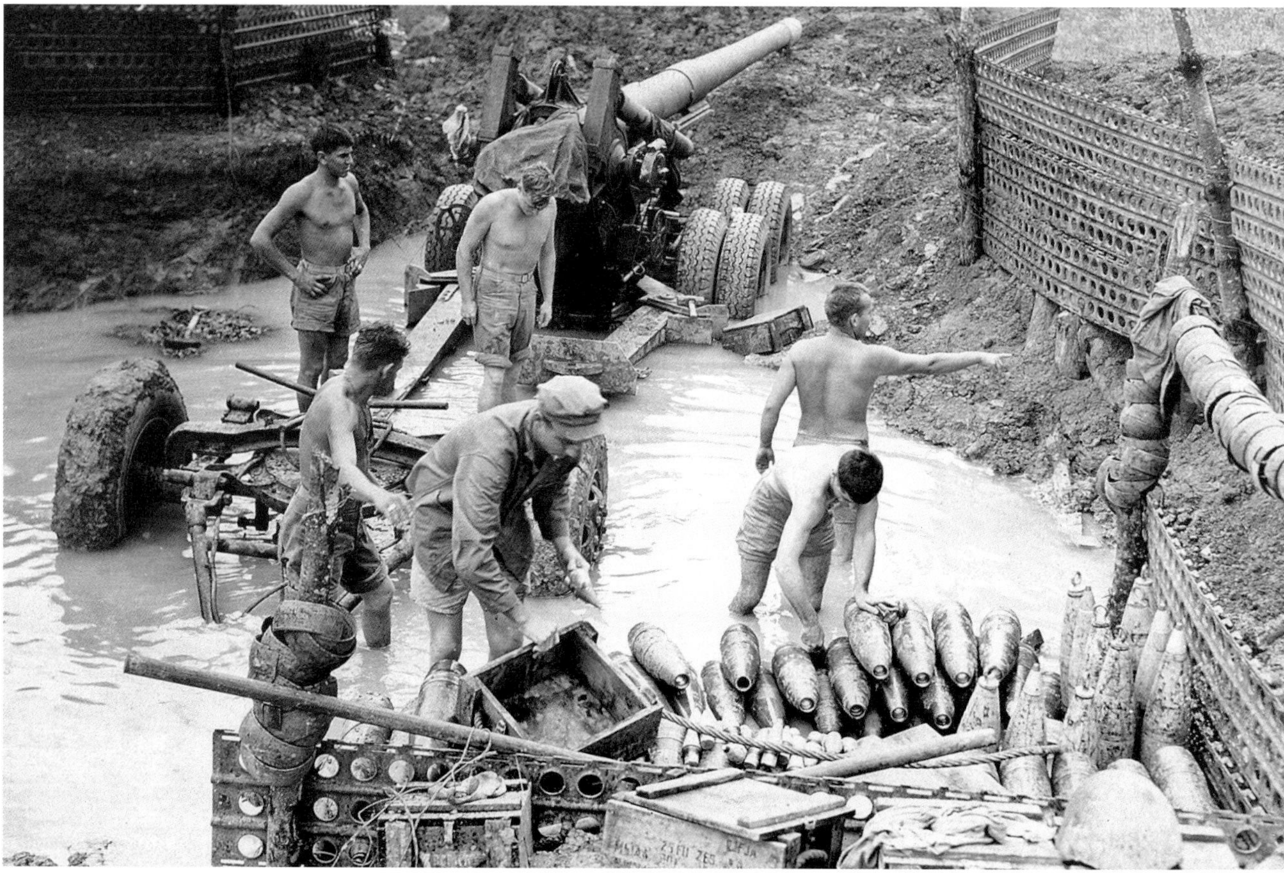

(**Opposite, above**) In action here on Okinawa is a Marine Corps 105mm howitzer M2. During the Okinawa campaign, Marine and US Army artillery battalions of the Tenth Army fired 1,766,352 rounds in support of the infantry. According to a Marine Corps historical publication: 'Coordination between Marine and army units was exceptional, and a pervading spirit of cooperation placed the protection and support of the infantryman ahead of all other considerations.' (*USMC*)

(**Above**) A new addition to the Marine Corps inventory by the time of the Okinawa campaign was the 105mm Howitzer Motor Carriage (HMC) M7 series, two of which are seen here on the island doubling as troop transports. The vehicle had a crew of seven: driver, chief of section, gunner and four cannoneers. It had authorized storage on board for sixty-nine main gun rounds. (*USMC*)

(**Opposite, below**) Adding to the misery of the Marines during the Okinawa campaign was the weather, often rainy as is evident from the water-filled artillery position in this photograph. The worst aspect of the rain on Okinawa was the fact that it turned every draw and gulley into a sticky morass of thick mud and made the hills and ridges impossible to climb or descend. Even full-tracked vehicles, including bulldozers, would eventually become bogged down. (*USMC*)

An enemy round struck this Marine Corps 81mm Mortar M1 position on Okinawa, killing one of the crew and wounding the other two. The Marine in this picture is no doubt checking the cross-levelling mechanism of the destroyed mortar to see if it could be salvaged for further use. The mortar fired an approximately 7lb high-explosive (HE) round designated the M43, many of which can be seen in this image as well as their metal carrying cases. (*USMC*)

Discovered during the fighting on Okinawa by Marines was this Japanese 150mm artillery piece Model 89 in a well-constructed dugout. With the Americans having complete air superiority over Okinawa, it was impossible for any Japanese artillery pieces to survive in the open. The Model 89 had a maximum effective range reported to be as great as 27,000 yards. Like other artillery pieces of this size, the rate of fire was limited to one or two rounds per minute. (USMC)

In this picture of Marines in combat on Okinawa is an interesting mixture of infantry weapons. To the immediate left of the Marine aiming the M9A1 2.36in rocket-launcher is a crouching Marine armed with an M1928A1 Thompson sub-machine gun fitted with a fifty-round detachable drum magazine. The Marine seen behind the others, armed with an M1 carbine, is holding an M9A1 rifle grenade with another lying on the ground near him. To the rear, the lead man holds a hand grenade; in front of the guy with rifle grenades is a Marine armed with what appears to be a BAR [note BAR magazine pouches]. (USMC)

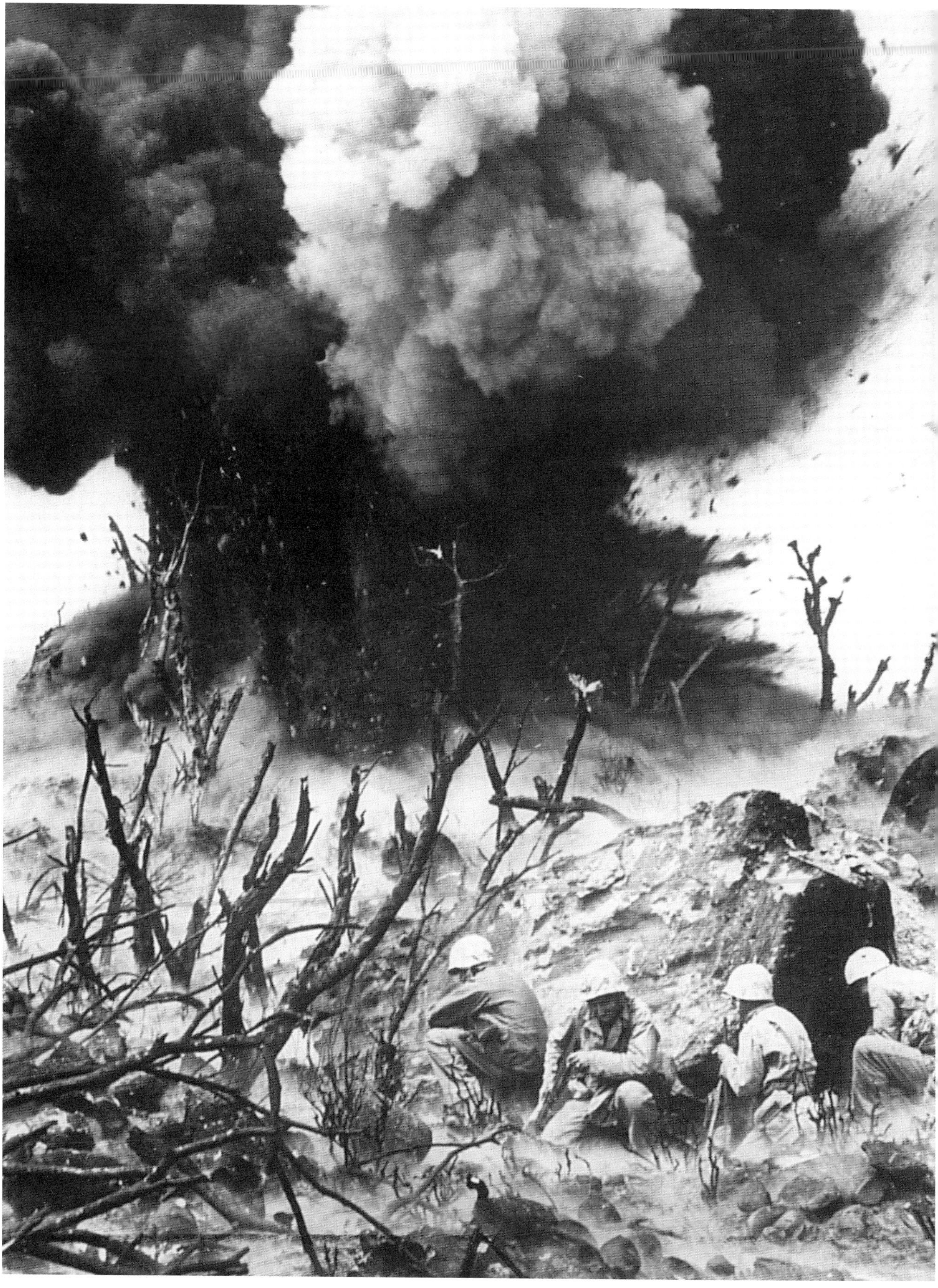

(**Opposite**) A massive explosive detonation marks another Japanese defensive position being destroyed. There could be enemy personnel in the position or it might have already been cleared and the Marine engineers are destroying it to deny it for future use by Japanese troops. Each Marine division had an engineer battalion of 875 men broken down into a headquarters company and three engineer companies of 200 men each. There was also a pioneer battalion per division and until 5 May 1944 each Marine division had an engineer regiment, but these were reduced to two battalions to save manpower. (USMC)

(**Above**) Keeping a steady flow of ammunition going to the Marines in the front lines was of crucial importance in every battle. When vehicles were not available or unable to reach the front lines, somebody had to do this as the two Marines pictured here on Okinawa found out. They are humping the fibreboard containers that each contained an 81mm mortar round. (USMC)

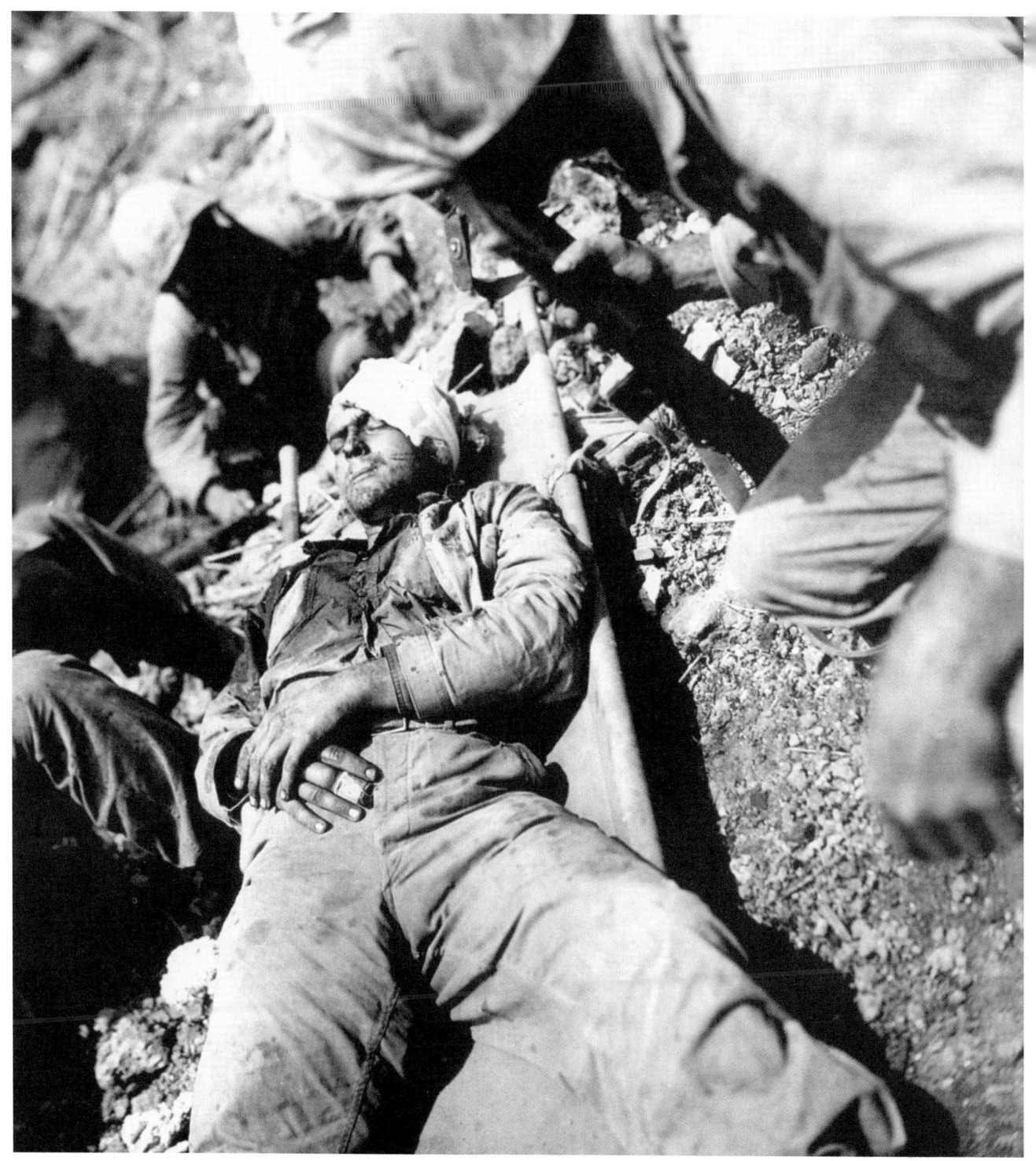

A Marine casualty on Okinawa has been treated by US Navy corpsmen and stabilized for the trip back to a battalion aid station. Major General Lemuel C. Shepherd Jr, commander of the 6th Marine Division, described the corpsmen that served on Okinawa as 'the finest, most courageous men that I know … they did a magnificent job.' Three corpsmen received the Medal of Honor for their service on Okinawa. (USMC)

The man on the right is a 28-year-old Korean labourer, with the other two being late-war examples of the Japanese military scraping the bottom of its manpower barrel. It was soldiers like these who lacked the typical fight-to-the-death attitude of the majority of Japanese soldiers and filled the prisoner-of-war (PoW) stockades erected by the American Tenth Army on Okinawa near the conclusion of the campaign. (*USMC*)

(**Above**) Marine aviators at Okinawa flying the F4U Corsair were tasked with both close air support (CAS) missions as seen in this picture, and protecting the US Navy fleet supporting the ground operations on Okinawa from Japanese suicide aircraft (kamikazes). From a Marine Corps historical monograph appears this gracious quote from a US Navy destroyer captain whose ship was saved from kamikazes by Marine Corsairs: 'When the leader was asked to close and assist us, he replied "I am out of ammunition but I am sticking with you." … I am willing to take my ship to the shores of Japan if I could have these Marines with me.' *(USMC)*

(**Opposite**) A Marine officer is shown here trying to comfort one of his men who had just lost a good friend in battle on Okinawa. The ferocity and duration of the bloody fighting on the island resulted in approximately 26,000 men of the Tenth Army, Marines and soldiers, being waylaid by what was then referred to as combat fatigue. Some would eventually recover and be returned to duty, with many others never completely recovering from their mental health problems incurred while fighting on Okinawa. *(USMC)*

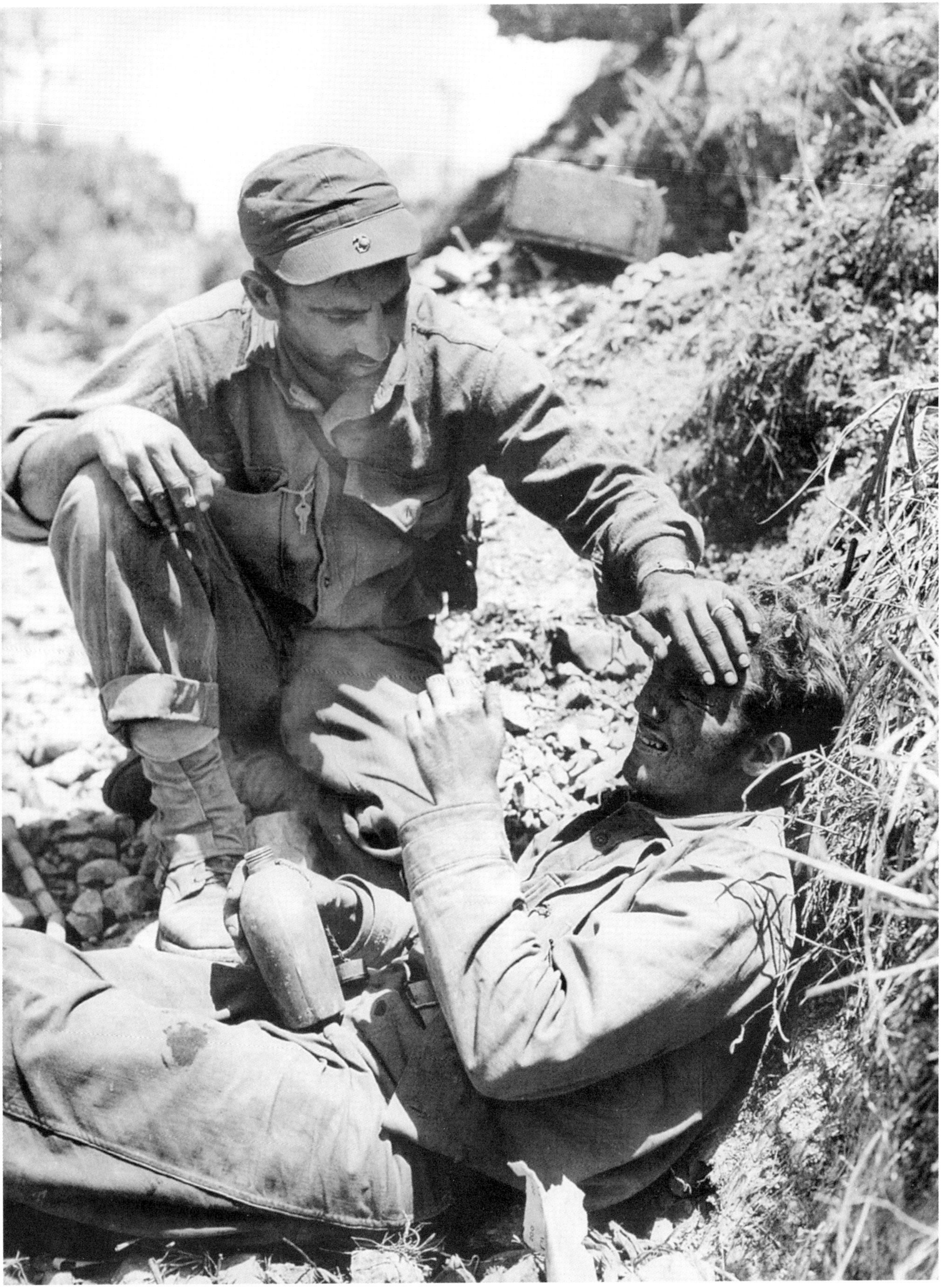

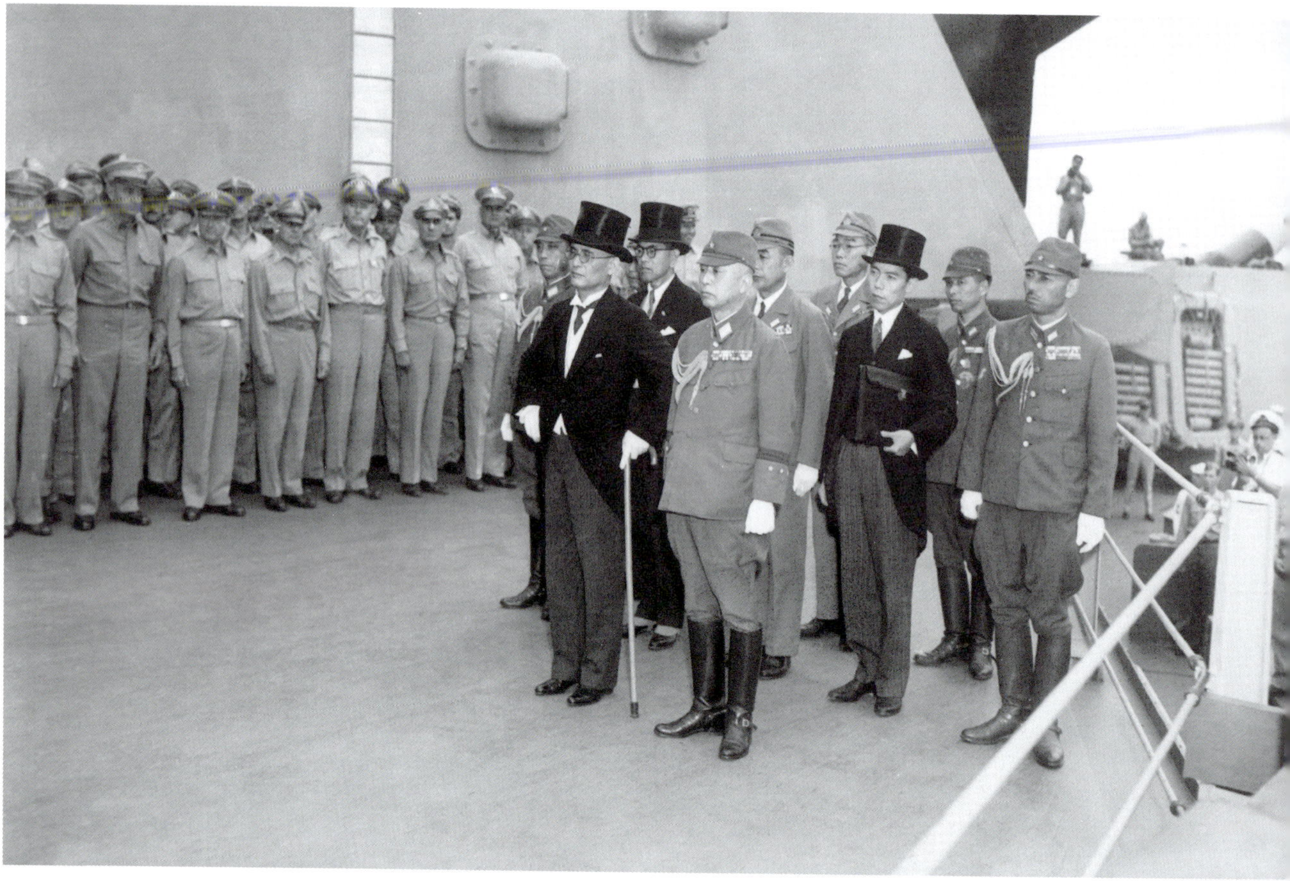

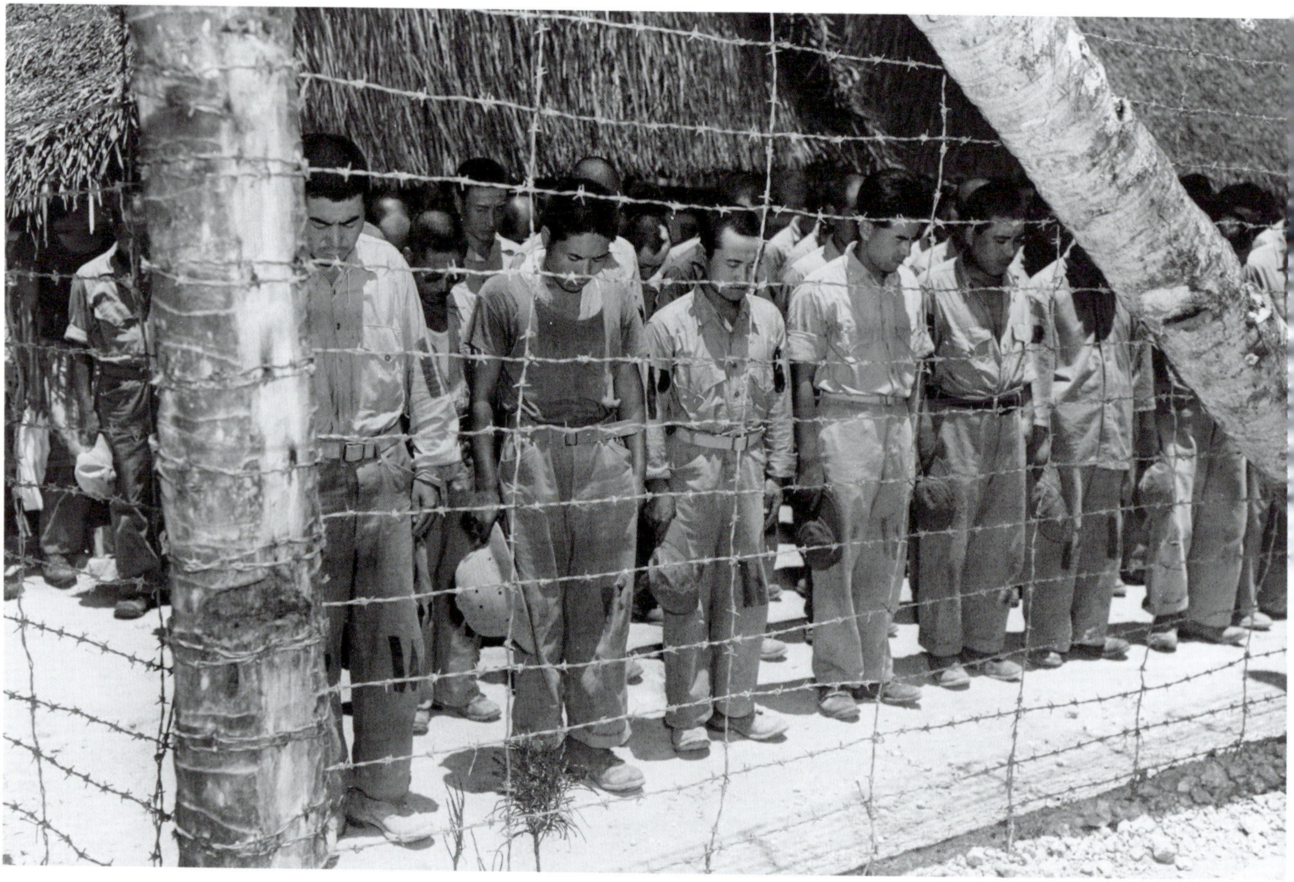

(**Opposite, above**) Faced with total destruction, the senior leadership of the Japanese Empire eventually decided to sue for peace on 15 August 1945. The ceremony marking their formal surrender took place on the US Navy battleship USS *Missouri* in Tokyo Bay on 2 September 1945. Pictured on the main deck of the USS *Missouri* prior to signing the Instrument of Surrender are the civilian and military representatives of the Japanese Empire. (*US Navy*)

(**Opposite, below**) Shown in an American military PoW stockade located on Guam are former Japanese soldiers bowing upon hearing of the surrender of their country. Total Japanese military losses between 1937 and 1945 are reported to be anywhere between 2.5 million and a little over 3 million. Broken down even further, approximately 486,000 were killed in fighting with the armed forces of the United States from 1941 to 1945. (*USMC*)

(**Above**) With the formal surrender of Japan, both Marine and US Army units were tasked with the occupation of the Japanese home islands and to ensure that the disarming of the Japanese military was carried out. In this picture we see two Marines, no doubt prompted by the photographer, pretending to be breaking Japanese small arms in a somewhat inefficient manner but no doubt very satisfying for those who had seen combat. (*USMC*)

Notes

Notes

Notes

Notes

Notes

Notes

Notes